# The Good Son

# The Good Son

SHAPING THE MORAL

DEVELOPMENT OF

OUR BOYS AND YOUNG MEN

## Michael Gurian

JEREMY P. TARCHER/PUTNAM
a member of Penguin Putnam Inc.
New York

Most Tarcher/Putnam books are available at special quantity discounts
for bulk purchases for sales promotions, premiums, fund-raising, and
educational needs. Special books or book excerpts also can be created
to fit specific needs. For details, write Putnam Special Markets,
375 Hudson Street, New York, NY 10014.

Jeremy P. Tarcher/Putnam
a member of
Penguin Putnam Inc.
375 Hudson Street
New York, NY 10014
www.penguinputnam.com

First Trade Paperback Edition 2000

*The Library of Congress has catalogued the hardback edition as follows:*

Gurian, Michael.
     The good son : shaping the moral development of
our boys and young men / by Michael Gurian.
          p.   cm.
        ISBN 0-87477-985-5
        1. Boys.   2. Boys—Psychology.   3. Boys—Conduct of life.
4. Child rearing.   I. Title.
HQ775.G82   1999
305.23—dc21          99-23765 CIP
        ISBN 1-58542-049-2 (paperback edition)

Printed in the United States of America

10   9   8   7   6   5   4   3   2   1

This book is printed on acid-free paper. ∞

BOOK DESIGN BY RALPH FOWLER

*For Gail, Gabrielle, and Davita,*

*whose love enfolds me,*

*and*

*For Jack and Julia Gurian,*

*my generous parents*

# Acknowledgments

This book could not have been written without the help of numerous colleagues all over the world, as well as families, clients, boys, and young men who cannot be mentioned by name. I thank the unnamed as much as the named for their generosity.

Mitch Horowitz has been editor extraordinaire. He is a man of vision and discipline who continually stimulates me to do my best. Joel Fotinos is one of those publishers whom writers dream about—supportive, wise, and inspiring. In Ken Siman I have found not only a publicist but a friend and ally. Thank you all so much. Lily Chin, Maria Liu, and so many others at Tarcher/Putnam have shown devotion and excellence in helping my work.

My profound gratitude goes as well to both Jeremy Tarcher and Phyllis Grann for their high-level confidence in my work, and for their individual visions.

My agent, Susan Schulman, and her staff work so hard so constantly to bring books of worth into the public dialogue. I thank them for sharing the idea that books exist to provide an important service to readers.

Many thanks to Alan Rinzler, father of four boys, for his extra editing help, as well as to Sheila Thomsen, mother of four boys; and Christine Barada, mother of Max, who read my manuscript and helped me shape my thoughts.

For special help with endocrinological issues, many thanks to both Drs. Joanna Ellington and Howard Lawrence.

For special help with neural science, many thanks to Dr. Mary Ann Sharkey.

For his very useful perspective and information on the state of boyhood in our culture, my thanks to Joe Manthey of Petaluma, California, who leads the school-based training program Kid Culture in the Schools.

My thanks also to Boy Scouts of America, Big Brothers and Big Sisters of America, the International Boys School Coalition, Court Appointed Special Advocates, and the National Mentoring Partnership for including me in their very important work with boys and young men.

A special note of thanks to the staff at the Michael Gurian Institute at the University of Missouri at Kansas City. Dr. Patricia Henley and her staff in the Department of Education have been instrumental in helping create school-based thinking, vision, and materials—this book would not be what it is without the support of Dr. Henley and the Institute staff.

# Contents

*To be a competent student of what is right and just, one must first have learned discipline and received a proper upbringing in moral conduct. A man with this kind of background has acquired the foundations of life. One who has not may one day be called useless.*

—ARISTOTLE

*To educate a person in intelligence but not in character is a crime to the human spirit.*

—MARTIN LUTHER KING, JR.

*What could be more important than making our boys into good men? Doesn't the whole human civilization kind of depend on it?*

—A TEACHER AT A WORKSHOP ON THE MORAL DEVELOPMENT OF BOYS

# Introduction

I was born in Honolulu, Hawaii, into a family that moved around the world and all over the United States before I was eighteen. My brother, Philip, with whom I shared a great love and a huge sibling rivalry, was two years older. In India, my parents adopted my sister, Maria, five years younger than me. Raised in broken homes, my parents shared similar, painful childhood experiences, and promised themselves they would make a different life for their kids: They worked hard to provide their children with "good values," including family loyalty, integrity, and ordinary decency. From both my brother and me, they wanted "good sons."

From my brother, they generally got it. On the other hand, I was a "hyperactive" boy (the old word for Attention Deficit Hyperactive Disorder), bouncing and bounding around the world like a little top, often resistant and rebellious. I presented my family with a powerful emotional and moral puzzle. No matter what culture they took me to—their jobs caused us to move every two years or so—one of my parents' primary concerns was my tenuous discipline.

In kindergarten in Hyderabad, India, when I was five years old, I kicked my teacher hard on the shin. A thin rail of a woman, she yowled in pain, then found her bamboo cane. Before my parents could even hear about it, she smashed the cane down on the back of my hands! I remember the pain to this day.

This incident was one of many in which I did things that demanded strong discipline and moral education—shoplifting, excessive talking, spitball wielding in classrooms, throwing snowballs with stones in them at car windows, smoking under the bleachers at the football field, lying to my parents. Back in Hawaii, in my late teens, my father had to take me to municipal court because I had received seven moving violations in two months! Three were for speeding, and four for making "California stops"—turning right without stopping at a stop sign. He and I sat with the judge in downtown Honolulu.

"What should we do with him, Mr. Gurian?" the judge asked.

"What are the options?" my father asked.

"Well, we could take his license away."

My father, without hesitation, asked where he should sign.

I was furious with my father and the judge for doing it, but of course they were right. When I got my license back again at age eighteen, I did not get another ticket for a very long time.

Now in their seventies, my parents recently discussed this book with me, sitting with my two children in the living room of our home. My mother laughed. "Do you remember what a wild little boy you were? We weren't sure you'd make it!" As I look back at my own life, at both the normal, "boyish" things I did and the illegal actions, I see quite clearly that behind any child's masks of rebellion, "troublemaking," or "hyperactivity" are emotional insecurity and moral fragility. One difference, however, between my generation and the generation of boys and young men I now work with is the extremity of moral crisis. More of our boys, at rates I see growing exponentially, live in moral confusion that is dangerous not only to them but to their society. Boys in our own homes, in our schools, and in the lives of our daughters are confused. If you have noticed an increase in ethical numbness, moral distraction, and spiritual emptiness among boys and young men, you are observing something we must protect our sons from. Our culture challenges all of us to come to grips with the experience of boyhood today.


## THE DECLINING MORAL HEALTH OF OUR SONS

In L.A., a group of four basically good guys, all between the ages of fifteen and eighteen, got drunk one night and threw bricks through the windows of parked cars. Their identities were discovered because, unbeknownst to them, a man and a woman were making out in one of the cars. They had a cell phone and called the police.

In Houston, a fourteen-year-old male walked into a convenience store and held a gun to the clerk's head, extracting money from the register. He was turned in by his mother, who saw the store videotape on television a few hours later.

In a suburb of Denver, two boys, ages seventeen and eighteen, planted bombs and murdered thirteen people at Columbine High School.

In a small, rural town in Arkansas, two boys, ages eleven and thirteen, opened fire in their school, killing a teacher and three children. Recently I heard the superintendent of that school district, a man in his seventies who had just retired, speak in tears to an audience of other superintendents of how powerless he felt to understand, or do anything, about the tragedy.

In New York, a sixteen-year-old boy, after just receiving his driver's license, drove home from work one night and killed a cat. A pedestrian witness saw that he specifically went out of his way to run it over. The police were shocked not by the accident but rather by the boy's mixture of feigned and very real indifference. "Whatever," he said. "I got thirty points."

In Chicago, a group of boys vandalized a pawnshop. When caught, they said, "So what—all the guys do stuff like this."

Incidents like these are happening in your town, and are increasing.

In this book, we'll rely much more on people's stories than on statistics; yet statistics themselves can be powerful. Statistics underscore the state of moral emergency that is gradually, and without our fully realizing it, becoming an everyday part of male life.

- We have the most violent non-war population of children in the world. More people in the U.S. per capita commit violent acts every day than anywhere else, and 90 percent of them are male.

- More of our children per capita get arrested for crimes than in any other country. Ninety percent of arrestees are boys.

- After Russia, more of our citizens are in prison than any other country in the world. Ninety percent of these incarcerated individuals are male.

- Our young males make up 80 percent of drug-addicted and alcoholic youth.

- Our boys constitute the majority of children who are homeless, murdered, in foster care, neglected, and institutionalized.

- Our rate of mental disorders in the male population per capita is one of the highest in the world. For instance, 90 percent of the Ritalin used on children in the world is used on ours. Approximately 3,000,000 kids are on Ritalin in the U.S.—90 percent of them boys.

- The child suicide rate has gone up over the last decade with increasing acceleration, mainly among adolescent boys.

- Our teen pregnancy rates are among the highest in the industrial world, and we provide the *least* extended family support to teens who have babies. Ninety percent of males who impregnate a teen girl abandon her and her family.

- Our schoolchildren are arguably the most undisciplined in the world. Ninety percent of the children who require discipline in schools are boys. As one educator recently put it to me, "After teaching in Hong Kong, Japan, and Australia, then returning to the United States, I felt something like despair when I saw what had happened to the American middle school classroom."

- Our boys and young men also comprise the majority of child-abuse victims and are the less likely victim to talk about and get help for their suffering. In a 1998 study of 7,000 children, 48 percent of boys, compared to 29 percent of girls, said they would never tell anyone about the abuse they had experienced. As psychologist Aaron Kipnis explains: "It is egodystonic—not in accord with their self-image and traditional gender identity—for boys to complain about pain." Thus our boys are becoming more and more at risk for abuse, neglect, violence, addiction, psychiatric illness, and all the pains of childhoods lived in broken homes and confusing worlds, pains that never appear in statistics.

The silence in which boys endure their suffering only perpetuates their moral fragility, since boys are ten times more likely than girls to act out their pain by being violent toward others. This reactionary violence is in turn criminalized, which is the most indicative sign of the crisis in boyhood today. *In the U.S., more boys and young men are incarcerated in juvenile detention, prison, and psychiatric hospitals than in any other nation on earth.* The legislative trend toward criminalizing boyhood is continuing at a fast pace. All fifty states now have laws making it easier to prosecute juveniles in adult criminal court. In half our states, kids younger than fourteen can be tried in adult court. In thirteen of our states, no minimum age exists at which a kid can be tried as an adult—the decision is made subjectively—and in some states boys as young as eleven have been tried as adults. The state of New York permits prosecution of seven-year-olds as adults for certain felonies. Bills intermittently come before the House and the Senate, like the Hatch-Sessions bill, espousing things like getting rid of the separation of juveniles and adults in prison.

Our boys are in trouble. Some lack basic impulse control; others lack what we would call a conscience; others lack the ability to articulate right and wrong; others lack empathy; others simply can't get understanding from a culture that has come to fear even normal male behavior. After almost two decades of my working with boys and young men—in classrooms, in prisons, in community agencies, and in my therapy practice—my fear for them grows. More and more they are in the obvious state of moral emergency that the media tracks through their stories of boys shooting up and placing bombs in schools, and of men shooting up workplaces. But there is the hidden emergency as well—the gradual decay in character education and emotional support systems for boys and young men.

As we will explore in part I of this book, our males live in a culture that commits both "sins of commission" and "sins of omission." Our culture directly poisons the character development of its males *and* neglects essential building blocks for that character development. While the moral development of any child is a complex enterprise, the moral development of a boy has unique complications. As we'll explore in chapter 1, male hormones, brain systems, and social acculturation compel males to push limits and request discipline and love in sometimes dangerous, even immoral ways. All children need clear and *systematic direction, well into the teen years*, and boys often need it in ways we don't notice. The male brain is structured and functions in ways that yearn for help with emotional and moral development. Male hormones and male acculturation cry out as well for certain, specific kinds of relationship and guidance, which we'll explore in chapter 1.

In chapter 2, we'll look at the exact ways our boys as a group are morally neglected. We'll explore how they are poisoned by the culture, how they receive too little childhood moral training in general and far too little *boy-specific* moral and emotional development. Based on these two foundational chapters, *The Good Son* is a call for moral and ethical revival in the raising of boys, and is a parenting plan by which to protect and nurture male development all the way to adulthood. The body of the book is comprised of the Good Son Parenting Plan, a practical blueprint by which to raise and protect our boys.

Both our exploration of the state of boyhood today and the parenting plan depend on our coming to agreement on what we mean by "discipline" and "moral development."

## TWO OF LIFE'S MOST IMPORTANT WORDS

What sense shall we make of the moral landscape our children live in? What would Plato think of the fifteen-year-old boy in Baltimore I saw the other day flipping off the driver of a car that nearly hit him while he played his boom box so loudly it shook the building near us? What would Jesus think of the boy in the department store in New York who called his mother, loud as can be, a motherfucker? What would Moses or Mohammed or Mahatma Gandhi or Mother Teresa think about the eleven-year-old boy who yells at the wrestlers in the ring, "Beat the shit out of him"? What should any of us think? Are these immoral acts? Do they show an egregious lack of self-discipline, or should they be considered "boyish" and "normal"? And what do we mean when we use the words "morality" and "discipline"?

For some people it is enough to literally go back to interpretations of the Bible and other sacred books for the whole moral foundation our contemporary culture needs. For others it is important to toss out all the old wisdom and embrace relativistic situation-based ethics. For me, neither course alone is enough. Ancient religious texts and religious traditions carry immense moral depth; new moral experiments have the qualities of freedom and egalitarianism that also are essential to contemporary life. In my own work in child development, I have tried to build a practical and tangible bridge between the past and the future. No task I've had as a social thinker, therapist, and educator has been as difficult as building this bridge between the cultures of Jesus, Moses, Rebecca, and Plato and the cultures of Freud, Darwin, Einstein, and Gloria Steinem. Yet to deal with our present moral landscape, we must find that bridge.

When I was growing up, I thought I had a clear understanding of "morality." Though I often acted in uncontrolled ways, I knew right from wrong, what the rules were, and the consequences of immoral action. In college, I earned a philosophy degree. It was in philosophy classes that I realized the paltriness of my boyish moral understanding—I learned countless different definitions of "values," "morals," and "good character." In graduate school and postgraduate work, I focused on physical and biological sciences, learning how nature affects human moral life. For years I searched through moral texts, traditions, and experiments by living not only in the U.S. but in Europe and the Middle East.

Then I returned to the U.S., where my wife, Gail, and I started a family. There is nothing like the creation of children to compel the heart, mind, and soul toward finally clarifying a moral system. Now as a parent, I saw the fruits of my own boyhood, my education, my years of research, and my work as a professional therapist and educator. As I became known as an "expert" in child development, I strove to hold myself and the many children, families, schools, community agencies, and other professionals I worked with to a high moral vision based on the following definition.

*Morality is and always has been the living human community's code of compassion.* Moral values are humanity's insurance policy that compassion will prevail in human interactions, whether parent-child, adult-adult, child-child, or nation-nation. Every rule, law, or honor code exists, at its most fundamental level, to ensure that we human beings act compassionately toward one another. When we act "immorally," we will always discover that we have acted *without compassion.* Whenever we discipline a child—whether we tell him to sit still or not to hit or not to watch too much television, or we put him in prison—we do so because either he has not been compassionate to others or himself or we are trying to teach him control of his impulses so that he will not behave with a lack of compassion. Even when we teach a young person to repress his immediate compassion in order to kill in war, we do so because the ultimate action of the war, although tragic, is thought to be necessary for ensuring a compassionate future. There is no act of human morality that is not based on some vision of compassion.

Almost every parent, educator, and caregiver knows how important it is to *consciously develop* a child's natural compassion by educating the child in morality. "In this house we share." "Do what's right." "Speak respectfully." All these lessons direct and sustain compassion. By consciously developing a child's natural compassion through moral education, we provide the child a focus for empathy and sensitivity, as well as frameworks by which to show honorable compassion even when he's angry.

*Discipline is the human being's ability to devote his own physical, mental, and emotional drives toward compassion.* Initially, it is by receiving the gift of discipline from parents and intimate caregivers that children learn how to contain, manage, regulate, and channel their physical and emotional energies. After years of childhood and adolescence experience, children develop *self-discipline.* They become their own conscience, their own physical and mental pilot. And when a human community teaches morality and discipline well, its children learn not just to control their own drives but to channel their physical, emotional, and mental energies toward the highest good: *the compassionate life.*

*The Good Son* culminates two decades of research and experience with individuals, families, and organizations; its ultimate goal is to help you direct your sons and the boys you know toward loving, wise, and responsible manhood—the compassionate life.

We caregiving adults have just less than twenty years of developmental time in which to accomplish this goal. I hope the parenting plan that makes up the core of this book will help you reach it.


## THE GOOD SON PARENTING PLAN

This book contains a blueprint through which you can guide your son from birth to adulthood. I have written the plan to be moving and inspiring to anyone who cares about boys—even if your sons are grown or if you have daughters and wonder about the boys they'll meet.

Information and wisdom from an "expert" isn't worth a lot, in my view, unless it resonates with everyday life. Every chapter of the plan begins and ends with stories I have lived, heard, or learned from parents, teachers, and other caregivers—stories of challenge, pain, and success. All of these teach from the heart.

The parenting plan presents a boy's life in three "developmental episodes"—birth to age six, ages seven to twelve, and ages thirteen to eighteen. Each of these is further divided into more specific time periods, e.g., infancy, the toddler years, kindergarten, and so on until age eighteen. The chapters provide you with information about what is considered normal for a boy of the specific age; what his developmental challenges are; how his family, school, and larger culture best interact to raise him well; and what you can do on a daily basis. You'll find suggestions for everything from when the toddler should go to bed to when the adolescent should be allowed private Internet access. You'll find subject headings that give you easy reference should you wish to treat the plan encyclopedically, like a parenting reference book.

While the parenting plan cannot cover every aspect of caring for a boy, if you follow its program, I believe you will raise a moral, well-disciplined, and well-adjusted boy. Even as your son's life is touched by pain and suffering, the plan will aid you in giving him a moral foundation. The aid it gives comes from the lessons of not only our own culture but the thirty cultures in which I have lived or about which I have studied.

Over the last ten years, I have conducted extensive surveys of parents, teachers, and other caregivers not only to learn their wisdom but to hear their most common questions. Throughout the parenting plan, I have included answers to many of these questions (e.g., "He is lying a lot lately—what should I do?"), questions that involve not only well-functioning boys but boys in trouble—boys who are withdrawn, addicted, or acting out in other dangerous ways.

The ultimate goal of all specific suggestions in this book is your son's development of these ten universally accepted moral competencies: *decency, fairness, empathy, self-sacrifice, respect, loyalty, service, responsibility, honesty,* and *honor.* These are the values that measure a good son, and they are the bedrock of compassion. Possession or lack of them makes or breaks a man. Ensuring that our sons develop them is one of the most important duties of not only an individual family but our civilization.

There will probably be aspects of the plan you find too extreme or too lax; I hope you'll use even these dissonances to inspire your own solutions and approaches. *The Good Son* is not meant to be the final word on raising boys. Rather, it is a guidepost directing us toward a happy, healthy boyhood for our sons. It is not meant as a substitute for your own intuition—for that, there is none.

## A CRUCIAL DUTY

The Greek philosopher Aeschylus hinged the longevity of a culture on how it is able to "tame the savagery of man and thus make gentle the life of the world." Every family and every culture is called to bring the beautiful but raw energy of a boy through the quest of boyhood into the moral center of the human community. Bringing him there, Aeschylus suggested, "we light his pathway to the very purpose of his existence." Aeschylus pointed to a crucial duty everyone in a civilization shares— to civilize our boys and *make* our men. These actions are not things that only one parent does, or even one isolated nuclear family. We all do them as a human community.

Today more than ever, few things are more important to all of us than to live with, produce, nurture, and enjoy good men. Many human moral systems and discipline strategies are in flux, religions hold less sway, extended families are in disarray, nuclear families are broken, schools are overwhelmed. Parents of daughters—I am one of these, with two daughters of my own—are just as concerned as parents of sons. Our girls live with boys, our women with men, inextricably linked in human community.

It should not be so difficult to raise a son as it has become. There are things we all can do to ensure the moral development and discipline of our sons, and thus to ensure the "gentleness" of our civilization. In providing our sons with these things, we help our children live lives of innocence as long as possible, and lives of experience that bring them happiness. In doing so, we find our happiness not only as parents of good sons but as individuals who unite to do the most important job of any civilization—the raising of children.

# Part One

## THE CHALLENGE OF
## PROVIDING DISCIPLINE
## AND MORAL DEVELOPMENT
## TO BOYS

# What Does It Mean to Have a Son?

The sun shined brightly that morning as I left home and walked the distance to my new school. We lived in Laramie, Wyoming, and I was entering seventh grade. We had recently moved to Laramie, so I had few friends yet. As I walked up the steps that day, I was one of a melee of boys and girls who still wanted to be kids but would never admit it, and wanted to be adults already but were scared of adulthood.

That afternoon, I went to my English class and sat at a desk in the middle of the room—not so far back that I was pegged as a troublemaker or stupid, and not right in front so I got called on a lot. A man of about thirty sat reading at the teacher's desk. He had close-cut black hair and a black beard, and he wore plain brown pants and a white shirt with a button-down collar. I couldn't tell his height yet, though he seemed tall. Behind him on the blackboard was written, "*The Adventures of Huckleberry Finn* by Mark Twain—Read it." Beneath that, in smaller letters, was the teacher's name: "Mr. Majors."

When the bell rang, he looked at us and smiled, his eyes lit up, his eyebrows curled like mustaches—big and black and expressive. He started talking about how he and his wife were going to have a baby any day now, and how he might try to take a day or two off (there was no official "family leave" for men in those days). He explained that this was his first child, and he thought it would be a boy. To our giggles, he said, "The reason I know this is because when my wife and I conceived this child, I was reading *Huck Finn.* Now, if there's a better story about boys, I don't know what it would be.

"But you know," he continued, rising from his chair and coming in front of the small desk, "there's nothing certain in life. You think it's certain that the sun will come up tomorrow, but it's not certain. You just believe it will because it always has." Then he pointed to his heart with a long finger. "But sometimes you just know something, and I just know I'm going to have a son, and I'm not sure what it means to have a son. It's a big deal. I'll tell you this—I'm not sure I want my son to have to live through everything Huck did, even though Huck had one heck of an adventure."

And so Mr. Majors went on about Huck, how he was a kind of metaphor, an "everyman," or, more literally, an "everyboy." He told Huck's story in brief, hoping to entice us to actually read the book cover to cover: Huck's running away from a bad lot, saving the Negro Jim, rolling down the river in the raft, the Duke and Dauphin, con men extraordinaire; treasure and Tom Sawyer, having to dress like a girl, another rescue. A happy ending, but not until after a lot of tragedy and pain. Without Mark Twain's humor, Mr. Majors told us, *The Adventures of Huckleberry Finn* might have read more like a Greek melodrama.

I did read the book cover to cover, and have since then a number of times. Not only because it was assigned, nor because it is a wonderful piece of literature, but because Mr. Majors was right: Every boy is in some way a Huck Finn. Boys are loving, good, and hungry for affection, for a pathway toward identity and importance, and for a personal journey through which to discover honor, honesty, empathy, decency, and all the other measures of a man. Like Huck's, each of our sons' "inherent goodness" is fragile: a family trauma, a disability, a rejection, a misconception about how someone feels about him can derail him quickly.

Like Huck's, our sons' road to self-discipline and moral life is confusing. With each new generation, it gets even more so. Like Huck's parents, we are often less available than our boy needs. Like Huck, who learns some pretty bad habits from people he meets on his journey, our boys get taught some immoral things by their culture. And like Huck, most of our sons do make the long, hard journey toward self-discovery, self-discipline, and a moral life.

Huck Finn had a tough go of it, especially when it came to learning right from wrong in a river society that itself wasn't clear about such things. Life was complicated for Huck, as it is for our boys. To whatever extent Huck's parents, extended family, and community did not ask the question "What does it mean to have this boy, Huck?" Huck, like our own sons, was forced to answer it himself. Mr. Majors, who *did* eventually have a son, didn't want his son to have to suffer a lot of what Huck did—the feelings of being lost, the isolation, and the lack of trustworthy elders. He wanted to protect his son, as we want to protect ours.

What *does* it mean to have a son? It is the question we each ask, even if only unconsciously, whether our boy has just been born or he is already moving through his journey toward manhood. It is a crucial question, especially in a culture today that is so confused about what to expect from its boys, so unclear on what they're made of, and how best to nurture them. I have recently heard this issue called the "male question."

## THE "MALE QUESTION"

Some thirty years after Mr. Majors's impassioned first day of class, I gathered with a number of adult professionals at a conference that explored themes relating to boys, men, and male development. The title of the seminar was "How to Get Males More Involved in Teen Pregnancy Issues." Because this was the keynote session, open to the public, the auditorium included a number of mothers and other parents and community members.

As I spoke, I brought up Mr. Majors and Huck Finn, and how confusing it can be to be a boy today. As we came to the question-and-answer session, a woman in her fifties raised her hand. She talked about Huck Finn from a woman's perspective, how she had liked the story but didn't get a lot out of it as a growing person. She said she had often wondered why boys like the book so much.

This statement led to a long discussion about how different boys and girls often are. Then one woman raised her hand and said, "All this is now very interesting, but I came here wanting to answer, for myself, the male question."

What is the "male question"? we asked her.

"It's pretty basic, and I hope it will come out right as I ask it. It's about how to make our boys and men fit, how to make them worthwhile, how to make them good people who care about others, and how to give them a purpose in life. I don't want uncontrolled, selfish, or unemotional men. I want useful, loving men. I've raised two sons and a daughter," she continued. "One of my sons really struggled with just not knowing what he was doing here in this life. He's grown now but still doesn't really know what it means to be a man. The way he put it to me was like this: 'Mom, as a guy, I don't quite know why I'm here.' This blew my mind, because I come from decades of feminism. I'm tuned to hear women saying they feel undervalued or unclear about their identity. But there was my son saying he didn't really know why he was born."

"The 'male question' is the same as Mr. Majors's question," another woman pointed out: "'What does it mean to have a son?' It's like our culture hasn't really asked this."

Another mom joined the dialogue: "The way I see it is, the world wanted my boys—they're grown now—to be quiet, kind, vulnerable, and controlled all the time, but it also wanted them to be strong, fearless, and aggressive all the time. We pull these boys in two really different directions and expect them to somehow figure it all out, pretty much all by themselves. I never knew if I did enough to help my sons pull both of these things off, and so I felt constantly guilty as a mother, too."

The woman who had started this discussion concluded it by saying: "If we don't come together as a culture and answer these questions— 'Why is a male here?' 'What is a male worth?' 'What does it mean to have a son?'—we'll create more and more of the very males we're at this conference talking about—the irresponsible ones, the violent ones, the druggies, the addicted, these guys who impregnate girls and disappear. It's up to us to look deeply into males and masculinity as we have into females and women's issues, don't you think?"

In this crowd of hundreds of mainly women, there was nearly unanimous agreement, of the type I have seen throughout the country over the last few years. Our culture has created the illusion that it understands its men and boys. But does it?

## MERILEE'S COURAGE

Merilee was forty-six, a lawyer, a petite woman with gray hair cut close and sparkling blue eyes. She had come to see me, she said, because she loved her three sons and her husband but felt so *different* from them. One son was having trouble, and it was his case she ostensibly wanted help with. But very quickly she admitted that she didn't think she could help him until she understood him, his brothers, his father, "and just men in general."

She continued, "Look, you must please help me understand these guys. I try to help Blake and I get stumped. It's like I don't have standards, or measurements, for how he should behave, or what to expect of him. What is he feeling? I don't know. What am I doing wrong with him? I don't know. And it's not like he or the other guys in my life help me understand. They don't tell me much, you know?"

Haven't we all felt like this? So many of us, whether parents, teachers, or grandparents, sense at some point that we have come to the tail end of what we understand about boys. We all know what it feels like to guess, or to gravitate toward a stereotype. We're all so busy we often don't even have time to sit down with others and ask, "Is what he just did normal?"

Merilee represents to me what seems to be happening all over the world right now: people admitting that we really don't understand boys and men. We haven't focused on them, despite the contemporary rhetoric that says, "The last three thousand years have been about men—we don't need to hear more about them." In fact, the last three thousand years have featured the accomplishments of a few men, but they have not featured the hidden interpersonal, psychological, and even moral worlds of our males in general.

Merilee is a parent who had the courage to admit: Guys can be confusing to us. They are well armored and in a shell; when they do talk it is rarely about their inner lives. It is difficult to say, "I *know* him." Sometimes, the males even talk a lot about inner lives just to make us think they're being revealing when in fact they're just trying to please us. Culturally, adult males remain so inscrutable that we end up labeling them inherently defective, or emotionally stupid, or morally reprehensible, or just not worth the effort.

I brought up Merilee's predicament on a radio show recently, raising the idea that we now understand our girls better than our boys. The radio host thought I came from the nineteenth century! "It's women who haven't had a voice," she insisted. Agreeing with her, I still pointed out that life now is not the same as it was thirty years ago. For instance, resources available for the understanding of girls and women—from academic studies to popular books to girl-power projects—outnumber resources available for understanding males by about nine to one. She still was incredulous, so I suggested she put this piece of the "male question" out to callers: "Let's ask callers if they feel human beings as a whole right now understand what's going on inside boys and men as well as we understand girls and women."

The talk-show host did generously put it to callers, and we were overwhelmed with calls, mainly from women, agreeing with Merilee. Since that first audience participation poll, I've raised this question throughout the country. The same results always come in: The majority of people are ready to admit that boys and men are too inscrutable to us right now, and we must change that in order to ensure the emotional and moral development of *all* our children.

In the rest of this chapter and in the next, I will be making a very simple argument: that our boys need a specific kind of love and attention, which they are rarely getting. That argument begins in our understanding of their hidden biology and of that biology's effect on their behavior not only as children but as *boys*.

## MORALITY IS SOMEWHAT DIFFERENT FOR BOYS

"My two sons," a mother told me, "seemed to come out of the gate having to figure out how to control themselves. My daughter just sort of knew."

So often, active, aggressive, and impulsive boys *do* seem different from girls. In some households, this activity makes for more discipline problems. In most households, when girls lose their sense of direction in life, their confusion does not show up as quickly in dangerous, immoral behavior. Males constitute the vast majority of criminals in any human culture; they engage in most of the violence in any culture; they constitute the vast majority of discipline problems in schools; they take the majority of moral and behavioral risks in any part of the world we study. While we all could argue whether boys or girls are harder to raise, I don't think most people would disagree that boys pose a special challenge when it comes to moral development.

A lot of moral development is, of course, the same for boys and girls. A lot of what you read in this book will work for girls. On the other hand, the difference is pretty significant. In my previous books, *The Wonder of Boys* and *A Fine Young Man*, I suggested that at the core of our emotional and social neglect of boys is the fact that a male experiences emotional and personal fragility in biologically recognizable ways, which we have neglected as a culture. In *The Good Son*, I will argue that we morally neglect our sons because we neglect male neurology and biochemistry. The deepening of our cultural understanding of our boys starts right here, in our biological and neurological inheritance and in its blending with culture.

Because I've covered a great deal about male biology and culture in *The Wonder of Boys* and *A Fine Young Man*, I won't repeat that material in *The Good Son*—I'll summarize and apply biocultural research to specific moral and discipline issues. And let's always remember that these are scientific and cultural generalizations and there are exceptions to everything presented here. The research into these biological and neurological clues is being done with brain scans—PET and MRI— by scientists, like Ruben Gur at the University of Pennsylvania. These scans show neurological differences between the ways a young female and a young male process the world and respond to its challenges. Scientists at the University of Iowa have now studied more than a million children and found profound brain-development differences between males and females. In research centers in England, Norway, Canada, and elsewhere, scientists have discovered differences in parts of the brain, like the hypothalamus, that create hormone flows in males and females. For people who work in neuroscience, these revelations are the most exciting stuff in life. In the references section for this chapter, I've listed a number of book and videotape resources you can access to increase your knowledge of this research. To some extent, this research helps us relearn what our great-great-grandparents probably always knew; but there are startling new developments as well.

Here are some key biological factors we must understand about the hidden nature of males and masculinity if we are to fully parent and raise good sons. Some of these factors may even frighten you—yet I hope you'll come to agree that their presence calls for us to modify the cultural influences on our boys that hurt their moral development. And at the outset, this very powerful biological material will also explain certain things about your sons and help you understand them, in ways that perhaps you have not experienced before.

### Aggression and the Brain

The male amygdala, a primary aggression center of the brain, is larger than that of the female, and creates more active aggression in males. When this fact is applied to male hormonal and cultural life, we find a deep and basic clue as to why a boy gets involved, so much more than the female, in morally at-risk behavior—more aggressive or violent behavior, for instance. He is more likely than a girl to hit, more likely to curse or otherwise compete with or one-up another person as a way of relating.

It is important to remember that aggression and violence are *not* the same thing. Boys all over the world have larger amygdalas and show more daily physical aggression than girls, but males in Japan, for instance, are far less violent than males in America. Japanese culture focuses more heavily on making sure children are raised to be nonviolent. Tightness of living quarters in Japan necessitates more antiviolence training of males. Japan is just one of the cultures that does more than we do to recognize that male biology needs close attention, training, and certain kinds of healthy love. Innovations from other cultures will help us direct our sons' lives in the parenting plan.

### Testosterone

Progesterone is the human bonding hormone. It exists biologically to bond its host body with the infant (and with others), to whom the host is required to give care. Driven by this hormone, females are more likely to seek "bonding outcomes" in the intricacies of relationship.

The dominant male hormone, testosterone, exists in large part to compel its host body toward increased sexual copulation and aggression. Driven by testosterone, males are more likely to seek a physically or intellectually competitive experience, wherein bonds are less direct. Testosterone levels have been studied in both prison populations and CEOs of companies. In other words, the higher the testosterone level, the higher the likelihood the host will climb the corporate ladder quickly, but also the more likely he will turn violent and hurt others and the community. Testosterone leads to both triumph and trouble. The "testosterone host" needs great care in his socialization if he is to channel his aggression into socially helpful tracks.

The increased testosterone—males have up to twenty times more than females—and limited amounts of progesterone and estrogen also make it more difficult for males to feel empathy as an *initial* response to an external stimulus. Males spend more time filtering through early aggression responses; females spend more time providing immediate and thorough early empathy responses.

The consequences for moral development are compelling. If families and a culture do not train males constantly and directly toward empathic responses, the male stands a chance of not developing them to the level of functionality his culture ultimately requires. Again, we'll look at this situation in greater depth in the parenting plan.

### Hormones and Stress

The male-female differences in behavior, moral outcome, and show of empathy increase when stress is imposed. As the female stress level increases, her female hormones (like progesterone) guide her toward more direct bonding responses with friends, family, and other potential emotional allies. When she is under the stress of depression, for instance, she is more likely to *attempt* suicide as a plea for help than to succeed at it, and she is more likely to verbalize her depression to a friend or caregiver than is a male. A male is more likely to *succeed* at suicide, and less likely to call or approach a friend for emotional help.

As the male stress level increases, testosterone guides him toward less direct, immediate bonding responses and more aggressive or, at worst, antisocial or isolative responses. She tries to pull close to others; he tends to pull away. Furthermore, when he is under heavy stress, his natural hormonal inclination is to directly *increase* his aggression and thus the environmental stress he puts on others. He is ten times more likely than a female to become violent. He is more likely to use his body destructively, employing the power of his muscle mass. His response to being abused or attacked or to other emotional stress—whether it is to punch a wall or yell at another person—is more often and more likely morally frightening to his community than is a girl's.

### External Behavior and the Male Brain

Males take longer, on average, to process feelings through the brain system than females do. The male brain—the corpus callosum, the limbic system, the prefrontal lobes—is not set up as well for internalized responses as for *externalized* responses. We see the externalizing impulse of the male brain when we watch kids at play. Male play involves more rough-and-tumble, more physical action, more climbing on objects, etc. We see it also in learning environments—boys are more physically impulsive in classrooms, and in the playroom are more likely to grab blocks or other physical objects with which to play and create externalized games. Girls are more likely to pick dolls and other objects by which to develop an internal dialogue, or even monologue.

Perhaps the primary reason for this difference is that the male brain system is more spatially oriented than the female. It is more of a "hunting" brain, one that for millions of years oriented itself in the universe by somewhat lonely journeys through external space—the savannah or forest or desert—in which it pursued objects of prey. In every significant test available, boys on average score better on spatial problems—depth perception, three-dimensionality, direction—than girls. This spatial brain system compels boys to act out, in external space, their feelings and to externalize much more of their human experience.

This brain difference becomes even clearer in a boy's prepubescence and is enhanced in adolescence, requiring middle school and then high school teachers to spend a great deal of time trying to train boys in personal discipline. As puberty hits, athletic activity becomes immensely important for many boys, as they themselves try to regulate their own personal energy and compulsion toward spatial physical activity.

This "externalization of experience" has profound moral consequences. "Use your words," we tell our girls and boys. It is often easier for girls. The male brain relies on less complex responses—many of which are aggression responses, like punches, that scare others in the environment. The female's more complex verbal responses are less scary to the community, and less likely to be labeled immoral and undisciplined. Our ancestors observed these male activities and responded to them with intense moral and discipline development, something we must do now, in ways that fit our times.

### Brain Flexibility

The male brain system is less neurologically "flexible" and "adaptable" than the female. It "lateralizes" its activity more. In other words, the female brain does its tasking in more places in the brain at once than the male. For instance, when a girl is producing words, there is blood flowing and more neural firing in more parts of the brain than when a boy is producing words. Similarly, when she is taking in sounds, more of her brain lights up. She is thus more flexible and adaptable and full-brained in her responses to the world around her. He is more narrowly focused, takes in less data into less of his brain, and ends up with a nar-rower emotional, behavioral, and therefore moral range of response.

We see this activity manifest in male problem solving. He often tries to problem solve quickly rather than fully delve into the problem. He often compels himself toward a singular task response, which may take the situation to an even more tragic end, rather than patiently and adaptably following a multitask response: "That man is hurting you," he might say, "so I will go hurt him for you." The more "moral" response is often the more multitasked response. The more disciplined response is, again, often the more multitasked response—one that involves pa-tience, impulse control, even walking away from the aggression. To a great extent, males more than females must be trained by parents and communities in multitasking their responses.

### The Brain at Rest

Blood flow in the male brain, when the brain is at rest, tends to set-tle in the brainstem, or what is called the *reptilian* brain, increasing male proclivities to aggression responses. The human brain is generally divided into three parts—the reptilian brain, the limbic system, and the cerebral cortex. The reptilian brain handles things like fear responses; the limbic system handles a lot of what makes up complex emotional life; and the cortex handles much of our intellectual develop-ment. When a male is at rest—e.g., "zoning out" in front of the TV or sleeping—a large amount of blood rests in the part of the brain that manages fight-or-flight responses. The female brain, on the other hand, idles in the *cingulate gyrus,* a part of the limbic system related to emotional life and expression. When at rest, the female brain is ori-ented more toward complex emotional response. Even in resting mode, the male brain is already set up for more dangerous and impulsive responses.

## Impulse Control

The female brain produces more serotonin than the male. Serotonin is an immensely powerful brain chemical that pacifies and calms its host system. In large part, because of their decreased levels of serotonin, boys have less natural impulse control than girls. Even in utero, male fetuses are already more physically impulsive than female, kicking Mom more from inside. This lack of impulse control continues throughout the life span of the male and female—males in boyhood, adolescence, and well into adulthood are more likely to be more physically impulsive more of the time, a neurological fact that has moral consequences. The less impulse control a child has, the more chance he has of getting in trouble. Thus, clear limits and discipline become even more essential for males, as does a certain forgiveness for boisterousness.

## Mental Disease

Of particular interest to neurologists has been the fact that males suffer the majority of brain disorders and diseases that result in immoral, amoral, or undisciplined behavior. Both girls and boys get mental diseases, but males get more of them (the majority of both juvenile and adult mental patients are male); and *the male brain tends more toward diseases and neurological conditions that directly affect self-control.* Tourette's syndrome, autism, schizophrenia, psychopathology, Attention Deficit Hyperactive Disorder, drug and alcohol addiction—all of these tendencies ranging from violence to overaggression are statistically dominated by males. In 1991, a team of researchers in the U.S. discovered the "dopamine receptor" (the D2 receptor), a genetic component found in higher quantities among victims of brain and thought disorders—most of whom are male. Research involving this receptor provides some potential information on a very distinct kind of male brain fragility—one that directly affects a male's conduct and thus challenges us to pay close attention to it.

I've outlined these biological differences in a necessarily general way. Yet they do show, I hope, how important it is for a people and a culture to more thoroughly address the discipline and moral development of boys. Our boys are nothing if not morally fragile, from the inside out. And there are ways in which our boys are simply more vulnerable than girls to moral instability. To neglect this fact is to neglect our boys.

## INSIDE THE MALE MIND: THE SEARCH FOR INHERENT WORTH AND VALUE

When people spoke at the teen pregnancy conference about how confused their sons were regarding their worth as males, they were talking, without realizing it, about a biological component of male-female life that perhaps we now can understand better. Here are two mothers talking about their sons.

> *Alex is into computers right now—he's learning everything like a sponge. He's like a thirteen-year-old who's trying to be Bill Gates. He's got a poster of Bill Gates up in his room, bigger than anything else in there. I showed him in the newspaper about some of the things that Gates may have done, the business practices, the lawsuits. Alex shocked me. He said, "Hey, Mom, whatever it takes to make it."*
>
> MOTHER OF ALEX, 13

> *He always has to be the best. When he loses at soccer, he can be depressed for days. I try to explain to him that it doesn't matter, but he doesn't buy it. I think he's desperate to make something of himself and make me proud. I think he will go to any lengths to be the best.*
>
> MOTHER OF T.J., 10

At a biological and hormonal level, boys and girls do not experience the search for self-worth in exactly the same way. While there are many similarities, there is a profound difference.

The human female is geared internally toward the ultimate possibility of creating and caring for her own new self—her child. Her hormones and brain system gear her toward emotional inwardness and relational closeness. Even with girls as young as six months old, we notice them tending more toward eye contact, more toward physical touch, and, in toddler years, more toward hands-on caregiving activities with siblings and dolls. Throughout childhood, girls naturally and by socialization practice the expression of inherent worth as they develop caregiving qualities. At puberty, the female hormonal cycle begins to present the female with the inherent potential to accomplish the most concretely worthwhile act in all of life—birthing and caring for one's offspring. Every month the female is reminded of her potential to conceive, carry, and birth a child.

Males undoubtedly enjoy certain advantages in our culture. But they do not have the advantage of being born with an inherent path to self-worth. Their early brain development pushes their lives more outward into the surrounding world than inward into their emotional development. They push and prod and hit and miss their way through obstacles and challenges. They know even from the first truck they hold that they must earn their place in the world. They compete and strive and can often appear to lack basic compassion as they try to do better, gain respect, and prove their worth.

Certainly some of this behavior comes from dads, moms, and others who push boys early toward competition. But so much of it comes from within human nature. Male importance in our human species is amorphous—it exists if there is someone to protect and a danger to protect that someone from. It exists if there is meaningful work or family life to focus on. It does not exist simply because the male exists. Simply impregnating a female does not give him worth—he has to receive status from the quality of their child. If he as a male has a weakness, an infirmity, an imperfection, a disability, his path to worth is even more desperate. A male born into a human society starts out with a longer biological road toward respect than a female.

Daughters have a choice sons don't have. As females, they can decide to have a child, and upon having that child, they will find many of the forces of culture marshaled toward the care and protection of them and that child. My daughters will be generally respected as mothers, and they will be told, with good reason, that they are doing "the most important job on earth."

For the boys in my care, I see a different future. Even when they become fathers, they must continue to prove that they are successful, that they are worthy of respect, that they can "make it." They will generally need external proof, even beyond their children. This is their fate as males. It is not better or worse than a female's fate—it just is.

One of the most moving three hours I've ever spent was watching, with my wife, Gail, the film *Saving Private Ryan.* I don't think any film in the last five years has brought so many tears to my eyes. Its plot is simple—Private Ryan's three brothers have been killed in battle in the last year of World War II. Military headquarters learns of their deaths and decides the fourth son must be saved. Captain John Miller, played by Tom Hanks, sets out with a few others on orders to find Ryan in France and bring him to safety. They find Ryan but are not sure he's worth saving. Toward the end of the movie, nearly everyone in Miller's group is killed in a battle. As Captain Miller himself is dying, he manages to let young Ryan know that he must now *earn* his life by living it as proof that he was worth saving. In the final scene, when Ryan is now in his seventies and standing over Miller's grave, he says to his wife, "Tell me I've led a good life. Tell me I'm a good man." As she replies to him that he has and he is, her face belies that she is missing how crucial this statement is to him. An elderly man, Ryan knows that if he has not been good and proven his worth, then his own life and the lives of all the men who saved him have been meaningless.

And so it is to be a boy and to be a man. Nature does not provide him with a blueprint for worth. The boy and the man must be raised to see the possibility of self-worth, then meet a few others who provide the vision of a road toward it, and then spend a lifetime pursuing that worth through action and relationship. One of the greatest tragedies in human life is to be born a male and not be guided toward the value of a man.

## BOYS DEPEND ON MORAL TRAINING

Understanding male-female differences provides an answer to a question that I once heard my own mother ask a counselor when I was a teen. In Durango, Colorado, the town we lived in during my first three years of high school, I saw a counselor who captured my attention during each session by playing chess with me. While we played chess, we talked. After one such session, I went back into the lobby while he spoke with my mom. My mother was a loud talker, so even through the closed door I could hear her ask, "Do you think boys just need more discipline and moral training than girls?" I could not hear his answer. Now, after years of life and research, I've found my answer.

*Boys depend on it.*

My mother was asking the "male question" in her way in that time of her life. She was discovering the challenge that is before every one of us: *Once we truly look inside the male mind, we discover that we must, as individual family members and as a caregiving culture, spend a lot more time providing love, discipline, and moral training to our boys.* Despite the fact that boys can display wonderful moral sense, they live as males at a potential moral disadvantage of biological proportions we now can summarize.

- They often don't control impulses as well as girls, thus they are, generally, not as naturally calm as girls.
- They tend toward more severe psychiatric disorders than girls, especially disorders involving physical anger and aggression.
- They tend toward more violence-causing disorders than girls.
- They tend toward disorders that cut them off from the kind of attention span that compassion and empathy require.
- Their hormones drive them toward greater physical, mental, and moral risk taking.
- When they are traumatized or depressed, boys tend more toward angry and aggressive ways of showing it.

- They have less natural sense of their own personal worth than females do, which compels them toward higher-risk behavior as they strive to prove themselves.

In this chapter, I hope I have shown you that our boys face some major challenges, especially where moral development is concerned. In the next chapter, we'll explore how boys live out their biology in a culture that often misunderstands them, and thus misdirects or even poisons them in the same way that many forces nearly poisoned Huck Finn on his life-journey.

# Are We Protecting Our Sons from Moral Harm?

Here is a fairy tale from India that seems to me a chilling allegory of the culture in which we raise our sons.

Once upon a time, there was a kingdom ruled by a king and queen so bent on making their world perfect that they were known for unflagging energy, and they motivated their people to the same. Legend had it that in their kingdom there were two matching diamonds of such richness that possession of them would ensure the people everlasting wealth and comfort. The king and queen were determined to find these diamonds. Because of their own and their people's intense efforts, the kingdom was very rich even without the diamonds. It had all the food it needed, for the people worked very hard. It was a place of immense inventiveness and power. Its armies were the strongest in the region. As the saying went, all the boys were born with stars on their foreheads, and all the girls with the crescent moon.

But one day the children started to disappear. First one family, then another, then another woke up to find their children gone. No one could understand why. Panic set in. Everyone searched for the children. They looked in the wells, they looked in the caves, they looked in the wilderness, where the animals were. The king and the queen themselves lost their two children, two young boys. Night after night, no one slept, keeping watch over their children. But the children would just disappear right in front of loving mothers and angry fathers and terrified siblings and startled aunties and grandparents.

As the population of children waned, the king and the queen ordered that everyone have more. The queen took over the sole rule of the realm while the king went to the high mountain, where the great Brahman was, to get advice. His journey took many days, and in tears he prostrated himself in front of the Brahman. "What have we done wrong?" he cried. "We have followed all of our dreams and found the good life. Why, now, when all was going so well, do the gods take our children? And what shall we do?"

The Brahman replied, "You are the victims of dark magic of your own making. Now a huge and invisible giant has descended on your kingdom. This giant eats only children. As the children go down the giant's gullet, they disappear. This is why you have watched them disappear before your eyes."

"Tell me what we must do to get rid of this giant," the king implored.

"You must forget your greed for perfection, and listen to your children."

"To what do you refer?" the king insisted. "I don't understand."

"Until you do," the Brahman replied, "you will keep losing your children."

"But we do listen to our children. We do all our work for them, to give them a perfect world."

"Listen better. Listen to their whispers."

Depressed and angry, the king did his ablutions and paid the Brahman gifts and returned with his entourage to the kingdom.

That night he had a startling dream. He stood with his two vanished sons and with the queen at the mouth of a cave. A huge giant sat behind the boys, ready to eat them. The king and queen were frozen. They watched their sons being gobbled up. Then the giant disappeared. In the spots where the boys were, the king and queen saw two glistening diamonds. They recognized them immediately as the diamonds legend had spoken of. These were as big as human beings, and perfect in light and design.

The king felt propelled toward them and began to move from his place to covet them. The queen cried out, "No! These are poison. Don't touch them." She ran to the side of the cave, where she found a stick. As she raised it to bash in the stones, the king did not worry, for what could a stick do against the hardness of perfect diamonds?

To his immense surprise, her first blow shattered one diamond, and her second the other. In their place reappeared the two sons.

The king awoke the next morning and understood what had to be done. As with most fairy tales, this one ends happily. As the king and queen spoke to the people of what they had learned, the people again turned to their children for their greatest sustenance. A trance seemed to lift from them, and their lost children returned. Life was good again—though not perfect as a jewel.

I often think of this story from India, where I lived as a boy. It makes me recognize that we have created a culture that, for all its innovations and luxuries, is also like a giant eating its children. In the Introduction we looked statistically at some of the crises our boys face. In this chapter we will explore in family stories how our culture presently eats our sons—does moral harm to them. Let's always remember that though we study boys in *The Good Son,* we know that when one child is feeling lost, so are all others; as the giant eats our sons, it eats our daughters.

## THE NOWHERE MEN

I recently visited a coed high school, where I spoke with boys in a general assembly. I asked the boys if they were men. They raucously yelled that they were. But when we became more serious, a number of them raised their hands to say they did not know what a man was. I asked them how they were going to become men. Some said, "By working hard," others, "By going to college," others, "By having a family." Most of the boys had no clear answer. They had, mainly, hope, as most young people do, but they could not articulate purpose in their lives.

I pointed this out to them, and re-created for them the lyrics to some songs—one an old Beatles tune, "Nowhere Man." In it is man's search for meaning, and the sadness of not finding it. I asked the boys to tell me if what I was about to say felt true to them. I told them I considered it one of the most important moral truths I have learned about male development: *If not before, then at least by the time he's about sixteen, a boy needs to become clear on fundamental principles of his own life-quest.* If he does not do this, he will wander unhappily for many decades through an unforgiving society. He will be a nowhere man, never content that he is worthwhile in the world.

"To become a man," I continued, "you must live your life as a quest for truth. You will know you're at the threshold of becoming a man when you realize you are now living your life as this search for truth. To be a man, you have to live your life like a mission.

"Do you do things just to get people's approval, or do you do them because your soul tells you to? Are you alive, or are you pretending to be alive? Are you ready to make a long, hard journey toward the adult's table, or are you so afraid of failure you hide your soul in inappropriate behaviors? Do you live every moment of your life as though it were a mission? And can you talk to people about the mission you're on—can you *show* them who you are and get their help?

"When you can answer these questions in ways that inspire you to be the most compassionate person you can be, that's when you'll know you're a man.

"Now," I challenged the 750 boys, "raise your hand if you know you are living truthfully. Raise your hand if you're on a life-quest you can articulate. You're in high school, so you don't have to have arrived at the adult's table yet, but are you on a man's quest toward it?"

About thirty hands were raised, then a few more, tentative, hesitant, then a few more. Perhaps fifty hands were raised in all. One of the raised hands belonged to Keith, a wide-eyed, blond-haired junior who told his story, quite passionately. Many of his classmates already knew it.

He had gotten a girl pregnant when he was fifteen. A little boy had been born three months ago. Keith and his girlfriend were not married but lived with her family above the garage of their home. He and the girl both were going to high school. Keith worked twenty hours a week at his "father-in-law's" construction company while maintaining passing grades.

"What are the truths you are living?" I asked him. "What is the quest you are on?"

"I live to do the right thing for my boy, no matter what," he replied. "I'll never give up on that dream. Even if it means I can't have a life like these others guys can have, with like all the freedom and stuff, I'll never give up doing what I have to do for my son. He's everything to me. He's made me into a man."

There was a brief hush among the 750 boys. The boys could see that Keith had a mission on which his life was hinged.

I asked the rest of the boys if they helped Keith on his quest. Not a single hand was raised.

Embarrassed, Keith said, "My best friend isn't here today, he's sick. But lots of these guys help." And yet we all could feel how Keith was different from so many of the boys around him. They were boys, and he was a half-man—they had other things they cared about rather than helping to nurture a new life.

"One of the best ways to become a man," I said, "is to start out by helping another man on his quest."

In this group of boys, as in so many, I experienced both the exhilaration of opening boys' eyes to greater truths and the deep sadness of looking into the eyes of hundreds of mainly decent boys who live in a cultural framework that does not spur them toward meaning and purpose. Many of the boys came up to me after the lecture and said no one had ever talked to them that way.

While no one hopes for their son the hard life Keith has, one does hope that a son reaches the end of high school with a sense of life-purpose. Why must a middle-teen boy experience the kind of immensely difficult life-circumstance Keith faces in order to focus on questions of purpose and personal truth?

## MARK: WHAT ARE THE TEN COMMANDMENTS?

"What does it mean to be a good?" I asked Mark. He was a month shy of fourteen. He had become a significant discipline problem by his seventh-grade year. School counseling, the principal's office, the loss of privileges at home—these and lots of other options had been tried.

"A good boy is someone who does what people say," Mark offered. I knew he didn't really believe this. His demeanor was oppositional, and his answer fit the moral development of a six-year-old. Twelve-year-olds think about morality and good behavior in much more subtle ways.

"What else?" I asked.

He tried out defiance on me. "A good *boy* is like a teacher's pet."

We went on this way for a little while. Finally, I changed tactics. "Is that the best you've got?" I goaded him. Sometimes young guys like Mark remind me of hostile witnesses.

"What do you mean?"

"I didn't ask what a good boy is. I asked what *good* means. What does it mean to be good?"

"Just, like, good, huh? You think I'm gonna just tell you what good means, like it's a quiz?"

"If you were king of the world, how would you tell people they should be 'good'?"

He frowned. He didn't really want to engage with me, but he liked the word game and he was a little curious to see where it went. "Like, you help people, I guess, or like, the Ten Commandments."

"The Ten Commandments," I repeated, nodding. "Okay. So, what are the Ten Commandments?"

"Don't kill, don't steal, don't . . . you know . . . adultery."

"What else?"

He paused in thought. "I don't know. I forget 'em." He said this with nonchalance, but in his deep brown eyes and beneath his buzz cut, I saw something more vulnerable.

"You knew them once, right? Your mom took you to church? You memorized them in Sunday school?"

"Who knows?" He frowned. "Maybe."

"How about the Golden Rule? You know what that is?"

"Yeah. Do to others what you want them to do to you."

"You believe that rule is a good one?"

"Sometimes."

"Sometimes," I repeated, nodding. "So, what else is 'good'? If you were king of the world. Teach me something."

"What else is good? I don't know. You tell me."

I steered back to the commandments, wondering something suddenly. Was it possible that Mark wasn't just being oppositional? Was it possible that he truly didn't have a clear internal compass for goodness? Was it possible he was truly unable to articulate what morality is?

"I don't know all the commandments by heart myself," I said, "but I can answer the question about what's good. You wanna know what I think 'good' is?"

"You're gonna tell me."

"Being fair, being kind, being helpful, being loyal, being honest, cooperating, controlling myself. These things are good."

Though he carried on his face the frown of his age and temperament, he also carried behind his eyes the brightness of his own mind. He was thinking as I talked.

"Ask me if it makes me feel good to be helpful, loyal, kind, and all that. Ask me if it makes me feel good," I continued.

He paused a moment, resisting, then said, "Okay, does it make you feel good?"

"Lots of the time it doesn't. But so what? I do it anyway. You know why?"

"Yeah, why?"

"Because it's right and I know it. It doesn't matter how it makes me feel to do them. I don't do them because they make me *feel* good. I do them because they're just *good* and I know they're good, and the thing I hate the most is when I do things that go against what I think is good."

He shook his head, a little engaged now. "There's no way. You're just saying that to, like, be Mr. Saint or something."

To Mark, something was "good" because it felt good; to do it just because it was the right thing to do was not normal. Though in other parts of his life he already could do some abstract thinking, he couldn't on moral and character issues.

"You know what character is?" I asked.

He shrugged.

"Your character is doing things right just because they're right. You think you've got much character? You think your character is pretty strong?"

"I don't know. I'm all right," he said.

"Does your mom think so?"

"Probably not."

"What about your dad?"

"Him neither."

"Do you think you have a strong character?"

One should never be surprised by the sudden honesties of adolescent boys. He thought a moment and said, "Nah, I guess not. Whatever."

I let there be some silence between us, then I shook my head at him. "Actually, I think you do, but I don't think you really know what good character is. You're fourteen years old, and you don't really have words for the rules you have to live by. You need to act a certain way, and you don't even know what that way is. No wonder you act like a nut.

"So, here's what I want to do. I don't want to nag at you about your misbehavior for the whole next month. All I want is for you and me to debate which of the Ten Commandments you think are good ones and why. You want to do that?"

He wasn't sure what to make of me, but he liked the idea better than the alternatives. I informed his family of my idea and asked them to hold off on coming back as a family for a month. Mark and I did indeed carry on discussions about each of the Ten Commandments, then the Sermon on the Mount, the Buddhist Sutras, and other basic rule-texts.

What caused the subsequent improvement in his behavior at home and at school? I don't really know. But fully engaging his mind in his own moral development played an important part.

I worked with Mark many years ago, and since then I have looked into the eyes of many boys capable of basic decency but who haven't, *in a concerted, planned effort by their parents and others,* been trained in the nature and articulation of decency. Mark's parents were good people but not inclined toward a religious doctrine, nor to a nonreligious substitute for moral and spiritual direction. Mark's peers and media were not high-level moral thinkers—in fact, just the opposite: Mark and his peers were heavily involved in video games and amoral television programs. Mark had gone nearly to middle adolescence without being nurtured in the basics of his own humanity. Why wouldn't he be a discipline problem? He was begging, through his discipline issues, to be granted a character by his caregivers, and to be taught what that character was and what it should be.

Just as the boys at the high school could not articulate what quest they were on, so many of our boys are not capable of age-appropriate moral thinking. All of us are to blame. Boys need constant contact with moral principles. They need these as foundations for both moral agreement and moral rebellion. As boys begin adolescence, as early as nine years old, they need moral debate and the increased sophistication of moral logic.

They receive far too little of this stimulation in our culture, and act out in search of it. The number of Marks out there is staggering. A helpful exercise is to sit down with a twelve- to fourteen-year-old and ask him questions about morality, engage him in debates. You may find that he is unable to describe morality with the clarity or articulateness that you know he should have.

## JONATHAN AND HIS FRIENDS:
## STRAIN ON THE MOTHER-SON BOND

Jonathan, at thirteen, was lean and sinewy, almost skinny, just starting an adolescent growth spurt. His smile started as one of sweet innocence but slowly broadened into a huge smirk, as if he'd decided he didn't really care what anyone thinks. His smile belied the fact that he had suffered a terrible tragedy. Jonathan's mother had died in a car accident eighteen months before. Up to her death, he had given no one a problem. Her death prompted a sea change in his life and in his behavior. He became a brutal young man.

"I beat the kid up because he dissed me in front of a girl," he told me. "He deserved worse."

Jonathan was disruptive, cursed at his teachers, and had been in detention twenty-five times in a few months. He called two girls bitches in front of the principal, finally prompting his fourth and last disciplinary hearing, at which Jonathan's father begged the principal to give his boy another chance. The principal felt sympathy but had no choice but to send Jonathan to an alternative school. There was little any of us could do by talking with Jonathan. He needed more serious help.

Jonathan's moral turnaround had a very obvious and overtly tragic cause—the *complete* loss of the mother-son bond in the boy's life. While Jonathan's dramatic circumstances are generally rare in the lives of modern boys, the strain on the mother-son bond is, unfortunately, quite common. The effect of the strain on the bond often can be measured by the extent of moral difficulties in the boy experiencing it.

Most boys lose their mothers not because of death but because the importance of the mother-son bond has been gradually diminishing in our culture, and thus in the home. Pressures on contemporary mothers are such that many mothers can't mother their sons as they wish and need to. Similar pressures have for years frayed the father-son bond, as we will explore in the next section.

As mothers spend less time with infants and toddlers especially, the boys' developing brains, and thus their behavioral systems, are affected. Over the last decade, researchers of parent-infant attachment have discovered that infant and early toddler brain development occurs more rapidly and more completely the more intensely bonded the child is with his primary caregivers. So, for instance, the greater a boy's bond with his caregivers, the more neural development can occur in the limbic system and other emotional centers of the brain.

One of the most clear neural disadvantages of contemporary culture is that we—especially our moms, who are generally the primary caregivers—often do not *hold* our babies as much as they need to be held. Our mothers and other primary caregivers do not have as much opportunity to *carry* our babies on our bodies as our ancestors did. Your ancestor would put her baby against her body while she gathered food, tended the field, went to the market, or worked at home. In ancient times, mothers went back to work right after giving birth, but they did not lose attachment to their children because they carried the children *on their bodies*. Moms today are not acculturated to do so, and often, for reasons of workplace practicality, cannot.

The "non-holding" problem can continue in child care settings if the infant-care personnel changes every few weeks or months. The mother-substitute caregiver doesn't bond with the baby and thus does not hold the baby much throughout the day. Yet that bonding process is worth a thousand pounds of later moral training or environmental influence. If the infant boy is raised in an environment of secure and loving physical attachment during the first one to two years of his life, he starts out on the path of good discipline and moral life. If he does not, he is more likely to start out on a path of later narcissism and out-of-control behavior as he compensates for his early deprivation. Studies show that a high proportion of our troubled adults, criminals, and antisocial individuals are males who did not bond well with their primary caregivers early in their lives. *Becoming Attached,* by Robert Karen, is a gold mine of information in this regard, and we will go more deeply into this issue in chapter 3.

As the parenting plan develops in the next nine chapters, we will address issues of mother-son bonding from birth all the way to age eighteen, and suggest specific ways to handle strains on the mother-son bond. Here are just a few of the strains we will be cognizant of.

- We have not realized how immensely attached boys are to their mothers—even adolescent boys—because we have mistaken boys' fierce or sullen attitudes for their true feelings. In our inability to see through our sons' masks, we have not noticed that much of our sons' misbehavior is often a response to feelings they have regarding a perceived lack of their mothers' love, approval, or respect. I continually see boys, condemned as discipline problems, who are in fact afraid of their mothers dying, or not loving them, or abandoning them. We exacerbate a boy's pain and his acting out by neglecting how primal and fragile is his bond with his mother.

- Our culture has not done well at educating mothers, fathers, and other caregivers on the neurological and hormonal development of their children, so they in turn don't know what is required of them to be good caregivers. In the area of boys' development, we have been especially circumspect in providing mothers and other caregivers with help.

- While adolescent boys have always hassled other boys about hugging and being loving to their mothers in public, studies at Harvard University argue that the "You're a sissy" acculturation may be pulling our sons farther away from mothers than is healthy, and starting the mother-son psychological separation earlier than many boys are ready for it.

- Boys are increasingly getting away with disrespecting their mothers—cursing at them, yelling at them, hitting them, calling them names in public. While a little of this kind of "dissing" is within the range of normal mother-son argument, the extent to which families are now allowing boys to get away with put-downs of mothers and women is dangerous not only to the self-esteem of women but also to the ultimate respect boys and men have for their loved ones. The disrespect we are allowing in our families is only encouraged by jokes, television shows, and movies that put mothers and women down.

- We have stripped extended family and other support systems from mothers' lives, often compelling a mother to take on, alone, the raising of a number of children when she alone cannot bond adequately with all of them.

Whether a mother feels her bond with her son has diminished because of strains on him or on her, the whole human community needs to pay attention to those strains. Jonathan had no choice in his separation from his mother—she died, and he was left feeling lost, which he acted out severely. Most boys do not face the extreme strain he faced, and they and their families have choices.

We begin our focus on the importance of mother-son and father-son bonds in the parenting plan with the idea that neglect of the primacy of the mother-son bond is equivalent to the invisible giant of the fable eating our children.

## GRANT, LES, AND TOMMY: THE TRAGIC LOSS OF THE FATHER

Grant, twelve, came to me as angry as a boy could be. He had discipline problems at home and at school. He lost his temper constantly. "I know there's an angel hiding in there," his mother said, "but all I see these days is the devil." A year before, Grant's parents had divorced and his father moved out. Grant was at perhaps the most emotionally and morally fragile period in his life, and he had been abandoned by the man whom he had assumed, in his deepest soul, would make him into a man.

Les, ten, was brought in after three shoplifting attempts, each of which he'd been caught for. He'd been detained overnight for the last one. Les already had been kicked out of one school. Just after Les's ninth birthday, his father had been arrested and jailed. His mother worked constantly and couldn't supervise him much. Les would be in juvie lockup by the time he was twelve—I was sadly sure of that. There was little I could do for him except try to find the right hard-edged program for him.

Tommy, fourteen, was already a gang-banger. He and most of his friends were in a gang. His truancy from school got him kicked out. One teacher had made some headway with him, but that teacher had transferred out to another city. Tommy had never lived with his father. His mother was raising three children by three separate men. None of these men stuck around.

Just as much as our diminishment of the mother-son bond is creating crisis for our boys and men, so too is the loss of the father-son bond.

According to numerous studies over the last decade, including the most recent one out of the Department of Justice, one of the most clearly definable causes of boys' acting out morally and antisocially is the lack of intimate relationships with their fathers. When I worked in the prison system, I did not need real insight to notice that nearly all of the inmates had been raised, at some point, without their fathers. One police lieutenant put the problem in these words: "On any given day, if we just poll the boys and men in our jails and in our prison cells, we'll find almost none had a father around."

Our boys need men for biological reasons as much as cultural ones. They need people of their own biology to help them control and cope with their inherent urges and drives. They need men to help them understand by example how a man is different from a boy.

Yet our culture systematically removes fathers from the lives of their sons.

- We have increased, especially with the prevalence of divorce, "parental competition" between mothers and fathers—many sons lose their fathers or see them only a few days a month, and many others grow up hearing how terrible fathers and men are.

- We have spent a few centuries, especially since the Industrial Revolution, pulling men's work so far away from sons' lives that the boys can barely model their own life-missions from their fathers.

- We have attached men's self-images to jobs that do not sustain them spiritually. Fathers pass on this lack of soul to sons (and daughters).

- We have created a society of male sports and entertainment figures who do not understand that it is every man's job to be a good role model.

- We have diminished the importance of the male mentor in the lives of boys so that many fatherless boys also do not have substitute fathers.

- We have diminished the importance of "male kinship systems"—male-male friendship groups and extended-family bonds—which help men deal with life problems and be better husbands and fathers.

- In jokes, television shows, movies, and even greeting cards, we have male-bashed for so long that many young males believe that men are not necessary—a message that leads boys to grow up with the sense that they themselves, as males, are failures-in-waiting, "just like dad."

Not every boy raised without a father acts out severely. Many other factors matter. But many boys do experience an increase in immoral behavior in the wake of losing a father, and the fault lies initially not with the boy but the fatherless environment he lives in.

## BRANDON: THE GRADUAL LOSS OF THE EXTENDED FAMILY

At nine, Brandon lost his father to a terrible car accident in which his mother was left paralyzed from the waist down. By the time he was twelve, Brandon's mother had begun to have serious mental problems—not only severe depression but also Alzheimer-like symptoms caused by scar tissue in the brain. Brandon had a sister, Holly, and an adopted brother, José. He became the de facto parent to these children until one day when a concerned teacher came to the house, found the door open, walked in, and discovered feces in a corner, the children malnourished, and José wailing, uncared for, after a fall down a flight of stairs.

The family was divided up and put into foster care. I heard about Brandon from a social worker, who told me about Brandon's perseverance in trying to get relatives to help him and his siblings. He called an aunt, he called cousins, he called grandparents. None came forth. The social worker, after hearing his story, called some of these relatives herself. Brandon, it seemed, had not explained to them how grave the situation was, perhaps being typically "strong," as many young males will pretend to be. Nonetheless, *even when the relatives had heard the full story, none came forward to adopt their own blood children.*

"It wasn't that these people didn't care about this family," my friend, near tears, remembered. "I could tell they did. But each of them had issues of their own, and none of them really had the time."

*None of them really had the time.* The words echoed in my mind. I myself had a client-family in which the fourteen-year-old son had gotten into drugs and needed an intimate, stable family situation. The best thing for him was to get away from his street friends and live in another city with people who cared about him. He had relatives all over the U.S., but none quite as appropriate as his grandparents, who lived two states away. He liked these grandparents more than any of the relatives, and when he finally agreed that they would be his best bet, not only did his parents and counselors ask for their help, but so did the boy himself.

Their answer was no. They were afraid the boy would bring trouble to their house. And they were not ready to give up their freedom to raise an adolescent. "He's not our responsibility," the grandfather said, "he's his family's."

So many grandparents and relatives these days are taking care of their children's children. Brandon's story and my client's story do not necessarily reflect the majority of cases. Yet they open a doorway to a crisis in our culture—the loss of the extended family that used to surround and protect our kids. Grandparents did not used to think of themselves as separate from "his family." They thought of themselves as family.

Our children often live far away from their own grandparents and relatives; family feuds often dispel extended family support; extended family members feel that each branch of a family should be "indepen-dent," as did my client's grandfather; and people in families have other time, space, and financial priorities than the giving of care and com-passion.

Our children are losing the human tribe that children have counted on since the beginning of humanity. Given our sons' biochemistry and neurology, the moral consequences of this loss are particularly severe—without the strength, character-building, and emotional safety of an ex-tended family, boys are more likely to form substitute gangs or peer "families" of their own. These peer families, who get their sustenance mainly from popular culture and peer direction, provide immensely in-complete moral guidance and emotional care.

When we combine a boy's loss of extended family with an absent father and an overworked, somewhat absent mother, the boy's isolation increases all the more. This morally and emotionally fragile child, who needs more bonding rather than less, more emotional and moral direc-tion rather than less, ends up with a hole inside him that has been dug by the very people who brought him into the world.

Cultures can eat their children by robbing them of lives of meaning, by deleting moral guidelines from their development, and by pulling mother, father, and extended family farther and farther away from them. All of these stunt a child's growth. In the case of males, all of them add to the male's lowered self-worth, ambiguity about how to be a self-disciplined man, and moral incompetence.

And there is another, very painful way we are betraying our own male children. When added to what we've already discussed, the be-trayal becomes even more compelling.

## WHEN THE MEDIA POISONS OUR BOYS

My wife and I walked up to the line outside the movie theater. *Saving Pri-vate Ryan* and *Blade* were playing. We were standing in the *Ryan* line.

Ahead of us stood a young man and woman, both about twenty-one, who held the hand of a three-year-old boy and asked for three tickets to *Saving Private Ryan.* Standing in the line for *Blade* were a woman of about eighteen and two young men, about twenty-two and twenty-five, who accompanied a five-year-old boy. My wife, Gail, and I both have worried so often when we see adults taking children to violent, gory movies. Standing in the movie line this particular night, we felt like this time was the last straw.

Once we got inside, Gail and I walked up to the manager and asked if she knew that a three-year-old boy was being taken into the realistically violent *Ryan,* and a five-year-old into the gory horror film *Blade.* She said she knew, and she agreed that it was terrible, but she said, "I've seen a lot worse. And if one of the people is over twenty-one, they can bring in any age kid. Our hands are tied."

Studies show overwhelmingly that visual media is potentially toxic to the developing child.

- If overused, visual media stimulants remove the child from reading, socializing, and other activities that develop his brain more fully than visual stimulants.

- Violent imagery "imprints" on the growing brain, causing everything from nightmares and phobias to desensitization and dehumanization of the developing male.

- Violent imagery can directly increase violent behavior among young males.

- Inappropriate sexual imagery sexualizes children earlier than they are developmentally ready. Some highly sexualized males show symptoms of sexual abuse, which include higher-than-normal incidences of sexual aggression toward females, and depression.

The young parents or guardians in those movies that night were either ignorant or selfish—it is hard to avoid being that blunt. Where did their ignorance or selfishness come from? From a culture such as our own that does not fully understand how the developing male brain works and how all stimulants can affect it. Even more than that, the ignorance and selfishness come from a culture that systematically poisons its children's minds so that adults can be entertained.

Recently, when I've seen adults take little kids into inappropriate movies, I've started confronting them, which is a very uncomfortable thing to do. The adults get defensive, just as I would if a stranger criticized my parenting at a movie theater. But on a night like that one, not to go up to the parents felt like an abandonment of my community responsibility. When I spoke with the young parents of the three-year-old going into *Ryan,* the young man told me in no uncertain terms to get out of his face. I said my piece and walked away, but sat near enough to tacitly observe the boy during the movie. He hid his face some of the time, stared blankly at other times, cried some of the time, and used the rest room a number of times. Gail told me after the movie that some of her own tears during the film were not only for *Ryan* but for the terror that the boy was put through.

Our children need protection from the nearly 100,000 violent images they will see in the media before they are eighteen. Because of the testosterone level in and spatial formatting of the male brain, males are more attracted than females to violent imagery. Males likewise have more trouble controlling violent impulses—which is even more reason for us to come to a better understanding of how the media affects little boys. Our culture profits immensely from betraying the development of its sons; its major storytellers do not spend enough time caring for our young in the stories they provide. Quite often they do just the opposite: they seek to exploit immoral impulses rather than promote healthy development. This exploitation wouldn't be a problem if the creators of media stories were like problematic relatives who lived far away and rarely saw our kids. But they are not—they have constant access to our children.

Our vigilance needs to extend to the sexualizing of our boys. According to the National Campaign to Stop Teen Pregnancy, 89 percent of sexual imagery in the media occurs without *consequence* of sexual activity shown. Our boys are absorbing 80,000 sexual images in the media by the time they hit puberty. Depending on where the boy is in his development, those images can be confusing enough to be considered dangerous. A seven-year-old boy's hearing about oral sex on television and trying to understand it is developmentally inappropriate. Sex, sexual pleasure, sexual intention, and the logistics of that sex act compel his brain to try to develop images and ideas that overstimulate him. The early sexualization is the very thing we do *not* want, especially given male biology, which is naturally sexualized enough. As we oversexualize it, we create a culture in which, once again, our sons are betrayed—they are set up for the kind of moral failure that inappropriate sexual behavior causes.

The Good Son Parenting Plan will provide suggested media use parameters for each year of a boy's development, and will be specific about how much time a boy may be exposed to video games, movies, cartoons, and other media. I invite you to modify it to fit your intuitions.

## THE MECHANIZATION OF BOYHOOD

Parents and teachers wonder what effect the Internet is having on our boys. Our culture's mechanization of our sons continues relatively unabated, as boys spend as much as five to seven hours a day in front of various screens. Robert Kraut, a social psychology professor at Carnegie Mellon University, recently published a landmark study showing that even though Internet connections between kids and others should "bring the world and bring people closer together," in fact, long-term Internet users feel more depressed and lonely, and their feelings of loneliness and depression escalate with their increase in time spent online.

"We were expecting exactly the opposite," Kraut said. He had expected that the more time people communicate via e-mail and chat rooms, the more they'd feel "together." Having studied his results, he sees now that *prolonged* use of the Internet leaves less time to relate to real people, family, and close friends. The energy of human love that transpires in a person's development cannot be supplied by machines, especially among children.

"People are substituting weaker social ties for stronger ones," according to Kraut. "They're substituting conversations on narrower topics with strangers for conversations with people who are connected to their life."

I've often heard parents say, "My son is so focused on his computer," or, "My son just seems addicted to his Tamagotchi," or, "My son is so bonded with his Game Boy, it's like an extension of him." Their language inadvertently reveals the truth. More and more of our boys are becoming addicted to television, video games, and the Internet. Jane Healy's *Failure to Connect* and Gloria DeGaetano's *Screen Smarts* are wonderful analyses of this problem. Many of our boys simply are not learning to read or relate to others at appropriate developmental levels because of their extended use of visual media.

And the trend toward the mechanization of boyhood extends into benign toys. More and more toys are being developed in which mechanical relationships connect children to the toy—a talking Winnie-the-Pooh, for instance, in which the child relates to a mechanical toy instead of verbalizing more with other children or adults. The kind of talk he develops with the toy is unsophisticated compared to the kind he developes relating to an adult or other living child. Does the talking Pooh hurt the boy? On the surface, no. Yet taken cumulatively with other mechanical toys and computer and television, it is one more mechanical object with which the boy "bonds" as a substitute for humans and other living beings.

Of course, anti-Internet or anti-TV zealotry ends up "turning off" our children. But in the Good Son Parenting Plan, we will err on the side of caution. My fundamental belief is that the moral development of our sons, especially our boys younger than age eight, depends to a great extent on our protecting them from inappropriate use of story-making machines and technology. Little moral development transpires through machines—moral development is a human occupation.

## THE MORAL NATURE OF BOYS

Our children's minds are fragile. Our boys often armor up as quickly as they can—their bodies look armored with the muscles that grow in adolescence, their emotions seem armored as they gradually use fewer words and more grunts—but they remain very fragile creatures. Thinking our boys are tough as nails, we believe they can take anything. We bring them into violent films at three years old; we mechanize them as early as possible; and we pretend they should be strong when they need to be weak.

Psychologist William Pollack, author of *Real Boys,* has a powerful phrase: "If we don't let our boys cry tears, they'll cry bullets." In understanding the fragility of our sons, Pollack recognizes also how they often respond to their own fragility—by hurting themselves and other people, even the people they most dearly love.

As we turn in the next chapters toward the practical work of raising boys into men, we must do so with the awareness that some of what our culture has done to raise sons will continue to work well, but some will not. Each of us may need to make changes in parenting philosophies. And we certainly will need to become advocates for boys in the larger culture. In order to provide the kinds of love and attention that boys need for happiness, we may have to alter long-held assumptions.

Before we move forward into the practical shaping of our sons' lives, let's summarize some of the keys to a boy's moral life.

- Boys and girls both want to be good, but boys more often need direct guidance in learning how to articulate and understand what "good" means.

- Boys whose nature is poorly guided during childhood are more likely than similarly neglected girls to hurt other people directly during boyhood and adolescence.

- There are very deep ways in which boys do not feel they have inborn self-worth and thus need help both in directing themselves to it and in avoiding unnecessarily dangerous and immoral paths to self-esteem.

- Boys get unfairly labeled as morally defective, hyperactive, undisciplined, or "problem children," when quite often the problem is not with the boys but with the families, extended families, or social environments, which do not understand their specific needs as human beings and as boys.

- Boys possess a natural aggressiveness which can be very nurturing of others but which often is misunderstood.
- There is a lot of unseen tenderness and compassion in each boy that is often very well hidden—the boy's moral development depends on our understanding and bringing it out into the open.

## GOOD SON PARENTING PRINCIPLES

The Good Son Parenting Plan comprises the next nine chapters of this book. Its spirit is captured, I hope, in Will Rogers's words: "Most of the time, things go better when you've got a plan."

This plan is based on the following philosophical principles.

1. Family closeness is the best way through which to raise moral, well-disciplined, and happy children.

2. Closeness must always be the first priority of the family except in profoundly unusual circumstances.

3. Much of what works for parenting boys can work for girls, yet some aspects of parenting will be very different for both sexes.

4. Wisdom about parenting can come from traditionalism and feminism, developmental psychology and religion, conservatism and liberalism, American culture and many others from around the world. Parenting is not an exact science; rather, it is an accumulation of personal instincts and social guidance adapted to fit the needs of growing children and applied consistently.

5. Boys want and need more structure, discipline, guidance, and training than our present families and culture give them.

The parenting plan you are about to begin will challenge, I hope, your finest gifts as a parent and human being. In so doing, it should bring you closer to your son, and bring your son closer to understanding himself as the "good son."

# Part Two:

**NURTURING THE EARLY**

**YEARS OF A BOY'S**

**MORAL DEVELOPMENT**

The Age of Obedience
(Birth to Six Years Old)

# THREE

# Infancy

NURTURING BOYS FROM BIRTH

TO EIGHTEEN MONTHS

I n Turkey, where my wife and I lived for two years, there is a saying: "You are not an adult until you have a child." Rather than seeing this statement as a judgment about the maturity of people without children, I understand it to mean that there are certain feelings in the soul that are reserved for children. You have felt those emotions as you gave birth to your son or in some other way received the boy who is now in your care.

As you gaze at the newborn boy, you embark on a sweet, spirited, rewarding journey. You need that boy, and he needs you. As writer Anthony Brandt has put it, "Other things may change, but we all begin and end with the family." The emotion of need for the child is very deep, and somehow different from any other. You have been dreaming about his existence for years, perhaps, and you have been planning his birth for months. The whole world changes its complexion during your pregnancy. Things take on more meaning. You become both afraid of responsibility and elated to feel fully alive. Perhaps you don't know the sex of the child until it is born, but then the "it" becomes a "he," and you stare down at your fragile son.

Every boy is like little Moses, who was adrift in the chaos of the river but, once taken up by friendly hands, welcomed the beginning of growth, direction, and tranquillity. Until he got older and sought the new chaos of his destiny, what he needed was order, as does your son, the kind of order that intuitive human love brings to any baby.

## YOUR SON'S FIRST DEVELOPMENTAL EPISODE: AN OVERVIEW

Child development is divided into three primary developmental episodes.

Birth to six

Seven to twelve

Thirteen to eighteen

These divisions occur because human development has distinctly different neurological, biochemical, psychological, and sociological episodes. It is useful for parents to have not only a year-by-year picture of their son's growth but also a "big picture" of the whole episode, so that they can guide their boy with the larger developmental picture in mind.

Because infancy happens within the larger context of the first developmental episode of human life—birth to six—let's focus on the six-year picture for a moment. In chapter 6, which begins the second developmental episode, and chapter 9, which begins the third, we will focus on those "big pictures" as well.

### He Is a Spiritual Embryo

Think about the young boy in his first years of life as a "spiritual embryo." This phrase was coined by Maria Montessori, one of this century's most gifted developmental psychologists. "Humans have two embryonic periods," she said. "One is prenatal like that of the animals; the other is postnatal and only humans have this one." Our infants are the most physically and psychologically delicate of the primate infants, needing more love and attention than any other to fully develop their brains.

### His Biggest Task

Probably the biggest task of the first phase of human life is to develop a distinct personality. Some of a boy's personality is set genetically. "He's just like his dad," we may say, or, "He's just like his mom." We're right. He is a lot like us, and that's how he was born.

Some of his personality is determined genetically by his gender. "He's so boyish!" we'll say. We're right. He is definitely male. Just as he won't be an exact copy of Mom or Dad, he won't be an exact copy of some stereotype of "a boy." But by the time he is six, we'll see pretty clearly that he's a lot like the other boys around, because of his biology and male brain system, as well as his socialization through imitation.

### He Learns by Imitation

Some of his personality will emerge as an imitation of his parents, nearby family, and larger culture. He's so malleable right now that any powerful presence can dramatically influence him. We see this influence in the way he copies even someone he just met. One mom told me about her two-year-old son who met his grandfather for the first time. His grandfather tended to wear "high-water" pants (pant legs high up on the ankles). The little boy followed him around the house hiking up his own pant legs to mirror Grandpa's. We see it also in the way a boy who has just watched a violent TV program goes out and hits someone in the exact same way the character in the program hit his opponent. The boy tries lots of things on for size in his daily life. While the flesh and bone of his personality is coded in his DNA, the costume and confidence he'll wear is very much a result of his learning by imitation.

### He Is a Literal Thinker

Once we can start noticing him think, a little boy will appear to do so very literally. If he learns that a big, white-haired man comes down the chimney at Christmas, the boy absolutely believes that's what happens. If there is a piece of cake on the counter and the boy wants the cake, he goes for it. He sees no reason to delay his gratification, especially in his first two years. Since this boy explores the world primarily through his *senses,* he believes what his senses tell him. He doesn't think out whether God exists. If he hears that God exists, then God does exist. If he is told that God is "in everything," he sees God in everything. The child does not make many judgments. The child absorbs like a sponge; he has few filters.

### He Is Delicate and Fragile

We have a tendency to prematurely believe our little boy is tougher than our little girl. Parents unconsciously breast-feed, hold, and cuddle infant boys less than girls. Because studies now indicate that our infant boys (and our grown males, too) are in some ways psychologically *more* fragile than our females, it's even more important that we discard any masculine stereotyping we might have about tough little boys. Save that for later, when it's important to teach each child as much toughness as tenderness. A good rule of thumb: In the boy's first three years of life, think, "This boy is fragile" when making *any* decisions about his care.

### He Sees Everyone as a Potential Nurturer

Well into kindergarten age, the child experiences even people and characters on television as nurturers. It is essential, therefore, that caregivers recognize how powerful every supposedly benign influence is on the child. A three-year-old does not see Barney or Big Bird or Walker, Texas Ranger as just a character on television. The child sees the character as a teacher, mentor, nurturer, caregiver. The child seeks to imitate the superficialities and overt actions of Batman, Spider-Man, Rocket Man, Scooby Doo, or the violent criminal he sees when his parents let him watch a police drama with them.

I'll never forget one mother of a violent three-year-old who took the advice to cut out all cartoons for a month, allowing only Disney movies. While the boy's personality did not change—he was still more aggressive than many of his peers—his acts of hitting dramatically decreased. Any parent can test this theory on her own—no academic study is needed. Stop a four-year-old from watching violent television—cartoons, crime shows, etc.—for two months. You will discover a different boy.

## The Age of Obedience

The first six or so years of life constitute the "age of obedience." This first developmental episode in a boy's life is the age in which morality and discipline are taught best by compelling the child to obey caregivers constantly. The boy must be allowed appropriate freedoms of exploration, play, education, feeling—but also, the boy is hungry to live an ordered life in which he does what he's told to do by parents who are patient in the telling and consistent in the follow-through.

This is not authoritarian parenting. This is *authoritative* parenting. Obedience is not about creating a perfectly mechanized boy. Some boys obey more quickly than others, some hear better, some process the instruction faster, so make sure your son does what he's told to do within a time period and in a way appropriate to his budding personality.

## DEVELOPMENTAL MILESTONES

Now let us turn to the boy's development in infancy, specifically from birth to eighteen months. While this time period is one of the richest in a child's developmental life, we will not explore every piece of infant development here. In the bibliographical section at the end of this book, I've listed specific developmental reference books if you want to go into more depth. Let me provide here the basics for giving constant care, attention, and love to your infant son. His future moral and ethical educations depend on his stability and attachment now. What should we expect of our infant son? What is normal for him? Let's answer those questions briefly but carefully.

## His Basic Needs and Cues

We can expect our infant boy to be sensorially interested in his immediate caregivers and environment—Mom, Dad, other caregivers, rooms, objects moving around him. From the time he is about three months to seven months old, we can expect lots of baby cues for "I adore you": looking the caregiver in the eye, cooing, wooing, even what we might call "flirting."

From about the middle of this period onward, we can expect him to be trying to communicate with us—concentrating on our own cues and trying to figure out how to relate, even if he can't do much more than stare and follow our eyes.

By the second year of his life, we can expect him to begin to see himself as a "me" or "mine"—in other words, an identity. It's really a slight push toward identity and self—he is still very dependent on us. It's normal for him even to do a little "disobeying" toward his second year. It is not disobeying that requires any kind of punishment; it is necessary developmental behavior. Thus, it's normal for him to test us, to walk away from us, look back to see if we're mad or afraid for him, then walk back.

It's also normal for him to play a lot and try to use his small vocabulary to elicit emotional responses. He likes being cute, sweet, and loving. Much of his play is directed toward feeling the unconditional connection with his caregivers. This period can be confusing for him, especially when, in the middle of trying to connect, he does something that makes us angry, like knocking something over.

## His Intellectual Growth

If we scan an infant's brain from its first few days of life onward, we will notice that intellectual growth activity is going on. When the brain is stimulated by contrasts of black and white in the environment—maybe the contrast of Dad's smooth cheek and beard—neurons move concomitantly in the brain. Different areas of the brain are beginning their journey of intellectual development. The infant boy is *completely* dependent on us to create the best intellectual environment possible for him. There is really no *wrong* way to set it up for him, because he will grow in these months of life from whatever is presented. We go wrong only if we put him in a room with nothing on the walls, no other sounds or sights—a sensory-deprivation tank. We go wrong if we don't respond to his intellectual cues—e.g., he points toward an object and we never bring it over to him. Our tendency in industrial cultures is sometimes to overfoster his stimulants, i.e., give him so many stimulants he can't keep up. Every parent needs to work out the balance between simple objects and tasks, and what is too much.

### His Individual Temperament

A child's temperament is a little different from his personality. When we think of temperament, we think of the child's "defining mood," his level of excitability or calm.

Every child's temperament differs from every other child's. Sometimes the differing temperaments don't seem very obvious, perhaps because we've had a number of kids and are used to temperamental differences. Sometimes they astound us because the difference is so vast. Gender can affect temperament, genes determine a great deal of the temperament, and stresses the mother experiences while the child is in the womb affect temperament—especially if she has imbibed dangerous substances.

Sometimes parents are shocked by basic differences in kids' temperaments. Don't be. It is always useful to remember that temperament is something to work with, not against. If your son comes out of the womb with a temperament that at first shocks you—one that is, for instance, far more excitable, boisterous, and demanding than your own—share your feelings of discomfort and confusion with others, and get support.

### His Necessary Narcissism

None of us wants our child to turn out to be selfish or self-absorbed. We sometimes believe that giving a child anything he wants in the first year or two of life will lead to later narcissism. One father put it this way: "When my kids were infants, I thought if they cried and we went right to them all the time, they'd be coddled kids. I didn't want them coddled. I wanted them to turn out to be good kids later."

Ironically, just the opposite is true. An infant child who is *not* coddled is much more likely to become narcissistic than a child who is. Because of the brain and biological development occurring in the early years of life, the infant needs constant contact. If he cries for food, he needs food. If he cries for attention, he needs attention. If he yearns, even silently, for cuddling, he needs cuddling. His neural web—the neural connections in his brain—develops specifically because it gets what it asks for. It sends out a signal and gets back a response. It is when the child *does not get back a response, on a continued basis,* that the child feels wrong in the world, defective, unloved. If that experience is branded into the neural web during infancy, the child will spend the rest of his life living out the brand and trying to compensate by getting others to love him in inappropriate and narcissistic ways.

There are a few small exceptions to the credo "Give the infant whatever he wants," which we'll explore in a moment. These involve sleeping and roaming habits. But generally, the path toward a well-disciplined, moral child lies in pre-empting later narcissism by encouraging it in the earliest phase of life.

### His Angels on Each Shoulder: Synchrony and Remedy

It's often useful for you to think of your son as having an angel on each shoulder: One appears when he and you are in perfect harmony, the other when he and you are not connecting well.

The time when caregiver and child are in sync is called *synchrony.* The natural and unavoidable times when they are not—the parent is distracted or doesn't understand the infant's cue, the infant sends out a number of cues at once, or the infant just becomes fussy—is called *dyssynchrony,* and dyssynchrony is very valuable. It leads the child to *remedy* its situation, by fussing harder to get help, or by modifying its cues, or by adapting to the caregiver's unavailability by becoming a little more patient. Both angels are good for your son.

Although we push ourselves to meet the child's every need, there is no reason to feel guilty when we've done everything we can yet he's still fussy. He is learning to adapt and remedy. If we know intuitively that we are doing all we can for the boy on a daily basis, there is no need for guilt. His fusses are as important as his cooing. And some fusses, like the evening fusses, are normal. Most kids get overstimulated by evening and just need to let off steam.

We feel guilty as caregivers if our intuition tells us we are not meeting the child's every need on a daily and hourly basis. We are basically all the infant boy has. If we've made anything more important to us than he is, we probably will feel good, normal guilt. The angels on his shoulders become angels on ours.

### His Moral Development

Even as an infant, your son is involved in moral growth and development. As he learns to cry for what he wants, recognize faces, and hold objects in his tiny hands, he is also observing moral patterns, and producing neural activity that inspires his knowledge of right and wrong. After about eighteen months, the boy's brain has developed enough to understand the concept of "I've done something wrong." But even before, an infant can "think morally" in these two unspoken ways.

- Right and wrong are based on what the authority figure thinks is right or wrong.
- The infant understands that he should do the things that elicit pleasure from the authority figure, not pain.

Later throughout his boyhood, his moral intelligence will get more sophisticated, thus our discipline techniques will get more sophisticated. During his infancy, simpler is generally better.

In each chapter of this parenting plan, I'll include a box of characteristics, which you can use to check if your son's behavior is within the normal range for a boy his age. As you review the characteristics of normal, it's essential to remember that just because a behavior, especially a disturbing one, lies within the normal range, it doesn't mean it won't require discipline. Quite often, a "disturbingly normal" behavior or action is actually the boy's way of specifically asking—with his body, developing brain, sounds, and hidden signals—for normal discipline and moral training.

## DISCIPLINE TECHNIQUES

How shall we use our authority in the boy's infancy years? How shall we help our infant son channel his formidable energy? How shall we provide him with the early rudiments of discipline and self-discipline?

### The Beginnings of Discipline

Discipline—the directing of a boy's energy toward self-control—begins the moment the boy is born. Subtly, we are constantly teaching him how to control his impulses by modeling good behavior ourselves, by our patience, by our responses to him. We intervene as he is flailing at a sibling, pet, or table, and hold his flailing hand tightly as we speak to him. We carry him away from a situation he is not handling well, and place him in his high chair. These all are necessary to infant development.

But when should we begin *punishing* him? Before he is about eighteen months old, there is no reason for us to punish a child. The infant simply does not have a brain that is developed well enough to understand what the punishment is for. Even if the child runs into the street, the parent's panicky grab is itself enough to scare the child. No other kind of yelling or swatting is really necessary.

### Creating Discipline in Your Verbal Interactions

Our little boy understands us more than we sometimes realize, if not in exact words then in tone and other aspects of verbal life.

**Repetition.**   Quite often, discipline of a boy in the first couple years of life means not reward or punishment, but verbal repetition. We have to patiently and repeatedly direct the boy through our words or actions. We say, "Please put that down," or, "Don't hit your sister." We say it once, then have to say it again, then again. By the third repetition, we want to

## The Range of Normal

It's normal for the boy to scream and yell.

It's normal for the boy to cry as much as he needs to.

It's normal for the boy to have flailing rages.

It's normal for the boy to throw tantrums.

It's normal for the boy to wail if he's colicky.

It's normal for the boy to be cognizant, by about one year old, as to what we want him to do, and then to purposefully disobey until we set him right.

It's normal for the boy to understand what we want but forget what we've asked him to do almost immediately; then to forget these instructions over and over again.

It's normal for the boy not to hear the instruction at all.

It's normal for the boy to take time to respond to us; children younger than three years old can take ten or more seconds to respond.

It's normal for the boy to become confused by multiple instructions and not do any of them.

It's normal for the boy to try to cling to us and yet try to get away from us also.

be very firm in tone, even loud—an authority putting the child in his place.

**Firm Tones.**   There is nothing hurtful about using a firm tone all the way through a child's boyhood. "Son, you may not do that!" By the time the boy is around eighteen months old, he will be accustomed to our firm tone.

**Praise and Admiration.**   We can overpraise a boy as he gets older, creating problems as we instruct his moral development, emotional strength, and self-discipline—but not in these first years of life. "That's great, sweetie." "You're so wonderful." "You're the best little walker I've ever seen." All of this and more is like a sweet song to the infant boy. He doesn't really understand the words—he understands the music. The music of our voice helps him learn an inward song, one whose refrain is: "I'm special, I'm wonderful," and, most important, "I'm good." If as an infant he is taught to be good and is praised as good, he is set up to act "good." While his development of discipline, and indeed of character, depends on far more than just self-esteem boosts, it is important for us to realize that a good son needs confidence. When the boy is an infant, we do an immense amount to ensure this emotional and moral confidence by never withholding appropriate praise and admiration.

### The Role of Adult Anger

Our anger as parents and caregivers is nearly useless in the first eighteen months to two years of a boy's life. In a sense, one of the great spiritual challenges of parenting infants is to face our own anger and quell it, as if we were monks taught by our religious tradition that to become fully one with God we must end our rages and tantrums. Only when the boy has done something immensely dangerous—like running out in front of a car—is it useful to frighten him with our adrenalized anger.

Anger on our part is generally caused by us, not by something he is doing. The boy is generally very normal, no matter his range of activity. Certainly none of us is perfect, and we will get angry at our infant. But the less, the better.

Once a grandmother confessed to me how she got angry at her eighteen-month-old grandson because he kept knocking things over in her "great room." The cures for his behavior (and her anger) were simple: Don't let the boy in the great room, or childproof the room. It was inappropriate for the caregiver to let a child of that age into an environment where he would make her angry. This grandmother's confession is an inspiration to all of us, I think, as we seek alternatives to getting angry with infants. Removal of the child from an offending situation is a good alternative; direction, firmness, instruction, distraction, and, most of all, a very forgiving patience all are better than a parent's or caregiver's anger.

### Using Appropriate Physical Discipline

How we use our bodies to control our son affects his development of self-discipline.

**Changing the Boy's Location.**    One of the most important discipline techniques for an infant is to physically change the child's location. If your son is hitting his friend, for instance, he may need to be moved to the other side of the room. We don't want the moving to feel violent— we might even be gentle, as when we pick him up from a nap—but we should do it whenever we need to.

**Avoiding Spanking.**    In no part of this plan will I suggest spanking or physically hitting a child. Many parents utilize this discipline technique to a greater extent after the boy's infancy, so we will explore it in more depth in later chapters. However, when a child is an infant, there is *never* a reason for a parent to spank. The risks far outweigh the benefits at this age.

### Using Bedtime as Self-Discipline Development

Often parents don't realize how much discipline a child learns as he adheres to established bedtime rituals. For a breast-feeding infant, parents must of course make the bedtime rules as they go along. Once the boy is ready for a consistent evening bedtime, however, I suggest 7:30 up until age eighteen months or so, then perhaps an increase to 8:00 P.M. If in your family parents and kids don't really get together at the end of the workday until around 6:00 P.M., then 7:30 is unrealistic and may negatively affect bonding between you and your child. You will probably want to insist that your child-care provider give the boy a long nap so that he can stay up later with you, say, till 9:00 P.M. A very useful book for anyone having difficulty with bedtime is *Solve Your Child's Sleep Problems,* by Richard Ferber, M.D.

**Making Tuck-ins a Ritual Activity.**    One of the most wonderful moral development episodes in a child's life is the half hour or so we spend with him at bedtime—reading, tucking him in, lying down with him, cuddling, cooing, chatting. In a way, this is prayer time for the child, even if he is too young to say prayers. This ritual can continue until the boy gets into the second decade of his life and feels uncomfortable with it. For now, it is the time of terrific love that enfolds the discipline of bedtime.

**Falling Asleep.**   After tuck-in time is over, it is very important for a parent to help the child fall asleep, though maintaining firm boundaries. Some parents get involved in two-hour sleep fights with their sons. These are not good for the boy. Sometimes these start very early in the boy's infancy because the parent feels guilty forcing the son to cry himself to sleep, or feels guilty being gone during the day. Falling-asleep rituals appear to be one of the very few exceptions to what we said earlier about making sure to give an infant exactly what he asks for when he asks for it.

In practical terms, I recommend the "fifteen minutes on, fifteen minutes off" rule. We finish our bedtime rituals with the infant. We say, "Okay, go to sleep now" (or the infant has already nodded off). We leave the room. The boy starts to scream for us. We wait fifteen minutes for the boy to cry himself to sleep; if he does not, we go pick him up and hold him for fifteen minutes, during which time he may fall asleep in our arms; then we lay him down again for fifteen minutes. After a few nights, unless they're colicky, most boys learn to go to sleep. As always, your own extended family, friends, and pediatrician should be consulted if your son is just not able to accommodate your reasonable ritual for sleep.

If you can push yourself through the pain of listening to the few nights of screams, not only do you end up with a good routine in place but also you've taught your son an immensely valuable lesson in self-control and self-discipline. He feels every night that he is making a choice to remain calm and go to sleep.


## MORAL TEACHING

In the first year and a half of a boy's life, his moral training comes to the greatest extent from his feeling of being unconditionally loved. We assure good moral development mainly by being very bonded with him. We don't do very much direct moral training yet. For now, as with discipline techniques, moral training goes by the rule "The simpler the better." Moral training has to be literal and consistent. We can't explain much—we have to show him physically how to act, and we have to do things for and with him.

We teach morality also by reading (and telling) him stories from sacred texts or other sources about people acting well. We praise him for acting well and redirect him away from acting badly. Using these techniques is a simple way for us to teach him to lead a moral life.

We can only hurt his moral development by letting him be exposed to things we consider amoral or immoral—most of these would come to him through media and video games. In a smaller number of cases, these would come to him through friends, relatives, or other people who are bad influences. And in all cases, both moral training and lack of it depend on the "sacred world"—the home and other intimate environments—we create for our infant.

## A HEALTHY MORAL AND EMOTIONAL ENVIRONMENT

Every chapter of this parenting plan will provide a kind of map for what environment will best produce healthy discipline and emotional and moral development for your son. I'll explore large themes like child care, schools, and parents, and suggest "regulations" like bedtimes, media use, and curfews.

### Child Care

One of the most important questions you'll face during your boy's infancy is that of child care. Attached to it is the issue of when and whether the mother should go back to work. Ultimately, this is a very private and intimate question for parents and families. I will discuss these issues here in the context of the mother being the child's primary and most intimate caregiver during the infant's first months of life. *In your family, if the father is the primary caregiver, or if the mother and father spend equal and shared caregiving time with the infant, please change the language as appropriate.*

Most of the time, when we try to understand the child's point of view, we come to the realization that in the first two years of his life he can rarely do better than have one consistent, primary caregiver with whom to completely bond. This person is generally the mother, though in some cases it may be the father or an adoptive mother.

As we discussed in chapter 2, since the beginning of human culture, mothers of infants have always worked—gathering, tilling fields, networking in their communities, helping with food preparation, raising their own and others' children. In many cultures, they did this work while carrying the child with them or keeping the child near them—attachment did not falter. They also relied on one or two other female caregivers, who became aunties to the child, so that in those moments when the mother was not around, an auntie remained the secondary female caregiver *consistently* in the boy's life.

The reason the question of working mothers and child care is so developmentally crucial now is that mother-child attachment itself has changed a great deal by force of culture. Our economic system forces many mothers to work far away from their babies, and the "aunties"— the child-care workers provided by our culture—are generally so slightly paid that they don't stay around long enough to form bonds. This situation is potentially dangerous to the developing child.

**Return to Work Later Rather Than Sooner, If Possible.**   If there is a general rule about when the mother (or other primary caregiver) ought to return to work, it is: If possible, the primary caregiver ought to try to remain at the child's side for one to two years. Perhaps the mother can work out of the home via online services, or take more than a few months of maternity leave because of the father's ability to bring in income. If there is a way to juggle family life so that primary caregiver and infant can stay in close physical proximity for one to two years, you as a parent will never regret it.

Many family systems are not able logistically to make possible a mother's one-to-two-year uninterrupted homestay, or many do not wish to have the mother home for the full one to two years. If a mother is going to work away from the "touch range" of the child—in other words, away from his physical proximity—that work hopefully would not begin at least until between three and six months after the child's birth.

**Work Shorter Hours Until the Child Is at Least Three Years Old.** Similarly, if the mother is going to work outside the touch range of the child, hopefully that work would entail a mother's spending only a few hours a day away from the child's proximity. It is important to remember that should the child have a grandma or father or other "second mother" in his life who keeps him in touch range constantly, the birth mother's constancy of contact becomes less crucial.

**Recruit Consistent, Trained, and Loving Child-Care Providers.** Generally, smaller in-home day cares are better than huge multiplex day cares because the in-home day cares assure the parents of at least one consistent caregiver. My wife and I experienced both large and small day care. I have visited hundreds of both. A great deal of clinical research has been devoted to day care and child care over the last five years, so we now have some basic facts.

Large day cares can be good places for infants, but generally they are better for older kids. To seek one that is good for infants, you must scrutinize them for consistency of caregivers. It is useful to remember that when child-care providers are not consistent, children are more likely to learn more about moral behavior and development from their little peers than from the caregivers. We don't want this circumstance until the male is near adulthood.

We need to spend as much time as possible at day-care centers to assure ourselves that our infant will be held a great deal during the day, stimulated as needed, and cared for *as if an auntie were loving our child.* If the provider isn't like an auntie, we might want to keep looking. We should also feel free to "drop in" to the day care at any time in the first few weeks or months. Any day care that frowns on drop-ins is set up more as a business than as our child's extended family.

**Pick Appropriate Nannies and Au Pairs.** In certain areas of the country, nannies and au pairs are used a great deal. Generally, I find two distinct kinds of nanny: the one that is nearly as primary a caregiver as the mother, and the one who is more peripheral. In the latter case, the mother is a stay-at-home mom and utilizes the nanny for "extra help." In the former case, the mother works full- or part-time, and the nanny is a profound influence on the child.

When the nanny is peripheral in the home, her consistent presence, discipline contribution, and touch is not as important. Often she will stay in the home a year or maybe two (or less), and act as a friendly auntie. There is little harm in doing so, since the mother (or father) is the at-home, primary caregiver. However, if the nanny is going to be the primary at-home caregiver, *it is very important the family exact from her a long-term commitment, and make sure she is trained to constantly touch and carry the infant.*

As in other child-care situations, there also needs to be consistency of rules and discipline. Sometimes nannies, especially young ones, are intimidated by a boisterous child and don't discipline the child well enough. The mother and father can help mentor the nanny. Conversely, sometimes the nanny is better at disciplining the child than the parents. Her wisdom may be something the mother and father need to listen to.

With nannies and au pairs, it is especially important that we make sure the prospective caregiver was brought up around boys or has experience with boys, especially if one or more of your sons has a boisterous temperament.

**Don't Worry Too Much About the Religion of the Infant-Care Provider.** My wife and I both worked part-time when our children were four months old. We traded having the kids every afternoon, and they went to day care in the morning. Their providers were fundamentalist Christians. I am Jewish by birth, and my wife Congregationalist. Yet the different religious/political orientation did not need to figure into our day-care choice. A six-month-old can only benefit from whatever religious conversation goes on. (In fact, when we select a child-care provider—whether nanny, au pair, day-care provider—it is useful for us to notice whether there is spiritual life in that day-care environment or caregiver's life.) The most important thing for my children was that their child-care providers—Marianne, Jennifer, and Sadarah—were wonderful, loving caregivers who understood child development, attachment, bonding, and discipline, *and* respected and modeled life's spiritual quality. As the child grows older, questions of common religious stories and political values become more important, and certain child-care choices might be made or not made depending on religion.

### The Role of the Active Father

I cannot overstate how crucial it is for a boy's emotional and moral development that a father bond quickly with his infant offspring—be at his birth, hold him during infancy, share child-care work like diaper changing, feed him when appropriate, and enjoy him.

In our ancestors' lives, this bonding was not as critical as it is now. Long ago, all children were brought up in large kinship communities— often children didn't know who their fathers were, or the fathers were away when the children were born. But the father's presence was not as crucial because the child had *many* "fathers" to take care of him: uncles, mentors, grandfathers, elder cousins, elder siblings, male religious figures. In our culture, most of the elder males are gone from our boys' lives. The father often is responsible for all or most of the primary male bonding. To neglect the boy's male-bonding needs is not only to decrease the love he experiences in infancy and early childhood but also to set him up for possible behavioral and social problems later. There comes a time in every boy's life when a primary male's presence and guidance is crucial for him to complete male development, as we have seen in chapter 2, and as we'll continue to explore in future chapters.

**Mothers and Fathers Often Bond Differently with Their Children.** Mothers become pregnant and secrete increased doses of progesterone, the bonding hormone. She and her child become hormonally inseparable, as well as emotionally close.

The father, the male who has impregnated the female and watched the progress of her pregnancy, has little of this hormone. His bond with his offspring depends on an *emotional* bond with its mother and with the offspring. If he lacks a deep-seated bond in one of these areas, he is more likely to abandon the offspring and, if other social factors permit, seek a new female with whom to bond. When we track teen pregnancies, we find a clear illustration of this lack of male bonding. Ninety percent of males who have impregnated teen females (these males are generally in their late teens and early to mid twenties) abandon their offspring. These males are not bonded enough emotionally with the females and do not bond with the babies.

Because it is so important to make sure a male bonds with the mother and then with the child, and especially in a culture that attempts to be monogamous, as ours does, many couples will wait for many years after marriage or early courtship before having a child. Unconsciously, the mother may be watching during this time, whether the potential father has enough of a bond with her to care for her kids. And because it is so important that fathers bond with their kids, mothers are becoming more and more open to males in child-care roles. "Get involved!" mothers are crying. Every mother, even if unconsciously, knows she must get the father to bond with the infant emotionally, through sensory and tactile contact, play, care, and time spent together.

Should she keep her bond with the man and should he remain bonded with the child, the ease of her life generally increases, as does the emotional and moral development of the child. In most cases, she is right about the father: Most men are good men who, once bonded, will strive to do what's right and give the care they are capable of giving. Even if the mother becomes bored with or unfulfilled by the man, in the vast majority of cases, if he bonds with the child he will be a good father.

During his infancy, the boy is utterly vulnerable, and the father's instincts to give care are heightened. If the father tends to be a resistant or stoic husband, enhancing his bond with the boy might mean finding subtle ways of helping him build love and attachment. You may want to let go of lecturing him to "Do the diapers!" but provide more time for "Look how he wants to play with you."

**Mothers and Fathers Interact Differently with Their Infant Sons.** T. Berry Brazelton's *The Earliest Relationship* and my own *The Wonder of Boys* delve into the unique ways parents interact with kids. Mothers and fathers interact differently with their sons. Where the mother might calm a boy down, the father might rev him up. Where the mother might hold him close, the father might toss him around.

Since both father and mother can see the flaws in each other's parenting work, hopefully, good dialogue techniques between them have been or can be established so that they will trust each other enough to give and take advice.

"Yes, you're right, he really can go to sleep by himself now."

"Yes, you're right, I am trying to push him too hard with the blocks."

Neither father nor mother knows best; they both do together.

## Adoption

When I was five years old, my family lived in Hyderabad, India, where my parents adopted my sister. Her name in the orphanage was Sujata. My parents renamed her Maria. Maria came into our home when she was seven months old.

As the brother of an adopted girl, and as a therapist, I have spent some of my most important hours in life helping people involved in the adoption process. If you have adopted or are thinking about adopting, you and your child will face some key issues. Awareness of them will, I hope, help your process go more smoothly over your adopted child's life span.

As you go through the process of adopting and then raise an adopted child, I hope you'll consider doing some of these things.

- Find support from others who share this unique life experience.
- Keep lines open, if possible and if healthy, with birth parents.
- Keep a scrapbook of birth-parent and adoptive-parent photos, writings, and other soulful objects that will help your child later on to deal with identity issues.
- If your child is from a different ethnic group than you are, expose him gradually to essential people and practices of that group.
- Learn everything you can about what adopted kids face—Internet sites on adoption are a very good resource for finding support and information.

### Psychological Issues of Adoption.

Generally, psychological issues that arise from being adopted fall into these seven categories.

Loss

Rejection

Guilt

Shame

Grief

Identity

Intimacy

These issues can appear in any child's life; an adopted child experiences them, however, in his own way. You will benefit by watching carefully for them.

As he grows up, he may fear ultimate abandonment, making it hard for him to fully commit to loving and being loved.

He may constantly anticipate rejection and always consider himself inferior, which makes it difficult for him to commit to tasks, academics, sports, or other challenges where he does not already have an inherent aptitude.

He may come to feel he deserves problems. He may live his life as if it were a constant struggle, unable to find happiness. He may make choices that keep him in trouble, behind, ostracized, and lonely.

He may feel ashamed of his very existence. A boy who has been "rejected" by his biological parents can feel that he is inherently defective. This sense of "I am flawed enough to have been abandoned" can distort all his relationships and commitments in the way deep shame sets up anyone for failure.

He will grieve the loss of his biological parents. His adoptive parents can help him through this grief as he becomes old enough to articulate it.

He may have trouble integrating his identity, especially during adolescence, because he feels like he doesn't fit in any world for certain. It is important to help him find teams, schools, extended families, and peer groups where he will feel he belongs.

He may have trouble being fully intimate, either as a child with his adoptive parents, or as an adult with his mate and children. It is crucial that his adoptive parents constantly teach him intimacy skills if he shows signs of having trouble bonding.

*Raising Adopted Children,* by Lois Ruskai Melina, is a wonderful re-source if you are raising an adopted child.

Adoption is as joyful an experience as the biological production of a child. I'm fully convinced of that. Yes, it is different. In a sense, it pro-vides parents with not only a particular set of worries but also gifts. One gift is that the parents of adopted kids often are challenged to give even more love and attention to these children than they had expected to give a child, and in doing so, they discover the depths of their own souls.

### Extra Attention the Boy Needs

There are ways in which boys sometimes need a little extra attention.

Because many boys naturally hold eye contact for shorter periods of time than girls, parents may stop eye contact, too, putting the boy down a little quicker than they might a girl. The male brain is a spatial brain, causing even the infant boy to watch objects moving in space through-out his immediate environment, and thus distracting him from long-term eye contact with his immediate caregiver. The male body is also, often, a more fidgety, pushy little body, so it's sometimes less comfort-able to hold than the infant female.

While all parents strive to give equal love to all children, it's still worthwhile to notice if your son is pretty "boyish" and how you re-spond. Is he one of those who is naturally fidgety and doesn't hold eye contact? If so, do you tend to stop holding him a little quicker than you might a girl? Perhaps you'll want to swaddle him very tightly when you hold him, which often will calm his fidgets down and make him feel safe. Perhaps, also, you'll want to hold him in a pack on your back even while you're doing chores or mundane daily things.

### Nutritional Issues

What your son eats is of great concern for many reasons that do not at first appear to include discipline, moral development, and emotional development, but do, in the end, affect all.

Many of the books I've listed in the Additional Resources section give very detailed analyses of breast-feeding and bottle-feeding. A mother's milk is generally agreed to be the most nutritious for the infant. The American Academy of Pediatrics urges mothers to breast-feed for at least a year because of possible advantages to the infants' physical and brain developments. However, should the mother have trouble with breast-milk production or with getting the infant to utilize the breast, formula and bottle-feeding are quite adequate. In these cases, she still should extract the colostrum into a bottle using a breast pump for four to six weeks after the birth of the baby. Colostrum is the nutritional chemical secreted by the mother's breast that helps keep the child's immune system strong. A sick baby often makes life for parents quite difficult, and parental impatience and anger can make the first years of a child's life morally difficult. On the issue of breast- and bottle-feeding, it is essential that each mother consult her pediatrician and, if possible, a lactation specialist (hospitals usually provide these to new mothers).

While the issue of breast-feeding tends to dominate our early-infant-nutrition dialogues, there are other areas that need our attention. Many of our children are born with allergies to certain foods. These allergies can create not only health problems but behavioral problems. Some of these appear soon after birth, though many do not appear until later. Dairy allergies, which can cause fidgety behavior, illness, and moroseness, are becoming more common. Again, it's important that you consult a health professional, whether in the traditional medical community or through an alternative venue. Chronic conditions during male life, from depression to addiction to mental illness to violence, are being at least partially treated through the monitoring of food intake. I can speak personally about this correlation. I discovered at age twenty-four that I am allergic to yeast. I believe now, in retrospect, that some of my own acting out as a boy may have been caused by the undiagnosed yeast allergy. Once I stopped eating yeast as a young man, my depressions nearly vanished and my irritability significantly decreased.

Sugar is also a controversial nutritional issue. Some boys just shouldn't eat sugar because it makes them jittery and affects their ability to control their impulses. I recommend very small amounts of refined sugar to infants, and indeed to children in general. It is certainly not useful, as children get older, to send sugar treats in school lunches, or to have children eat sugary snacks before school.

**Hormone Disruptions in Foods and the Environment.** New research has shown that "endocrine disruptors" found in the herbicides, pesticides, fertilizers, and plasticizers that dominate our children's immediate environment—in the lawns, weeds, and plastic cartons—and in many foods, including meat from cattle raised with hormonally augmented feed, can alter the way human hormones work and can affect male sperm counts, creating more potential for infertility among our sons as they become adults. In addition, testicular cancer is rising in part because of these disruptors in food, fertilizer, and other products.

This issue has profound moral implications for individual boys and, in the end, for the culture. You'll find in the notes to this section a number of resources for getting further acquainted with this issue. The Environmental Protection Agency is aware of the link between increases in endocrine disruptors and male health concerns, but so far no government policy of sweeping proportion has been forthcoming. So parents and caregivers of boys cannot rely fully on outside help. We need to look carefully at our sons' food and environment ourselves.

It is very important that you study the issue and come to your own conclusions. There is certainly no harm to your son if you eat organically grown vegetables and meats. The more you can cut out endocrine disruptors in your boy's life, the better you'll protect him from possible reproductive trouble later.

### Media Use

As we explored in chapter 2, the amount of time our children spend absorbed in TV, video games, movies, and the Internet is substantial. This time is not spent with a benign pal but rather with a complex set of machines that affect brain development, emotional development, and moral development.

Violent images imprint on the developing brain, dehumanizing and desensitizing it, to say nothing of frightening the boy. Years of violent imagery will create a more violent male.

Constant use of visual media decreases your child's attention span and ability to learn and perform other tasks.

Fast-moving images in visual media retard healthy brain development.

Especially in the first six years of life, the boy's brain is generally not mature enough to understand or successfully process many of the images and moral messages on screen.

In every chapter of this parenting plan, we will look at media use, how it affects a boy, and how to monitor, contain, and utilize it effectively. I will suggest specific media use rules—rules for TV, video games, movies, and the Internet—that I hope you will either apply directly or use to create your own rules. The media are stimulants to your son's brain, and their influence changes as your son develops. Thus we will look at different rules *for every developmental period of your son's life.* More and more today, discipline of media use is an important job for parents and caregivers.

The first and most crucial point we can make about infant media use is this one: *The less, the better.* If your infant has little or no exposure to television or other visual media stimulants (video game, computer), you will not regret it. He will in no way "fall behind" his peers. The American Academy of Pediatrics suggests that children younger than two years old avoid visual media stimulants altogether, and I agree with their suggestion.

If, however, you are going to provide your son with limited media use, here are some guidelines.

The infant's developing brain is fragile and does not process information at the speed of most visual programming. It is a bad idea to have an infant watch anything on TV other than slow-moving programs. *Barney* is a good example. *Sesame Street,* which is appropriate for older kids, is much less appropriate for infants. Its images change and move too fast for comfort for an infant's brain.

The infant brain *cannot process aesthetic complexity—it is a literal-minded brain system.* Thus it should be exposed only to programming with clear moral or behavioral messages. Again, *Barney* is an example. There is no ambiguity about what is being taught—act well, care about one another, clean up after yourself, learn a new thing every day. These are simple messages, without ambiguity, that the infant can process.

### The Rituals of Life

The daily and weekly rituals we develop during these early years of a boy's life can become foundational. The more we develop rituals for the small child and ourselves—bedtime rituals, reading rituals, family meal rituals, taking drives together, getting together with family and friends, telling the family's story—the more we'll be inclined to create rituals later in life—rites of passage for the adolescent boy, extended family gatherings and sports activities, going to church together, and other family outings.

One very valuable ritual is the Weekly Clan Gathering. Perhaps a few months after the birth—after everyone is sleeping a little bit more again—it's nice to find an evening or time during the weekend when the extended family can get together. In my family, we use Thursday evening. My family and a couple of others with kids, as well as some older people and our children's godparents, come together at Clancy's house—he is a man of seventy who has a Ping-Pong table in his basement. We talk for a while, we play Ping-Pong, the kids go to bed between 8:30 and 9:00 (a splurge for all of them); we adults chat some more or watch a little TV, eat some dessert, then pack everyone up and go home. This same group has been doing this ritual since my children were born.

Modified as needed by every family to fit its circumstances, this kind of ritual is a complete celebration of child, family, and community. There's something in it to keep the men busy when they get antsy—the Ping-Pong—there's a lot of attention paid to children and family, and it becomes a way of directing the growth of the children. As the children leave infancy and grow older, they have people to turn to, they have a night to look forward to, and they have a big family close to home.

### The Role of Godmothers and Godfathers

One of the greatest gifts we create in the boy's environment is god-parents. These people will be mentors, friends, and moral and emotional allies all through his life. If possible, they should be present at the birth, so they bond immediately with the boy. Even if we can provide only a godmother or godfather, I believe we should do so from day one. If we move across the country, our children and these godparents can keep their bond via phone, letters, e-mail, and visits.

Generally, we intuitively know who we want to fulfill this essential role. The people can be blood kin or not. The godparent tradition is ancient, one each culture has practiced differently. In many matrilineal tribes long ago, mothers chose the godparents, and generally she chose her own brothers as godfathers. In many patrilineal or patriarchal tribes, fathers chose. Now both parents can choose. The godparents don't have to have kids of their own. Our children can become like their own.

## EMMIT'S STORY

We'll conclude each chapter of the parenting plan with a success story. These stories have come to me, generally, from personal interactions with parents and teachers, and from mail I've received over the years. This chapter on infancy ends with the story of Emmit.

Emmit was a little blond boy who came into the world only ten months before his sibling, Lisa. Emmit wasn't quite ready to let go of complete control over his mother, Lynn, but he had to. By the time Emmit was walking, Lynn had little Lisa to breast-feed, too. Emmit protested in many ways. One of those involved finding objects around the room and hitting his infant sister with them.

Mild-mannered in comparison to her brother, Lisa took most of the hits in stride, but then Emmit—as if frustrated that he couldn't get a screaming response from her—would instinctively find a harder object, a Lego stick, and hit her with that. Little Lisa would wail, and Lynn would come running in, yank the stick out of Emmit's hands, and place him over on the couch. Emmit was no dummy—he knew how to wail, too. Lynn was stuck trying to comfort both children.

The success moment that Emmit's mother shared with me happened at just one of those times, as she had Lisa on one side of her and had gone over to explain to Emmit what he had done and give him comfort, too. Once he got a hug, he stopped crying pretty quickly. He looked up at his mother with his big brown eyes, then he reached his little one-year-old hand over to his sister. In a gesture that his mother just knew, intuitively, was a foreshadowing of how he would take care of his sister later in life, he caressed her blond hair with his little hand. Lynn hugged both her children, and Emmit seemed to be trying to say something. His mother couldn't understand it *verbally,* but "heard" him say, "I love you, Sissy." Lynn broke down and cried, hugging them both. This was the kind of moment, she told me later, that she had wanted a family for. Her son's sudden compassion made her feel whole and serene.

# FOUR

# The Toddler Years

NURTURING BOYS OF

EIGHTEEN MONTHS TO FOUR YEARS

I met Janet at her day-care center one day in the spring. The children were outside on the swings and other playground equipment. Janet held an infant on her arm as she wiped the nose of a three-year-old boy. Two other toddlers rolled around on each other, giggling. The other children were sliding and swinging and playing in a sandbox. Janet's assistant, her younger sister, pushed one of the kids on a swing. Janet had asked me to stop by and talk to her about what was going on with her boys in the day care.

As it happened, Janet taught me more than I taught her. She was preparing a talk for parents and wanted to show me the materials she had developed. Her day care specializes in toddlers, so she wanted to engage the toddlers' parents in exploring their environment. In the set of materials was a drawing of a big circle with four pillars in it. In the center between the four pillars was a little child. Janet was going to have parents write down what they thought the circle and the pillars around the child were. She showed me what she considered to be the circle and the pillars for the children she cared for.

The toddler boy, she said, stands within the circle of love that parents and the rest of the human community provide him. Inside that circle are four necessary elements to healthy, happy development.

The First Pillar: The Activity of Learning (Play, Stimulation, Creativity)

The Second Pillar: Coaching Him in Tenderness (Empathy and Sensitivity Training)

The Third Pillar: Moral Training (Development of Self-Discipline and Responsibility)

The Fourth Pillar: Helping Him Be a Hero (Development of Strength and a Sense of Justice)

Janet's four pillars are handy ways of looking at basics in a toddler's life. Perhaps your own definitions will differ a little, but you would probably include most of these elements. And as you prepare to handle your toddler, you'll most likely gravitate naturally toward creating methods of organizing your care for him. Chaos is confusing for him; circles and pillars and a diagrammed life work better.

Every toddler boy wants a lot of creativity and activity; he needs to learn to enhance his natural tenderness; he needs to be taught discipline and moral competency; he needs to be brave and just and fair. It's good to remember that in the everyday caring, training, coaching, and loving we give our toddler boys, we are preparing them for not only their present circumstances but their *adolescence,* then adulthood. As we'll see throughout this chapter, *much of what transpires in the toddler years is a foreshadowing of adolescence,* so it's very important we spend a lot of time and energy organizing our toddlers' volatile lives. This chapter will suggest a number of methods for guiding and organizing their formidable energies.

## DEVELOPMENTAL MILESTONES

What are the key developmental points to remember about your toddler boy? Much of what he experienced in the first eighteen months continues here.

### His Basic Psychological Development

From about eighteen to thirty months old, toddlers begin to do the immense amount of pretend play that continues well through childhood. Not only through interaction with caregivers but now through pretend play they learn about their own feelings—how those feelings function, and how to put budding language to them.

From about thirty months to four years old, they are hungry to test the limits. They seek limits set by caregivers, and they are also trying to figure out how to set limits internally. A toddler boy will wander down the sidewalk, trying to figure how far away to go. He *wants and needs* his caregiver to help him set a limit—to the next house—and if she doesn't, he himself will try to find one. It's hit and miss for him to do it alone at this age, which is why we watch over our toddlers like hawks. We want them to learn the limits *we* set, so that they will incorporate them and not get into danger.

### His Intellectual Growth

As he did in infancy, your toddler boy is developing his intellect like one of those movies of fast photography following clouds from dawn to dusk. In the movie, it takes only about ten seconds to show a whole day going by. So it is with a boy's brilliant little brain. It is starved for stimulation to help its frontal lobes and other sections grow tissue and neurotransmission. This brain may often get overstimulated, making the child cry or become "unruly." It will often need break time, running-around time, a safe place on the floor to throw its overstimulation tantrum—but then, soon, it will show its hunger again, and it will learn, learn, learn!

Among toddlers a very likely cause of tantrums will actually be the *lack* of appropriate intellectual stimulation. Tantrums are quite often the child's way of saying that the environment is not meeting his intellectual needs.

### His Hunger to Explore

You may notice that your boy is a little Columbus, exploring all over the place. Exploration is one of the most important ways he learns. We help him by responding to him, opening new doors for him (providing limits, too), and spending lots of time exploring with him. One way we help him is by putting important things in front of him so that he can grab them. While toddlers will move around the house a lot, they don't tend to need to explore far away for their development—exploration is often more of a tactile sort and involves play and manipulation of new objects nearby.

Reading to the toddler is *one of the most crucial ways* he explores.

In a toddler's exploring years, you may see a distinct difference between a toddler boy and toddler girl. You may find him more physically aggressive, and you may find he uses more physical space as he plays, learns, and explores.

### His Hidden Biology

In boys' toddler years, we often start to see them becoming very "boyish." Perhaps we give them dolls and they turn them into guns, or they throw objects or take them apart. Perhaps we notice them picking up a twig or other similar object and turning it into a tool, drumstick, or weapon. Perhaps we notice that they need a lot of time outdoors or in large spaces to run off steam. Perhaps we notice that when a toddler boy and toddler girl are given similar tasks—to make a cut-and-paste piece of artwork—the toddler boy spreads his materials and activities out over more physical space on the table or floor.

When we discuss biological differences between males and females, we generalize, and there are always exceptions. We may not notice all these differences, but we will see some. Much of what we're noticing are inherent differences, rooted in human nature. In *The Wonder of*

*Boys,* I countered the recent notion that differences between boys and girls are the result merely of acculturation. Some differences are, but the ones that show up in the toddler years are largely differences in brain structure, brain functioning, and hormonal development. How the biobehavioral differences exactly manifest themselves is dependent on culture. For instance, before guns existed, a little boy would not have formed a gun out of the twig as he sought to fulfill his inherent push toward aggression play. He might have formed a sword or other object taken from his time and culture. His push toward aggressive play, however, was not dependent on society only.

**Testosterone, the Aggression Hormone, and the Developing Male Brain.** "His testosterone, his aggression hormone, won't come in till puberty," a mom said to me. "So why is he so rambunctious and aggressive already at three?" If you watch your little boy bounce around the world like a bungee jumper, or hit his sister more than she hits him, or yell out aggressively, or hit friends with toy weapons and kick them karate-style, you are seeing, in part, his endocrine system (hormones) and neurological system (male brain) engaging in a primordial dance. Male biology is, in large part, about the emergence of testosterone. The human sex and aggression hormone, testosterone is, to some extent, humanity's life insurance. Without it, the human species would not survive. Both our males and females need to be aggressive. Our males have up to twenty times more testosterone than our females for reasons of biological evolution—throughout the course of four million years, labor had to divide in order for our children to grow to adulthood: Females needed to birth and care intimately for children, and thus had less sex drive because for months on end they would not be able to have sex; males needed to hunt, build, and protect territory, and had more sex drive so that as many females as possible could get pregnant. It's a "basic" scenario, one we tend to think is beneath us, but that is how it has been for 99 percent of human history. The male brain system, like the female, had to be structured in such a way as to accept the wash of the adult hormones at puberty. So, the male brain already in the toddler years evidences more aggression-type behavior. If it weren't set up as such from day one, the male organism would fail at puberty.

We actually see examples of this kind of "failure"—this conflict and rejection between neurological and endocrine systems—to this day. You may have seen the case made famous by the media recently, of the child who had a rare condition at birth that required the doctor to hazard a guess as to which sex to make him. The doctor made him a male, but he always "acted" like a female. Finally, at fourteen years old, he was told what had happened. He had male genitalia and even hormones, but just never felt like a male. In fact, his brain was female formatted.

In the end, much of your son's aggressive activity in the toddler years—stuff that might make us uncomfortable, especially if we didn't have brothers and this is our first boy—is probably quite normal. This doesn't mean we don't guide and discipline it. It simply means we smile with more sereneness at it, and we educate others around us who are not used to it.

### Attention as Discipline

Here is the story of a little toddler, Terry, as it appears in psychologist Kathleen Berger's study of human development. It paints a wonderful and useful picture of what many toddler boys can be like.

Terry is pulling books off a bookshelf, making a mess. His mother comes in from the other room and tells him, "No! Stop!" She pulls him up and across the room, slapping his hand. Terry ambles back over to the bookshelf and touches the books again. She repeats, "No!" Terry whines and throws himself on the floor. After a little while, he gets back up and takes a doll off the shelf, throws it on the floor, then he goes back to pulling more books down. His mother again yells, "No!" and goes to remove him. He escapes, marching around. He grabs a framed picture off a table. "Terry!" his mother cries, "Don't touch!" She grabs the picture, replaces it, and removes Terry. He laughs. She says, "Terry, I'm not playing with you!" He grabs another picture. Somewhat exasperated, his mom tells his big sister, who is watching by now, to get the picture. His sister gets in a tug-of-war with Terry for the picture. Their mother reenters the fray, removes the picture, puts it back on the shelf, and tells Terry, "Don't touch it again. Don't laugh. You're being fresh." Terry laughs and walks over toward the TV.

What mom of a toddler has not faced something like this? It is normal behavior, yet its normality reveals so many secrets of the boy's psychological sense of who he is and what he's trying to be.

The books are *his* to play with, until his mom lets him know they are not. Just so the picture. The books are also his way of getting the attention of his caregiver. The whole interaction is play to him unless he's forced to see it otherwise. When another party—the sister—enters, he becomes territorial. He is exploring his own sense of personal power. He comes to enjoy the power struggle with his mother, and learns from it.

In very simple terms, Terry's mother made a mistake. Much of all the fighting might have been avoided if she had simply noticed, in the first instant, that he probably wanted her attention—wanted her to read to him—when he pulled the books down. Had she asked him to select a book, and had she read to him, the power struggle and need to reprimand and punish probably would have been averted.

While she could have "improved" the situation by noticing what she missed, still she and all of us learn a lot about Terry from the prolonged incident. We learn something about his stubbornness, his sense of humor, the fact that he feels secure with his mother and does not fear that she will abuse him. We also learn, should we see a number of incidents like this involving him, that Terry's innate temperament might be one in which he is harder to distract, quicker to complain, and easier to anger than other children. This information is good to have as we later consider what kind of discipline he needs throughout the toddler years.

### His Toddler Search for Independence

Throughout his toddler years, the child seeks independence from the caregivers in little bursts of behavior. When we talk about the "terrible twos," we are talking about a child's desire for self-determination, which can permeate family life at around two years old (though some kids don't really begin it till three or so), and which lasts for a year or more.

The boy wants to be boss. He wants to be able to do things that are independent from his parents. He gets very frustrated that he can't do most things without them.

He will go through another one of these independence-seeking episodes at around five or six, then again in prepuberty, then again at puberty and at adolescence. As we notice our child pursuing independence in these toddler years, we get a foreshadowing of how he will probably do so in adolescence. And we can have a great effect on it now, so that it will go smoother both now and in the second decade of life.

### His Moral Development

Our toddlers are becoming moral creatures. They are thinking morally now. While much of their morality still is based on whether they anger caregivers—"I know I did wrong because Mom is mad at me"—some of it also is becoming a little more sophisticated. They are beginning to see life as a *marketplace,* in which they themselves have to try to be fair.

Billy's three-year-old friend might try to "steal"—take away—Jamal's Animorph, and after the tumult subsides, we might find four-year-old Jamal saying, "Give me that Animorph. I'll give you my Power Ranger." These boys are developing their own, sometimes very sophisticated, sense of fairness in the late toddler years. We'll cover how language is used in this process later in this chapter.

Often these boys will have enough "moral sense" to work certain things out for themselves. Just as often, however, they'll need us to give them moral options: "Maybe if you and Billy tried this . . ." Or: "Why don't you give Billy that for five minutes, then when the timer goes off, you get it back."

In the area of hitting and other physical aggressions, many toddlers

## The Range of Normal

Much of what is normal in the toddler years was normal during infancy. Some of the behaviors become more frequent, some less. For instance, a boy who bit people a little in infancy might bite more now. A boy who cried a lot might cry less now.

It's within the range of normal for the boy to throw tantrums, very physically, hitting the walls or floor, or even others, with fists.

It's normal for the boy to emotionally manipulate you with guilt, sadness, and everything else at his disposal.

It's normal for the boy to pick on older or younger siblings.

It's normal for the boy to scream and yell.

It's normal for the boy to cry as much as he needs to.

It's normal for the boy to roughhouse the pets.

It's normal for the boy to bounce around the room (it's also normal for him to be very quiet and unaggressive).

It's normal for the boy to purposefully disobey until we assert our authority appropriately (he is in the "testing twos" now—I prefer this phrase to the "terrible twos").

It's normal for the boy to forget our command or instruction if he gets distracted by something else. It's normal for the boy to forget these instructions over and over again.

It's normal for the boy not to hear the instruction at all, or to hear it differently from how we gave it.

It's normal for the boy to become confused by multiple instructions and not do any of them.

It's normal for the boy to take five to ten seconds to respond to us, especially if we're calling from another room—i.e., not right next to him.

It's normal for the boy to get in little yelling and pulling fights with other kids and, once in a while, with his caregivers.

It's normal for the boy to do or say anything he has modeled from our behavior or another's.

will need to learn, over and over again, that hitting, scratching, and biting are unacceptable. Some toddler boys will need us to teach them this with very intense discipline, which we'll explore in a moment.

All these things are within the range of normal and can be very challenging, but they are balanced by our adult influence over the behavior. The list of behaviors within the normal human range for a toddler is not an invitation for us to allow the behavior to go unchecked.

## DISCIPLINE TECHNIQUES

So much of providing discipline to children is about helping them learn to *regulate their urges.* With a toddler, this is obvious to us. We are charged with helping a growing boy learn how to regulate and handle the flow of his own massive energy.

As we proceed through topics like "Discipline Techniques" in this parenting plan, I'm going to avoid repeating things from previous chapters by asking you to look back at previous chapters as needed. If you find something missing in the chapter you're reading, you'll probably find it covered already in the previous chapter. So much that is covered in a previous chapter applies to the present one, because raising our children is a cumulative experience.

### Creating a Family Discipline System

By the time a child's infancy ends, it is crucial for a family to create a *discipline system* by which to raise him. This systematic approach teaches a child appropriate behavior by building character, testing self-esteem, and teaching social skills.

This system is laid out by Mom, Dad, and the other caregivers; its basics are agreed on and applied consistently. For instance, if you are not going to spank but someone else in the intimate caregiving group is, the system goes awry. While there will always be "style" differences among disciplinarians, it's important for toddlers to get the sense of continuity in the fundamental beliefs and practices of the disciplinarians.

Here are the key elements of a working discipline system. I hope you can agree to practice them in consistent ways.

- As developmentally appropriate, we will provide our son with both increased freedom *and* increased responsibility, rarely giving him more of one than the other.

- Because discipline and moral development are much less effective if the child does not feel loved unconditionally, we will show disappointment when he does something wrong, but we will never withhold love.

- To build character in our son, we will have to make him feel guilty, ashamed, and even "bad" at times, not overdoing it but practicing it carefully, when he has significantly upset family trust.

- In order to develop his discipline and moral system, our son needs to know who the leaders are. We must carry the confidence—and support other caregivers in developing the confidence—to be strong models of moral and parental authority.

- Boys need to see their daily lives as paths toward the accomplishment of a mission. Because this sense of mission is so important to them, we will provide our son with developmentally appropriate duties, even as small as picking up a spoon he drops.

**The Family Mission Statement.**   For some families, a "family mission statement" is a beautiful way to augment a discipline system. Long ago, our ancestors used to have built-in traditions and extended families who provided unspoken family mission statements. For some of these ancestors, a religious text provided such a statement. The Torah, Bible, Koran, or other text was read every day in the family, its mission statements seeping through.

For most of us, our extended families and lineal traditions are not omnipresent enough to comprise the energy of a family mission statement. We need to write our own, gathering the best of all traditions and creating something both old and new.

We can write:

"In this family, we believe . . ."

"We have decided to . . ."

"We aspire to . . ."

### Creating Discipline in Your Verbal Interactions

In a child's toddler years, language becomes one of the primary ways we interact to help the boy regulate his energy. When our son was an infant, we cooed at him and chatted with him, but not with the sophistication possible now. Our new use of language is like a rite of passage for our son. Robert Coles, in *The Moral Intelligence of Children,* writes: "With language comes possibilities, opportunities, responsibilities, burdens—comes the life we know as talking, interpreting, conceptualizing creatures, creatures who can also be given now to moral introspection."

**Using Language Effectively with Toddler Boys.**   Each of us knows intuitively how to talk to our child. But we may not be as good at understanding the subtleties of communication about discipline and moral life. We may ask questions like "Why did you do that?" to a three-year-old and expect an answer. We may get mad when an answer is not forthcoming—yet the three-year-old's brain has not developed well enough to answer.

Boys' verbal abilities often come later than girls', so language interchanges that may have worked with big sister may not work with the boy. His brain may not be as well set up for processing verbal-emotive material as early or as quickly as the female brain. It is much more common for boys to be held back a year from kindergarten or first grade and for girls to outperform boys verbally in preschool. This discrepancy shows up not only in the U.S. but throughout the world in countries where both boys and girls are given early educations. Our boy may be a normal child whose brain isn't ready to respond with the words we're looking for.

A good tool to use with toddler boys is to ask the question "Do you know what you did wrong?" and wait between five and ten seconds for an answer. If no answer comes, then give two choices.

"Did you make me mad because you cried, or because you knocked the chair down?"

If he chooses one, tell him yes or no and then explain what you didn't like.

If he can't choose, choose for him: "You made me mad because you knocked the chair down. You can cry when you need to, but I told you not to run through the room and you did anyway, and you knocked the chair down. It was wrong to run like that in the room; it was wrong to disobey me, and when you knocked the chair down, it finally made me angry. Do you understand?"

He will probably nod or murmur yes.

"Will you listen better next time?"

Again, he'll probably nod.

Throughout this process, don't be afraid to put your language in the context of how the boy affected *you*. He's a toddler. Most of his sense of doing something wrong comes from his caregivers and how they react to him.

**Touch and Talk at the Same Time.**   It is also very useful to have tactile contact with him while you are using language to discipline him. In nearly every circumstance, you only enhance his brain's reception of the language and the discipline if you hold him on your lap or hold his hand or touch him gently in some other way as you speak with him. This methods works even later in a child's life, when tough moral conversations are needed. A five-, six-, or seven-year-old will benefit from your holding his hand as you lead him through tough paces. This technique combines the first sense, aural, with the second, tactile. That sensory echoing makes it easier for the child's brain to process the linguistic statements. The combination of words and touch provides a positive reinforcement for the brain.

**Be Concrete.**   As the toddler boy gets to be three or four, he may be able to answer questions like "Why?" and "What did you do wrong?" with whole sentences, though still not long speeches. We do best by expecting short, concrete answers, and by providing him with explanations of how his behavior affects us. If we give him these explanations, he will develop not just an "I did wrong" response in himself (healthy shame) but also an "I hurt Mom" response (healthy guilt), so it's very important we give him the opportunity to *confess, apologize, and be resolved.* Generally this means an "I'm sorry" and an embrace from the caregiver.

**Firmness and Name Use.** In nearly every case of instruction, it's good to be firm. Studies show that small children consistently respond better to commands—e.g., "Tell me what you're doing there, son"—than to questions like "Would you like to tell me what you're doing?" Research confirms that older children also respond better to commands. The command "Tell me what you did in school today" works better than the question "Do you want to tell me what you did in school today?" The more firm, concrete, and even gently commanding we are, the more we enhance our child's ability to verbally interact and socialize.

When there is no choice, don't offer the child one. This action precludes a lot of need for punishment. Rather than saying to a two-and-a-half-year-old, "Would you like to put that toy hammer back in the box?" we say, "Please put the hammer back in the box," or, "Put that hammer back in the box, now." We might also use the boy's name aloud: "Mitch, please put the hammer in the box, now."

In that sentence we have four elements: the instruction, a time to accomplish the task, mature politeness in our command, and the name of the child. There is no way he can be mistaken as to who we're speaking to. If we have to repeat the command, we repeat it. Generally, by the third, firm, concrete repetition, the two-year-old boy should be expected to accomplish the task.

**Praise and Criticism.** "I love it!" "That's great!" "That's so hard, but you did it so well!" Toddlers need a lot of praise. And they need a lot of it to be specific. As much as it helps them to hear how generally wonderful they are, it is essential they hear how they did well at *a specific task.*

Sometimes we overdo the praise, thinking that we build self-esteem only by praising, or fearing that if we don't keep a lot of praise in his environment, he'll grow up robbed of self-esteem. Our intuition has to guide us to the fine line between how much praise and criticism every child needs. While for a toddler the majority of our interactions will be ones involving praise, there's an art to criticism, too.

Our boys get as much self-esteem from well-accomplished criticism as from well-accomplished praise. We'll get deeper into this idea in later chapters, because toddler criticism is pretty straightforward. For toddlers, usually it's enough to say, "No, Billy, you can't do that," or, "That hurts your brother."

**The Power of Permission.** Parents often underestimate the power of their own permission giving. They miss useful tricks in the language. For instance, "Sweetie, you may carry that tray over to the table now," is a powerful giving of permission to fulfill a task. "Sweetie, do you want to carry the tray somewhere else in the room?" is probably confusing to the boy, and misses the trick of permission language. A little boy who is repeatedly told, "You may do this . . ." "You may do that . . ." gains a sense of being given something important to do by someone he trusts and loves. I often have watched teachers employ this trick. Instead of asking a preschool toddler if he wants to clean up a mess, the teacher says, "You may get the broom and clean up that dirt, now." It's kind of hard for the little boy to refuse.

**Repetition.** How many times should we repeat an instruction or show a toddler how to accomplish it? In a given five-minute period, three times is generally adequate. If he is not getting it, or doing it, after three repetitions, either something is wrong in the way we are instructing him or he may be involved in a power game with us. If he is two years old and playing a child-parent power game, we need to provide the discipline of consequence—generally a "time-out" or the threat of the loss of a toy or privilege.

Tone of voice matters a great deal with little boys. If the instruction—"Pick up the paper from the floor"—is spoken in a normal voice the first time, then we may need to use a stronger tone the second time. If you have to say it a third time, you may need to use a very firm tone, with eye contact, and perhaps gently hold the child's arms. This is not only a give-three-chances rule, it's also a *use-three-senses* rule for getting the boy to attend to you. In fact, if you think of it, applying the three-senses rule the first time you give an instruction can help avoid the frustrating repetition process—the child gets it better the first time.

As discussed in chapter 1, there is interesting biology behind using more than one sense to communicate with boys. The male brain does not take in as much sensory data as the female, nor as quickly. While there are always exceptions, it's not unusual for a parent to find that sometimes her daughter seems to hear better than her son. When we use three senses to communicate with the boy—touch (holding the arms), sight (eye contact), and hearing (saying the instruction firmly)—we adapt to his brain system. He gets a chance to fully hear our instruction.

**A Step-by-Step Verbal Interaction for the Discipline of Toddlers and Boys of Later Ages.** Here is a step-by-step verbal process to incorporate into your discipline system when your son or another boy in your care has done something wrong.

1. Approach the boy's bad action from a position of authority and control. The child who needs discipline is the disciple of the authority providing it.

2. Verbally identify to the child the mistake he has made and explain yourself very concretely: "You were told not to hit your sister. You hit her."

3. If the child is old enough, engage him in preparing his own punishment. If not, tell him what the punishment will be, and stick to it. Too many second chances can lead to loss of authority on your part.

4. Make sure to verbalize to him what moral principle or competency he has not upheld in his actions. The development of his conscience occurs not only because he's punished but because he sees how his "bad action" affects something larger—for instance, "how our family behaves." "You took those cookies

when you were specifically told not to. That is wrong, and it goes against how our family loves and trusts each other."

5. Compel the child to apologize if necessary or make restitution.

6. Talk to him after the experience about what has occurred

7. As age-appropriate, engage the child in a plan to prevent the "bad action" in the future. Especially if a child is committing "bad actions" in order to get attention, we can make some promises to give more attention to the child in the future.

8. End the discipline incident with a reassuring gesture—a hug, a game, or an activity together.

When discipline is a conscious process in this way, it is not merely a set of random reward/punishment acts: It is a sophisticated way of developing a child's character and conscience.

### Using a "Time-Out" and Loss of Privileges

Throughout a boy's childhood, most of our discipline of him will not require more than a "time-out" or privilege loss. Exceptions to this rule may be made for a boy who suffers family trauma of some kind—deaths, divorce, abuse, neglect—which he may act out with regularly uncontrolled behavior.

Time-out is the practice of having the boy sit in a specific place or go to a specific place for a period of time to "think about" what he's done. Usually, we give children time-outs for as many minutes as they are old. It often helps to set a timer.

Loss of privileges can include the loss of a toy or an event or outing he's looking forward to. Sometimes you will just take the privilege or toy away, and no explanation will be needed. Your son will know very well what he has done wrong. Often, however, you will need to make very clear what the offending act was, so that the boy understands the fairness of the punishment.

### Showing Him How to Do the Right Thing

The toddler years are prime years for a caregiver to *show,* not just *tell. No matter what we've told or asked him to do, we should probably show him how to do it the first time and be ready to show him more.* Showing the boy what to do is essential for his brain development. While he is definitely using more language now, he's still not a deeply verbal creature—he remains a very *sensory* creature. He's learning by sensory observation and experience. So often we punish a little boy because he didn't do what we told him. Yet if we haven't first shown him what to do, we shouldn't punish him.

By the time he's about two, your son will probably have a number of daily and personal tasks. One of these might be to clean up a section of his room. In order for him to clean the little section, you can't rely just on telling him (not till he's nearer to four, and even then he'll need help). You have to clean the room with him yourself so he can model the proper behavior. It's best to break the job into little tasks, because the one big task—"Clean your room"—is too unwieldy to him.

One approach is to segment his messy room into four parts and direct him to one part, getting down on your knees and showing him what to do. It is crucial to teach a toddler to imitate us till we're satisfied he knows what we want. Hopefully, as we have brought new toys into his room, we have had him choose which particular shelf area they will go on, so he has a personal sense of his own spaces and some of the "stuff" in each space.

### Raising Your Voice

Often we have to stop our toddler from a potentially dangerous or bad behavior. Using a loud, even harsh voice is a good idea.

Sometimes people will equate a harsh "Do it NOW!" or "That's very bad, never do it again" with psychological abuse. They will feel that verbal harshness, and even being very close to a boy's face, is the same as a hit. I would caution people against equating these things. A harsh voice, used as needed, like a drill sergeant's voice, is authoritative and no-nonsense. It's not abusive unless you use insulting words or name-calling.

### Dealing with Repeated Offenses

Often toddlers get involved in a repeated misbehavior. They keep running through the room when they're not supposed to. They keep taking books off the shelf when they know it's bad behavior. They keep hitting or biting.

Generally, the repeated offense is occurring because (1) the boy needs our attention, or (2) he's in an environment that stimulates the offense. So he needs either our attention or to be removed from the environment.

He keeps running around the room because it's only a room—he really needs to be outside. He has so much energy but doesn't know what to do with it. He needs us to guide him to a physical activity in a larger space. Generally, guiding him to this activity—helping him put his coat on, putting him out in the backyard with the dog, or taking him to the park if you live in an apartment—will reduce needs for discipline and punishment.

He keeps pulling the books off the shelf because he needs our attention. He misses us, he wants us, he needs us, he can't understand why we're not there near him and will make trouble for us rather than verbalize his longing. If we have the time—hopefully, we can make the time—we generally will solve his problem and reduce our need to punish.

Other times, however, his repeated behavior is evidence of the child's inability to self-regulate his energy. How do we deal with that? He can't control his impulse to hit his brother or bite his mother or pull the dog's tail.

In these "repeated-offense" cases, we often gain by (1) providing an equal but harmless environment for the activity; and/or (2) showing the negative result of the behavior. These options won't cure his misbehavior, but they'll go a long way.

For instance, a boy gets angry and hits his mother. Mother brings him to the couch and tells him to hit the couch. Mother is a living object. The couch is an inanimate, nonliving object. The boy learns to take his anger out on the couch, or with a Nerf bat in the dirt. He learns not to hurt or harm a living thing in anger. Training him in this way will make his adolescence easier. Later in life, perhaps he'll shoot hoops when angry or punch a punching bag.

Even beyond initially redirecting his angry fists and voice, we can redirect his whole-body activity. In other words, we get him to dig, work with sand or clay, tear newspapers for a collage he'll make later, or tear up cardboard that's going in the recycling bin anyway. We teach the toddler to redirect his energy from anger to usefulness.

This point speaks directly to a second technique for dealing with repeated negative behavior—namely, showing him the painful result of his behavior.

Because of differences in male and female hormones and brain systems, males are often less likely to notice the depth of harm they bring. When researchers watch empathy behavior among male and female children, they often find that boys "move on" more quickly after knocking someone over, or hitting someone, or even being hit or knocked over themselves. They don't as naturally move to what's called an "early empathy response."

Because we want our boys to learn empathy, we *show them how their behavior affects others.* We don't let them off the hook about what they've done until they actually *feel* another's pain, sensorially and emotionally.

If a boy hurts his brother, we say, "Look, Justin's crying. You hurt him. He doesn't like to be hurt; neither do you."

If a boy bruises another boy, we show him the bruise.

If a boy repeatedly pushes his sister into the wall, we might—in a safe and controlled manner—push the boy into the wall. "Does that feel good to you?" we ask. He will generally see that it does not. He will experience the sense of powerlessness and the pain. Things like this must be done carefully and must remain safe.

If a boy repeatedly yells at others in the day care, we might try matching his yell. We might go right up to him and let out the same disturbing yell. "Did you like that, Ronny? It hurts your ears, doesn't it? It hurts ours, too." If talking to the boy firmly and ordering time-outs and loss of privileges are not working with repeated behaviors such as these, it will not harm the boy to try this somewhat more dramatic kind of solution. Sometimes, getting him to empathize, through his senses, will solve the repeated problem.

### Spanking

There is great disagreement among parents about when and whether to spank toddlers. Some say, "Go ahead and spank as you see fit." Some say, "Spank only as a last resort." Some say spanking as a last resort means you're doing it when you're angry, which is risky. There is an immense amount of wisdom and controversy about spanking toddlers which I, as a professional and a parent, have filtered in this way: *The risks to hitting a toddler outweigh the benefits.*

With infants, there is absolutely no reason to spank, ever. They can't understand why they are being hit. Toddlers may understand why, and every once in a while a quick swat on the butt may help them realize you are the authority. But to spank also means to choose a way of relating that is, ultimately, violent. We try to teach our children not to hit, yet we hit them.

Will swatting a boy once a year or so teach him that to handle his own anger, aggression, and power he should choose violent means? No. Will hitting or spanking him once a month do so—very possibly. Will hitting a boy in the face teach violence? Yes. Will taking a whip to his behind and humiliating him by pulling his pants down teach him that later in life he has the right to humiliate others? Yes.

I suggest never hitting a toddler, but here are some guidelines if you are going to.

1.  Swat once with an open hand on the buttocks (clothed).

2.  Do it to regain authority and stop a dangerous situation—not simply because you are impatient, frustrated, or angry. If you feel these emotions and want to hit, leave the room for a time.

3.  Don't do it more than a few times in a year.

4. If you find yourself needing or wanting to spank frequently, ask yourself and your family and community system why you need to.

If your son is, in your mind, "acting out" constantly enough to need corporal punishment, generally, you'll find that

- he is involved in seeking *negative attention* devices from you because he's not getting enough positive attention;

- he is experiencing a trauma in the family or in day care—perhaps a new sibling has been born; perhaps a divorce is occurring or his parents are very tense;

- he has a congenital behavioral problem (extremely rare in toddlers); or

- his caregiving system has not provided enough authority, rules, structures, and limitations—i.e., he is being raised too permissively. *Boys often act out to get spanked or otherwise to be "put in their place" when they are not naturally being shown their place in their families and communities.*

**Other Kinds of Physical Force Often Are Needed.** Having argued against spanking, I would not say that *all* use of physical force is to be avoided. We've already looked at how you might, sometimes, want to *show* your son, physically, how his actions affect others. You might also need to physically and forcefully—but always carefully—pick him up and put him back into his time-out chair, or into his room, or out of a room in which he is causing trouble. A friend of mine picks her toddler son up by his two biceps, while he is screaming and wrestling, and places him forcibly on his bed in his room and then shuts the door. She said to me once, "Sometimes he just needs me to be as physical as he is." She never hits or inappropriately shakes her son. She simply uses her parental force to show him that she is the authority. Boys whom you consider "more aggressive" may need more of this kind of authority.

**An Angry Place.** If you are dealing with an excessively aggressive or angry toddler, he may need an "angry place"—a place he can go or physically be put into when he is too angry to control himself. The place should have a carpeted floor or a mat. It might contain a few soft Nerf bat–type items in it. He can throw his tantrum there.

Without realizing it, we develop this intimate environment pretty intuitively for all our kids. "You're being too loud and whiny right now," we say. "You may go to your room until you can get control." If we have a child who needs this instruction every few hours, his own bedroom is the wrong place for him to go—he will associate his angry place with his bedroom, and he'll be confused. But for the less bellicose child, we can make his room his angry place.

### Using Bedtime as Self-Discipline Development

Once the boy has grown enough to be sleeping long nights (eight to ten or more hours at a time), which generally happens when he is between one and two years old, 8:00 P.M. is an appropriate bedtime. Eight P.M. is probably good until he is about ten years old. A growing child needs ten to twelve hours of sleep per day. Nap time often is not included in this figure (nap time generally ends when he is about four years old). As we saw in the previous chapter, there are good reasons to adjust this 8:00 P.M. suggestion—for instance, if you don't get home from work till 6:00 or 7:00 and need more bonding time with your toddler.

Also, for some boys' natural temperaments, 8:00 P.M. is unrealistic. Some boys just don't fall asleep early—metabolism, genetics, and other factors apply here. Every parent can adapt this time to fit his or her life.

It's important to be vigilant about bedtime. Going to bed at a certain time helps a child develop self-discipline. Many boys don't fall asleep late in the evening because they were not trained to do so by parents and caregivers, not because their temperament requires a chaotic bedtime schedule. These boys are missing an opportunity to learn discipline.

Beyond the advantage of an 8:00 P.M. bedtime for the boy is the advantage for his family. You as parents need the time after 8:00 to make your house run. If your son is not able to fall asleep around 8:00, let him know clearly that as of a certain time (between 8:00 and 8:30), he is not to leave his room and bed except to go to the bathroom.

**Stalling.**   Often the boy will go to bed, then come out of his room and say he's hurting or hungry or . . . you name it. If he is stalling, he needs to be told, "No stalling, son. Go to bed." And we have to mean it. He'll finally get the message.

### Toilet Training

It's quite normal for a boy of even four or five still to wear pull-ups to bed. In general, boys potty train for both night and day later than girls, so our expectations ought to be a little different. A boy usually can be day trained between the ages of two and three, but there are frequent exceptions. *In nearly every case, potty training should not be an issue for punitive discipline.* A toddler's life is basically not in his own control—it's in adults' control. But there are a few things in his control, and potty training is one of them. The best success with potty training comes by gently prodding, reminding, reading books to him about potty training, and modeling off bigger siblings—not by pressuring. If we're subtle, consistent, and patient, he'll get trained on time for his body.

From this chapter forward, I will include a box of Rules to Live By (see pages 112 to 113), a kind of culmination or summary of what we should expect from and make sure of in our son's life.

## MORAL TEACHING

We teach a toddler morality, to a great extent, by loving him uncondi-tionally and by providing him a well-ordered life. In addition, it is cru-cial for us to tell and read moral and spiritual stories to toddlers. Our toddlers love to hear our voices when we read and tell these stories to them, and though the toddlers don't understand the meanings exactly,

## Rules to Live By

1.  A toddler boy should learn never to hit his caregiver, even when angry. If he is throwing a tantrum and hitting you, he can be redirected to hit the floor or a suitable couch or other soft object.

2.  A toddler boy should learn that there is a difference between aggressive play and angry aggression. If he's hitting other children in anger, we need to intercede. He is crying out for help in disciplining and regulating his own angry energy. If he's involved in fake wrestling, fake punching, or other kinds of harmless pretend play, we generally don't need to intercede.

3.  A toddler boy should learn not to bite anyone, anytime.

4.  A toddler boy should learn to guide his body in physical games and in spontaneous play. If he's very awkward and clumsy—he bumps into others—we need to help him pay more attention to physical dexterity and give him more parent-child training and game time.

5.  A toddler boy should learn to negotiate the use of toys and objects, rather than take or steal them from other children. The toddler boy can be taught to trade toys and create time limits for toy use. If his belligerence becomes bellicose, he should lose the use of the toy. If all parents and child-care providers taught children better about respecting their own and other kids' workspace and toys, adolescents would have fewer discipline problems.

6.  A toddler boy should learn profound respect for his authorities—this means no sticking a tongue out at a parent or calling names.

7.  A toddler boy should not curse or use words inappropriate to the family and community. In my house, children are not allowed to use any curse words or use the Lord's name in vain. They have to say, "My gosh," not "My God." When I err, and a child imitates, I quickly correct him, reminding him that he need not do as I do.

8.  A toddler boy should learn the magic words "Please," "Thank you," "Excuse me," "I'm sorry," and learn to use them frequently. He actually wants to be polite—it brings him the reward of positive attention from others.

9. A toddler boy should do independently those small tasks he can do independently.

10. A toddler boy should help us with our chores. If he is standing by a counter and can reach the apple we need to cut, we can ask him to bring us the apple. Generally, he'll enjoy helping us and accomplishing the tiny task.

11. By three and a half to four years old, the toddler boy should be able to repeat to us, with some help, the basic rules of his house or school.

12. A toddler boy should not significantly disrupt an adult area of interaction. For instance, a toddler should be disciplined if he carries on in a grocery store (perhaps by being removed). If he can't stay still for the weekly shopping, you may not want to take him to the store for a while—it is too public a place to have a weekly power struggle with a toddler.

13. A toddler boy, by age three, should learn not to interrupt. His repeated interruptions should be considered a pretty big offense. The boy may not be getting enough general attention from the caregivers—something that must be addressed. Also, the toddler may not have learned that interrupting is wrong. "You may not interrupt" is an important response to a toddler who interrupts inappropriately, as are time-outs and loss of privileges.

14. A toddler boy should expect to play independently for a significant period nearly every day. "Alone" play is very good for the boy—it helps him get destimulated from other interactions, it shows him that his parents aren't necessarily his only recourse to self-stimulation, and it gives him time to grow on his own.

15. A toddler boy should learn to pick up after himself. In most cases, there's little need for his mother to pick up an item he dropped, or to constantly clean up after him. "Son, you dropped that Kleenex; please pick it up." Perhaps we're singing this kind of thing ten times a day—but it's a good refrain.

they get a great deal more than we think they do. We know a three-year-old boy understands the themes because we'll hear him say to his friend, "That's wrong," and perhaps give an example of a character from a book or program who did wrong.

### Letting Toddlers Experiment

Much of toddler behavior is really just experimental behavior. Much of a toddler's "lying," "cheating," "stealing" are not those things— they are developmentally appropriate experimental behaviors by which the boy is gaining, even self-teaching, moral education.

The toddler yanks a toy away from Billy. He's learning how he feels and how Billy feels. He has to yank the toy in order to learn.

When we correct a toddler, we usually don't need to come down hard on him for *stealing,* but rather for "taking that toy from Billy." The boy is too young to be labeled a morally defective creature. We do well by protecting boys from being labeled for as long as possible.

Simultaneously, our vigilance about making sure kids are fair with one another is absolutely essential. If we are dealing with a toddler who "just doesn't get it"—who always yanks toys away—we will want to find out if he has a deep resentment toward other children. If his misbehavior is temporary—e.g., his parents have just had another child and he is trying to adjust, or his mother has just opened a day care and he's suddenly got a lot of competition for her attention—we can be patient, give him more alone time with a caregiver so he doesn't have to be jealous, and/or discipline the behavior until it passes from his experimental path. If his misbehavior seems to be becoming permanent, we need to get help from the rest of our family and, perhaps, from professionals.

### Helping Toddlers Make Good Choices

Toddlers start having to make choices. Should I run that way, or this? Should I talk back, or not? Should I wear that shirt, or this? Many choices are unconscious, but they get made nonetheless, and helping the toddler to make choices is essential. *Moral training of a tod-*

*dler involves training him to make right choices rather than wrong ones.*

Simultaneously, while choice making becomes a new part of a child's development in the late toddler years, too many choices can be overwhelming. We want to let our child make little choices—what to wear, for instance—but not try to force our child into a moral dilemma where he has to figure out what to choose: "Do you want to watch TV with your big brother, or come to the store with me?" The older brother will probably watch something morally inappropriate for a toddler boy, but the younger boy may well want to stick around just to be with him. He'll end up choosing material morally unsuitable for himself in order to have the emotional closeness with his brother. When it comes to overt or covert moral choices, it's often best to *show* him the right choice yourself. "You'll come with me to the store."

### Finding the Spiritual in Everyday Life

Toddlers, especially as they understand language better, can grasp the existence of spirituality in everyday life. To some extent, they can understand stories about God and angels. Especially as they near four years old, they can begin to grasp Aesop's fables.

William J. Bennett's *The Children's Book of Virtues* is a good resource for moral stories to read to children. Marianne Williamson's *Emma and Mommy Talk to God* is another. Though the unannotated Bible is generally too wordy and its language too abstruse, the stories will intrigue and teach the late toddler. Certainly the reading of any sacred stories will only help the child begin to set within himself a pattern of expecting those stories to be a part of his life throughout his development.

Spirituality—the child's connection with hidden mysteries—is not a matter just of books for toddlers. In fact, to make it such would be to miss completely the toddler's developmental universe. He is developing sensorially, so he needs to sense God everywhere around him.

"It's raining," we might say. "Do you think maybe God is crying?"

"I look at your smile, son, and I see God smiling."

"Look at that flower. God is so good."

"Mom," he might ask, either with words or just with his eyes, "why did Grandma die?"

"Because," we might answer, "that's the way God planned it."

We will explore spiritual development a great deal more as this parenting plan continues. It is essential to remember that moral training will be more difficult if we don't provide the child with a way of understanding the mysterious. Little boys want to believe in God—please substitute your words and philosophy as needed when I use that word. They want to have answers to mysterious things. They feel lost without such answers. That which we can answer for them in the toddler years is less they have to feel scared about, and more they can use as ballast for their own good behavior.

It is also very useful to use God as our parenting ally. "God wouldn't like you to hit the way you did." This kind of statement can be overused, but if we use it a few times, surgically, it will be successful with cognizant toddlers.

## A HEALTHY MORAL AND EMOTIONAL ENVIRONMENT

We've explored what kind of discipline will exist in a healthy environment, and what kind of moral focus we want. Now let's examine a number of other crucial elements in home and child-care environments.

### Changes in the Caregiving System

As the child becomes two to three years old, his immersion in his mother's caregiving remains very strong, but it does dissipate a little. Should she have had the choice or opportunity to stay home since the child's birth, the mother might be starting plans to return to work. The boy wants to socialize more through day care, preschool, or co-op environments. The dad may find the boy easier to "hang out with." The late toddler years especially are different from the infant years, and the whole caregiving system does alter itself intuitively.

**Choose Child Care and Preschool Wisely.** Many boys will enter day care, nursery school, or preschool in the toddler years. Some key things to look for in toddler care and education are

- caregivers who themselves are raising or have raised boys, or who clearly understand "boyishness";
- a day-care environment we think our child will enjoy long-term. A recent study of day care showed that boys who change day cares frequently—for instance, boys in six day cares in eighteen months—end up more unnecessarily aggressive and more prone to develop attachment disorders;
- a preschool/day-care environment where there is a lot of kines- thetic learning—artwork, coloring, blocks, moving toys. It is impor- tant to remember that often when little boys get into a lot of trouble in child-care environments, it is because the environment is not appropriately stimulating;
- an environment that provides order and discipline.
- an environment with no television in it (or, if there is one, it's rarely used);
- an environment where the staff appears happy (this suggestion is also very important for nannies and au pairs—if they are not happy, the child will suffer);
- an environment that can become like your extended family—for instance, if appropriate, you can go in and volunteer once in a while, and you can drop in to see how the toddler is doing;
- a preschool environment that provides parent-teacher conferences regularly;
- a preschool with an appropriate ratio of boys to girls—i.e., your boy is not the only one in it;
- a day care where the infants have a room to themselves, separate from the toddlers during parts of the day (like nap time)—often

toddlers will bump, hit, or sit on infants and be scolded for being too loud when the two groups are together; and

• an environment that allows lots of outside play time, weather permitting, and allows appropriate male fantasy play.

As always your intuition holds the key to success with day care, nannies, and preschool. Some of the "brand-name" preschools, like Montessori, when taught by qualified and passionate teachers, can be superb for a little boy. Some of the small in-home preschools have school-type activities that adequately challenge your toddler. Making many visits to a day care, nursery school, or other child-care environment before deciding on one is appropriate. Before purchasing a home, we go look at it many times. Choosing child care deserves at least that.

**Give Fathers "Tickle Time."**   Noah is three. His day-care providers take him to see a parade. He comes home and tells his parents about how fun it was.

"What did you see?" his mother asks.

"I saw elephants."

"What were they like?" his mother asks.

The boy says, "They were big, they had big ears."

"Let's read *Jimmy the Elephant* later, okay?" the mother suggests.

"Yeah," the boy says gleefully.

His father gets down on the ground and says, "Climb on, I'll be the elephant. You wanna ride?"

The child jumps on, laughing.

This is a true story and such a wonderful illustration of something many toddlers experience. Often, women and men react to their toddlers differently. Mothers often direct themselves toward what are called "verbal-emotive" responses, and fathers tend to direct themselves to what are called "spatial-action" responses. Both ways of relating are natural to the different brain systems, and both are positive *and important* for that toddler boy.

Since so much of what's in this chapter is directed to moms, let me just take a moment to say to dads and moms both that it is so important dads get "tickle time" with the toddler—my nickname for that wrestling and other active playtime (right before bed is probably not the best time!) dads so often love with their children, and children love with their dads.

**Coming Home from Work.** There's something that a mom or dad coming home from work may miss—in my observation, it's especially something dads miss. Its lack often shows up with toddlers.

Say we come home and our child wants our attention. So often, rather than doing something transitional before arriving home, something that will help us be fresh for our family—a little drive, a little walk in the park—we come home exhausted. Because we are exhausted, we try to avoid the stimulation of our toddler. He comes at us hard, and we pull away. Unconsciously we think, *I'm too tired. Leave me alone for now. Later, we'll do something.* "Later" arrives, and sometimes we do something and sometimes we don't. One thing that often does happen between now and later is that we have hassles with the boy—he emotionally manipulates, or he acts out in some way.

We've missed the boy's reality and a chance to manage it smoothly. *All he really needs when we first come home is a few minutes of our undivided attention.* If he gets this, he'll go back to what he's doing, and we'll get a brief respite and some time with our spouse. If we don't give him this five or ten minutes, he'll actually be pressuring us, in overt and covert ways, all evening. He'll create lots of tension in order to get our attention.

The trick is to give him the few minutes of undivided attention when *he* asks for it, so that we don't have to give him varying degrees of negative and frustrating attention as a family for the next two hours.

**Give Messages of Love to Moms Taking Care of Toddlers.** I was speaking in a city one evening when a mom came up in a crowd afterward and immediately started crying. She had three children, one a very spirited three-year-old boy. Her husband's work took him out of town a lot, and she felt overwhelmed and unsupported. She was not blaming him—she was sympathetic to how hard he worked—but she felt very sad about how difficult it was to care for a toddler in the father's absence.

"He needs his father!" she said. "*I* need his father."

Men often cannot understand how difficult it can be to give love and attention and care to any toddlers, to say nothing of more than one at a time. Especially if we are not an active, hands-on father—if we are gone a lot or if, even when home, we don't provide much hands-on care—it is so important that we constantly send messages of love and support to the mother. If this means calling her every night from out of town and listening to her day, it's essential we do so. Our whole interaction with our family will be happier because she will be happier, and we will be modeling compassionate marital behavior for that little boy.

### The Importance of Motor Activity

Susan, mother of two, once said to me, "I have a two-year-old and a three-and-a-half-year-old, both boys. I just try to stay serene, even though my house looks like a war zone." Her solution: "When they start getting wild, I send them outside, all bundled up, if need be. There's nothing better than to run around."

Joanna, a microbiologist by profession and a mother of two boys, put her experience this way: "In our house it is an *absolute requirement* for the boys to get outside for physical activity. Letting young boys have place and space for 'uncontrolled motor activity' is so important. When my boys get their energy bottled up, we make them do 'forced activity time.' If it's too hard for one of them to go out because of the weather, we time him running around the house, like a game. What the young male needs is activity that forces large muscle mass movement. I have many friends with boys who keep them in confined spaces, and the boys just keep getting into trouble. It's very sad."

Motor activity is indeed essential for these little guys. As early as possible, it's worth starting these "activity times." Everything from emotional to moral to discipline development goes better in environments that give boys controlled, and also safe and uncontrolled, gross motor activity.

## Media Use

Some people like to start two-year-olds on computers. If you are one of these, you might reconsider. Attaching his developing brain to a screen at two years old is less useful to him than reading to him, talking to him, doing a tactile project with him, giving him friends to play with, and tossing his little body up in the air in adult play. All of these build his brain development better than staring at a screen. Toddlers need hands-on manipulation of *real* objects in order for the brain to become fully capable of abstraction later. Toddlers need to be read to in order to increase a number of capacities, including verbal skills. Toddlers need lots of socialization time in order for the human brain to learn how to interact with others. A learning-oriented CD-ROM *once in a while* is a fine thing, but on a list of important activities for the developing toddler brain, computer use should go near the bottom.

Sometimes parents will worry about this point of view. They'll say, "But this is the information age—my son's got to compete; he's got to get started on computers as soon as possible." It is actually a myth that toddlers who do a lot of computer activity compete better later. In fact, a child who learns to use the computer at age six or seven or ten can actually compete just as well as one who learns at two or three. It is not difficult for the brain to learn to use a computer; it is difficult for it to learn verbal skills, social interaction skills, and so on. These are the great priority in brain development for young children. I *highly* recommend Jane Healy's *Failure to Connect: How Computers Affect Our Children's Minds—for Better and Worse* to anyone with any questions about computer use and children.

**Be Careful with Television Use.**   Some people like to plop infants and toddlers in front of the television for hours at a time. Again, this activity not only retards brain development but it cuts the boy off from actual relationship. The American Federation of Teachers recently published a landmark issue devoted to how reading affects the brain. Their study shows that while television viewing does little to stimulate complex neural firing and development of dendrites and tissue, reading does a great deal to effect growth in all the brain-development indicators.

It is, quite simply, better to spend the "TV time" reading to the boy. *Since television actually serves no useful brain or self-development function for the toddler, a policy of no or very limited TV in your toddler's life can't hurt.* For many of us who come home from work tired, or during rushed morning routines, television can be a useful way to occupy kids so we can have a half hour of free time or "getting ready for work" time. Thus television can serve a useful function in the lives of toddlers, but much beyond a half hour to one hour per day of TV time is not ultimately useful for your family.

**Be Aware of Media Morality.**   One of the primary storehouses of both moral and immoral teaching in our child's environment is the media. In their toddler years, children ought to be watching *only* programming that teaches values and has good messages. Just as in infancy, a three- or four-year-old does not have a brain well enough developed to do anything except absorb what it sees. A toddler's brain will absorb amoral or immoral stories, and the child will seek to imitate them. Likewise, it will absorb stories with morals or "lessons," and neutral, beautiful experiences—as in *The Magic Schoolbus* or *Reading Rainbow*—and the child will imitate those as well. Once I was at a day care and heard a three-year-old boy talking about sticking his hands down the throat of his play companion "to pull out your guts and choke you on them." This boy had older siblings who let him watch horror movies with them. According to the day-care provider, this media imitation happened a lot. We put our boys at a moral disadvantage only if we allow inappropriate media use.

On the other hand, for a three- or four-year-old, Disney animated movies, like *The Lion King* or *Pocahontas,* can teach moral and emotional development.

I would advise against placing a toddler boy in front of Saturday-morning cartoons without heavy discernment on your part of which ones are worthwhile. Most are basically worthless to his developing brain, and many cause him moral ambiguity.

## TERRENCE'S STORY

A mother of three told me this wonderful story.

*We were at big sister's soccer game. Terrence, my three-year-old, was watching his sister play and yelling to her, trying to get her attention. He just really wanted her to notice him. She tried to once in a while, but I could tell he was being distracting. I took him away from the game. Well, this made him wail and carry on.*

*"Will you be good?" I asked. "If I take you back to the sidelines, will you just watch and not yell out at Sarah?"*

*He assured me he would! But sure enough, as soon as we got back there, he carried on again. By now it was a way of getting attention, it was a way of testing me, it was just all sorts of terrible twos stuff. I took him away again; we replayed the whole thing again.*

*I was getting very frustrated with him. Fortunately, the game ended and we got out of there. That night I was thinking about what to do. I thought about how little boys do love to have a mission, an important thing to focus on. So the next day, when we had Sarah's next game (her team made it to the next round of the tournament), I said to Terrence, "You know, this game is so important for Sarah, and she really needs you to help her. Do you want to help her?"*

*He nodded his head vigorously. Sarah helped by saying, "I really need you to, Terrence."*

*"So what you have to do," I told him, "is cheer for Sarah when something goes well, like I do. If you do this, she's going to play even better, and maybe she'll win. Because you and I cheer, she might do something really great, and won't that feel good?"*

*He was into this now. He really wanted to help. And he felt like he was a part of it.*

*So when we got to the game, we acted like we were really on an important mission. I got down on my knees with him and talked to him about what the players were doing, and he clapped and cheered and really focused on his sister's actions. Between this and him having a mission, Terrence just really got into the game. By the time he finally got bored and distracted, he was ready to kick a ball around behind us rather than make trouble.*

Terrence's mother made his sister's success part of his *mission,* and modeled the activity of mission with him: She drew him into the larger world of the game, and he responded with less negative attention getting and ultimately an interest in the game. In this small set of interactions, the boy learned a lot about how to live his life.

# FIVE

# The Boy Emerges

## NURTURING BOYS OF FIVE AND SIX

This sweet story came to me from a mom of two, off the Internet.

*Last week I took my children to a restaurant. My six-year-old asked if he could say grace. As we bowed our heads, he said, "God is good. God is great. Thank you for the food, and I would even thank you more if Mom gets us ice cream for dessert. And liberty and justice for all! Amen!"*

*Along with the laughter from the other customers nearby, I heard a woman remark, "That's what's wrong with this country. Kids today don't even know how to pray. Asking God for ice cream!"*

*Hearing this, my son burst into tears and asked me, "Did I do it wrong? Is God mad at me?" As I held him and assured him that he had done a terrific job and God was certainly not mad at him, an elderly gentleman approached the table.*

*He winked at my son and said, "I happen to know that God thought that was a great prayer."*

*"Really?" my son asked.*

*"Cross my heart." Then, in a theatrical whisper, he added—indicating the customer who had disliked the prayer—"Too*

*bad she never asks God for ice cream. A little ice cream is good for the soul sometimes."*

*Naturally, I bought my kids ice cream at the end of the meal. My son stared at his for a moment and then did something I will remember the rest of my life.*

*He picked up his sundae and without a word walked over and placed it in front of the woman who had disliked his prayer.*

*With a big smile, he told her, "There, this is for you. Ice cream is good for the soul sometimes, and my soul is good already."*


## DEVELOPMENTAL MILESTONES

So much emerges in our children during the "kinder years." Our kids are five and six years old, generally in or soon to be in kindergarten, perhaps some of them already moving into first grade. Immense kindnesses emerge in children during these years, especially when their basic needs are met and they are treated well. Immense frustration also can emerge. The German poet Goethe was famous for saying, "You can never satisfy an intelligent man." He could very well have been speaking of the little boy emerging into the realities of post-toddler life. His intelligence is just budding in new ways, making him capable of trying to save an angry customer's soul in a restaurant, and just as capable of confusing himself with many little thoughts at once.

### His Intellectual Growth

Don't be surprised to find your little boy a very kinesthetic learner—a toucher, a holder of things, a boy who learns letters better by tracing them than by memorizing them. Your boy is soaking in the world through his senses, and wanting to do it in more organized ways than he had in the first four or so years of life. He wants to follow through with projects a little more. He focuses for a somewhat longer period of time now. He becomes immensely proud of his accomplishments and needs you to be proud of not only the product but the process he followed. In fact, the product—a picture, for example—may often seem silly or unfinished to the caregiver, but it is *always* an indication of hard work by a growing mind and heart. While the boy can take some soft criticism about what he makes, he rarely needs criticism for his process of making it—he's doing his best. Intellectual guidance is better than criticism: "Here, do it this way; this might work."

### His New Sense of Gender Identity

Sometimes parents will worry that their five- or six-year-old starts really focusing on his own gender for playmates and for social interaction. Boys and girls mix very well in school and on social occasions, but especially at play, kinder boys and girls start gravitating toward their own gender. Sometimes there is even tension created between genders because "she doesn't know how to play like we do," or "we don't want those girls around."

It is completely normal for boys to seek out boys and girls to seek out girls. It's also a wonderful teaching opportunity to lead boys to *appropriately* show their gender preference—not with "I hate you" or "You're just a girl!" As with just about everything a "kinder" boy does, there is opportunity to teach him social skills so that he learns to be *kinder*—and learns now, so that he does not have to be punished later for inappropriate behavior.

The gender identity that the boy experiences during this time will extend to a new curiosity about his father and other men. You might find the boy following Dad around more than he did a year or two ago. This action is a foreshadowing of the gender identity surge that will occur in adolescence, when the boy will go through a very critical search for the father's (and other men's) attention. In the kinder years, we should notch up the father's participation just a little.

### His Moral Development

In the kinder years, remorse in our son may seem to break his heart, and as he weeps, may break our own. When he notices that he has done something very wrong, he might simply break down in tears because he's so sorry. Kahlil Gibran, the Lebanese poet, wrote in *The Prophet:* "How shall you punish those whose remorse is already greater than their misdeed?" Often, faced with our kinder son's remorse, we may well not punish at all.

This boy is becoming very moral, from the inside out. He is able to think morally not only because he is obedient but also because an inner voice—his conscience—is beginning to develop. Often he still will be too late to catch his impulsiveness. But he more often will know when he is wrong and have some sense even of why. This conscience is just budding and needs our constant encouragement.

The boy is also moving toward a clearer sense of justice. He's beginning to understand that unfairness does exist. He'll try to get everything to be even: "Jake got a treat, so why can't I?" He wants things fair, and he can think out what would be fair from his subjective point of view. But he's also able to handle it better if you say, "Jake gets a treat today because he did so well on that test. On another day, it will happen for you, too."

Perhaps the greatest development in his moral thinking is his development of self-consciousness—his sense of himself as an accountable moral actor. Even if he has trouble controlling impulses, we can use his new self-consciousness to train him in everything from impulse control to good manners to following instructions to acting compassionately toward a sibling.

The end of toddlerhood and the beginning of boyhood is a time of such transitions that nearly anything the boy does can be within the range of normal (see page 129).

## DISCIPLINE TECHNIQUES

By now, if you have not established a clear discipline system (see chapter 2), you may be having some real troubles with your son's ability to regulate his own energy, handle his impulses, and feel comfortable in the family. If you haven't already, now is the time to look back at the two previous chapters and set up such a system.

Here are techniques to advance and add to your developing discipline system.

## The Range of Normal

It's normal for the boy to lie a little or stretch the truth.

It's normal for the boy to whine, and still have a few tantrums.

It's normal for the boy to jump and bounce around a lot from sheer pent-up energy.

It's normal for the boy to increase verbal expression of and questions about spiritual thoughts, especially if spiritual life is important to his family system.

It's normal for the boy to be bossy at times.

It's normal for the boy, in one mom's words, "to want to conquer everything and everyone."

It's normal for the boy to tell people to go away—he wants quiet, individual playtime; it's just as normal for the boy to feel rejected when other people aren't around.

It's normal for the boy to still say "No!" but with much less frequency now than in toddlerhood.

It's normal for him to excel at emotional manipulation, playing authorities against each other, and getting other siblings in trouble.

It's normal for the boy still to grab and take others' toys, though with much less frequency than two years ago.

It's normal for the boy to seek not only positive attention but also negative attention—to do things that bring our rebuke. Both feel like "attention" to him.

It's normal for the boy to be a know-it-all, pretending he knows answers when he doesn't even fully understand the questions.

It's normal for the boy to notice bullies now, and become scared of them.

It's normal for the boy to do lots of things wrong so that we will show him how to do them right.

### Providing Adequate Love and Attention

A grandmother once said to me: "If a child gets enough love and at-tention, he won't need as much criticism and correction." This is a very useful dictum. If we have found ourselves having to reprimand a boy—"Stop doing that!"—ten times in the last hour, what's probably most wrong is not what he's doing but that he has to keep doing this undisci-plined activity *in order to get our undivided attention.* If we stop what we're doing in the other room and go tickle, hug, play with, and guide him, he will often cease doing the irritating thing.

### Providing Natural Consequences

When your son was two years old and crayoned the walls of his room, his brain had not developed enough for him to realize that he shouldn't. The parts of his brain that can disconnect impulse from ac-tion hadn't really formed. After you got angry at him, he really wanted to never do it again, but his memory still hadn't developed well enough to remember, so three days later, it happened again. By the time he was four, this behavior changed. He was able to make better connections and he had a better memory—thus when we discussed discipline for toddlers we talked about the importance of natural consequences.

Now that he's five or six, these consequences become even more im-portant. The vast majority of the time, he *can* remember the instruction, and he knows what's wrong. If he does draw on his wall, we enhance the development of his brain, his morality, and his self-discipline by as-sociating his wrong action with a *natural consequence:* e.g., he scrubs the wall. Natural consequences now can become more useful than time-outs and loss of privileges.

### Providing Natural Rewards

Not only do we give him the natural consequence when he does wrong, but we give him a natural reward when he does right. For in-stance, if he cleans up his room one day without our asking, we give him a hug and lots of loving and also a reward of time: "You cleaned up your room, and I didn't have to nag you. That nagging would have taken a half hour. So now you have a half hour with me, just you and me, to do whatever you want." Creative, natural rewards build love, connection, and a desire to please in the future.

### Creating Discipline in Your Verbal Interactions

There are a lot of wonderful "talk tools" we can use to strengthen our communication with the kinder boy and to teach obedience and authority in creative ways.

If the boy is resisting or dawdling, give him two choices: "You may get in the car right now, or you may go sit in time-out. Which do you choose?" Generally, he'll choose to get in the car.

If he avoids fulfilling requests, make sure to give firm directions: Say, "Get in the car now," rather than "Would you get in the car now, please?" especially if he's showing resistance to request-type directions.

Don't explain your instructions all the time.

Son: "I don't want to! Why do I have to?"

Mom: "Because I said so."

"Because I said so" is enough much of the time. Explanations are needed when they will help the boy grow up, not when they will lead to an unnecessary power struggle.

On some occasions, you can make commands into games: "See if you can get in the car before I tickle you!" Kids love games, and many commands can be just those. Multiple-choice games often work: "Do I want you to . . . dig a hole twenty miles wide? . . . stand on your head? . . . or get in the car?" The boy will generally cry, "Get in the car!"

**The Two-Times Rule.** In our discussion about how many times to repeat an instruction in the toddler years, we agreed that the boy might get three repetitions. If that was a part of our discipline system then, in the boy's kinder years, we may want to scale the repetitions back to two.

"Please put your coat on, son."

Some time passes.

"I asked you to put your coat on. I won't ask again."

Indeed, we should not ask again. If these two times don't work, we employ a discipline technique—a natural consequence: He doesn't go to the place he wanted to go; he receives a time-out, a loss of privilege, etc.

By five years old, the boy is quite capable of remembering instructions and mediating his own natural distraction.

**Praise and Criticism.**   In our child's kinder years, we must praise a great deal but also be more critical. While we still should praise our son about nine times more than we criticize him, we must critique accurately, directly, and concretely.

"Son, you spit at Jimmy. That was rude." We don't couch our comments. We say exactly what impulse was inappropriate, and we name its bad quality.

"Son, you sneaked those marshmallows when you were told not to. That was wrong, wasn't it?" We are using criticism to teach impulse control, so we must be very specific about the offending impulse.

So often, tears will come and we will embrace the boy. Just after the criticism, we may also want to immediately redirect his energy to a constructive way of making amends. "I see that you're pretty sad about doing that. What if you help Mommy bake this cake, and we'll use some of those marshmallows in it?" He's been criticized, and then redirected toward a practical project.

Critique often involves teaching empathy and compassion quite directly: "You remember how you left Heather out of your games and made her feel bad? That made her feel the way you feel when I put you in time-out. Do you like that feeling?"

"Son, when you push the back of my seat with your feet, it really hurts my back." It is often as important to show the boy how he's hurting us as it is to say, "Don't do that." In fact, generally, it creates a better-disciplined child.

"What did you do wrong?" is a constant question to ask. It is critical, and increases the boy's thinking ability. If he can't answer, we feed him the answer. "Do you understand?" can be followed by a request for him to tell us in his words. He'll often get close to what he did wrong. That's generally enough. And as usual, when our critique is done, we embrace him in some way to show him that he is always loved.

In the boy's kinder years, try asking, "How do you feel about what just happened?" but don't expect an entirely articulate response. The boy's brain still is not fully set up for that task. Better is often to say,

"Are you sad about _____?" and fill in the blank, trying out different things you think he might be feeling. Once he's been helped by you into the area where he is feeling something, he often can be more talkative. This technique builds greater emotional vocabulary and more moral connection.

### Limiting Whining and Backtalk

It is difficult to teach self-discipline when the discipline system allows a lot of uncontrolled whining and backtalk. The boy is in the age of obedience; letting him backtalk hurts his sense of your authority and his own safety. Three books I like that help flesh this problem out are *Backtalk,* by Audrey Ricker and Carolyn Crowder, *Win the Whining War and Other Skirmishes,* by Cynthia Whitham, and *Taming the Dragon in Your Child,* by Meg Eastman and Sydney Craft Rozen.

If you've gotten tired of the boy's whining, you may infer that he is tired of it, too—he just doesn't know how to stop and needs your help. Putting him in the time-out spot is appropriate; or, if you're in a public place, take him out to the car.

While nearly every boy will experiment with backtalk—and we don't need to overreact to it—he nonetheless wants his parents' authority to remain strong. He actually develops better self-esteem by depending on a strong, loving authority. So if we allow him to backtalk a lot, it gives him too much power, and gives us too little, which utterly confuses a five-year-old.

Sometimes, in dealing with backtalk, the parent who is the more authoritative has to support the parent who is getting most of the backtalk. If, for instance, the boy is backtalking Mom but not Dad (perhaps he is more respectful of Dad's authority), Dad must step in for a time and fully support Mom's efforts to cut it out.

### Providing Behavioral Limits

Just as his brain has developed to understand, suffer, and enjoy natural consequences and rewards, he has also developed enough to be incredibly hungry for experiences he now can see on his expanded horizon. If limits are not imposed, he will voraciously overstimulate himself.

For instance, if your boy has a sweet tooth, he will eat all the sweets he can. He's mature enough now to figure out how to manually or emotionally manipulate his environment to get what he wants. He is not, however, mature enough to realize that he'll rot his teeth and get overstimulated (and then depressed) by the sugar. Once in a while we might hear him mimic us—"Sugar just rots your teeth. I shouldn't eat it." But for the most part, he'll eat all he can.

It is our job to impose the limits he needs for safety and happiness. One sweet treat per day is an appropriate limitation. He'll adapt to it relatively quickly. Even if he fusses a few times, he'll adapt. Our own continued firmness will ensure that.

### Giving Permission

It is highly appropriate for your five- or six-year-old son to ask your permission to go to a friend's house nearby. It is appropriate for him to ask permission to stay after school for a snack. *The more permission you notice your son asking, the more in control you are and, therefore, the more in control he is of his own life.* He is building self-discipline.

We don't want to be unnecessarily rigid or overly punitive with him. But at five or six, a boy ought to be seeing his everyday life as a plot that has been written, for the most part, by his trusted caregivers, not by himself.

### Teaching Appropriate Response Time

When we ask him to do something, how much response time does the boy need? Often, whether it is a chore we want him to do or some other of a thousand instructions, we notice that our son does not do it immediately. He gets distracted, or he just doesn't want to fulfill the request. We noticed this lack of response more in his toddlerhood, but still we see it in his kinder years.

Some delay of response is normal, simply because the five-year-old gets distracted by new stimuli or new opportunities. You may ask him to make his bed and get dressed, which he starts out doing, but then he gets distracted playing with some toys as he puts them away. As our discipline system shifts from a toddler system to a kinder-years system, we will gain a great deal by keeping him on task and guiding him to appropriate response times.

To help with this shift, we might give him one instruction at a time: "Son, make your bed, now." We follow through by checking that it's done. Then we say, "Get dressed in your jeans, now." We're concrete and chronological, and we clearly expect him to fulfill his obligations as we set them. We make it clear, as well, that they are to be fulfilled when we ask, not two hours later. It is perfectly appropriate to insist that the five- or six-year-old boy does what we ask him when we ask him.

---

### Rules to Live By

Because in this chapter the list of manners to teach boys is so detailed, we will not repeat it with a list of Rules to Live By.

---

## MORAL TEACHING

The boy's kinder years are a good time for us to grow more ambitious in the directness of our moral training. Now we take it to the next level. Here are some key ways of accomplishing that.

### Building Spiritual Life

Polls continually show that 90 percent of Americans believe in God or a divine force. Even atheists feel that there is a larger physical force. Whatever your family's sense of mystery, it is a special moral tool in the boy's young life, for it gives a large background to all the small rules you teach him.

**Help Him Build a Relationship with God.**   As boys enter kindergarten, they can already do some pretty sophisticated thinking about what God is, where God resides, and God's role vis-à-vis themselves. We need to work with this understanding as much as possible.

A recent study by the National Science Foundation showed that people who are actively engaged in spiritual life live around seven years longer than those who are not. Among African-Americans, those who are spiritual live up to fourteen years longer than those who aren't. What seems wonderful to me about the study is not only that people live longer who engage in spiritual life, but that males—who die on average seven years younger than females—can make up those seven years. White females live about fourteen years longer than African-American males, so could deep commitment to spiritual life help these males make up for their lost years? Unable to prove my "theory," I am nonetheless stunned by the symmetry in the dates.

Statistically, boys and men do not tend to involve themselves as much in religious and spiritual practice as girls and women. The majority of churchgoers are female in most denominations. Given how healthy spirituality is for a human being, those of us who give love and care to boys are challenged to find ways to incorporate spirituality into the lives of our sons. In this and the next chapters, we will focus on ever-expanding ways of doing so.

For the kinder boy, an intimate relationship with the natural world is an immediate method for knowing God. Regular church, synagogue, or mosque attendance also provides a traditionally strong way.

"Home-churching" is also a means of developing the child's relationship with God. By this term I mean the parents' and extended family's instruction of children in spiritual language and practice that takes place outside of an institutional environment. The telling of the world's sacred stories—orally or through books—builds the child's relationship with God.

If we model spiritual life, our children will imitate it, so we must be involved in spiritual life ourselves—whether by going to church, meditating by a river, and/or praying before bedtime. If you have not felt spiritual life or spiritual institutions to be important to you over the last few years, now is the time to assess whether you may want to investigate them for the sake of your children's development.

The benefits of a strong spiritual life are quantified not just in longer life spans. The same National Science Foundation study also found that people involved in spiritual life have fewer "vices" and addictions, and are less involved in antisocial activities, whether as adolescents or as adults.

A child who feels he belongs in the universe, in nature, in life's greater patterns does not have to search as hard through every interstice of life and attempt every moral experiment to figure out where he belongs. A child who feels accepted by a spiritual community does not have to work so hard to find other communities—some of them antisocial. A child who engages in a conversation with God does not have to search far from his own soul for a language of feeling, emotion, and happiness.

Spiritual life is not a panacea and can be grossly abused and overly dogmatic. But parents and communities who try to raise moral sons without it will, if both the research and human intuition are true, start their boy off with a disadvantage.

Because five- and six-year-olds are gaining intelligence, they are able to absorb spiritual direction as never before. The more dynamic and concrete the spiritual teaching, the more tied to everyday emotional and moral questions, the more fascinating it will be to them. Boys are able to hear God speaking through a river's sounds in ways we adults can't—but they need us to lead them to the river.

**Giving Thanks.**   The kinder years are a very important age for saying grace at the dinner table and at other times of bounty. If it doesn't fit one's spiritual sense, one doesn't need to indoctrinate a child in "I thank God for . . ." One can teach "I give thanks for . . ."

**Prayer.**   Kinder boys have a deep sense of the invisible world. It's not a leap at all for them to imagine that they are talking to God. Therefore we teach kids in their early years of life how to pray. It is important to teach *your* language of prayer in these kinder years. Some of it may be the rote prayers of your own religion. Some of it may be your own innovations.

Bedtime prayers are good opportunities to model for the boy. "When I pray, son, just while I'm falling asleep, here's what I do and say.

I ask God what His plan was for me today. I ask if I did it well. I ask how I can do better tomorrow." Concrete prayers are generally the most useful to the boy. He will gradually engage in his own form of asking if he's been good and trying to find ways to be better tomorrow.

Prayer is, of course, one of the most complex and intimate human experiences. A boy simply asking if he's been good is not satisfying enough for the human spirit, but it is a place to ground his moral development.

### Modeling Adult Responsibility

When the authority models responsibility, the child learns it. The same goes for all aspects of honor, commitment, and hard work, *and* for mistake making. Our boys learn an incredible amount when their parents and other authorities proffer apologies.

"It was my fault, son. I'm going to fix my mistake."

"That was my fault, son. I'll clean it up. You can help if you want."

Taking responsibility teaches responsibility. Apologizing teaches the boy to apologize when he is wrong.

When our son takes responsibility and apologizes, we need to show *admiration* for his moral effort.

"Good job, son, for apologizing."

"That was really good how you cleaned up your own mess when you spilled that."

When he is eight, he will be expected just to clean up his mess without our having to encourage and admire him each time. But when he's five, he really needs this admiration and encouragement.

### Teaching Delayed Gratification

Toward the middle and end of the boy's toddler years, we were able to teach him delayed gratification. Now his brain is developed well enough to fully control the impulse, though we may have to repeatedly teach the lessons.

"Not now, sweetie, I'm on the phone."

"Don't interrupt."

"I'll be right there."

"You'll get that later."

A good and reasonable amount of that message helps the boy develop the value of patience.

"Dad, can I watch now?"

"No, not yet."

"Grandma, I want to go play outside now."

"Okay, but first let's see if you've finished the job I gave you."

"Grandpa, can I have my dessert now?"

"Not till we've all finished our dinner."

"Mom, let's play ticklebug!"

"After I'm finished with this, son."

Good parent-child dynamics rely, of course, on follow-through. *We have to come through for the boy when we said we would.* If we say he can watch his Disney movie after the football game is over, we have to keep our word. If we said he'd get five minutes of our undivided attention after the chicken is set up on the stove, we have to sit down and tickle his tummy and give him love at that time. Kinder kids keep an internal moral ledger sheet like St. Peter at the gates. They don't forget our promises.

### Teaching Good Manners

A boy in the kinder years is starved to learn good manners. Sometimes he doesn't seem to be, especially if he's very rough-and-tumble, but in fact, he wants the routine, ritual, and social skill of doing what is right. Having good manners brings more opportunity for tranquillity, love, and respect.

Here are some good manners to teach him.

**Table Manners.**  No interrupting; use silverware; no more eating with the hands or playing with food or sticking hands in your water to play with the ice; no more talking while chewing; eat the food in front of you before you're allowed dessert; ask to be excused from the table; bring your plate to the kitchen sink. As with all "manners training," we don't overreact if he makes a mistake. Over a year or two, we repeatedly, and patiently, teach good manners.

**Verbal Manners.**  We discourage verbal bad manners. We don't allow him to say, "I hate Jimmy." Only by accident or angry impulse does he use the word "hate," and it gets corrected.

We continue our training in "Please, Thank you, Excuse me, I'm sorry." By age five, our son should speak "magic words" with decreasing necessity for us to remind him. We will, however, have to keep reminding him to say he's sorry and to shake hands.

He is not allowed to "diss" parents or teachers and other authorities. In other words, he does not verbally disrespect Mom, Dad, or any adult with "You're stupid" or a scornful "Whatever." The boy is in the age of obedience when much of his self-respect grows from being compelled to respect authority.

Children gain a lot by having verbal limits put on certain sacred words: "Don't use the Lord's name in vain." Even if you are an atheist, it is very useful to determine sacred words or phrases in your house, and to compel the boy to control his impulses regarding them.

Discourage excessive competitive talk. While it's normal for boys to talk competitively with siblings and friends, and even with authorities, it's important for us to monitor and guide this talk. For instance, if a boy often tells his mother or father, "I know about that; you don't know about that," this kind of "I'm better than you" attitude is to be discouraged. Also, if the boy is verbally bullying—"Mine's better than yours; yours is ugly"—it is appropriate to say, quite firmly, "That is rude talk. It hurts Joe's feelings. Now, stop it."

A kinder boy should not be using curse words of any kind. Boys model them off older siblings or parents or the media and thus experiment with them, but then we must discourage them. Cursing control is one of the primary verbal ways we can teach a boy verbal impulse control. If we or older siblings are modeling cursing, we must stop ourselves and them. Expecting the five-year-old not to say "shit" when others around him do is a wrong expectation. Allowing the six-year-old to say anything he pleases or finding his cursing "cute" actually robs him of good development. The kinder years are a time when he actually *wants* to learn what is off-limits.

Belligerent, angry, or disdainful tones from kinder boys also are something to monitor. It's important for us to teach him verbal impulse control, how to control his own tone of voice.

**Gestural Manners.** No disrespectful gestures are to be tolerated, even if they've been modeled elsewhere—like flipping someone off or sticking the tongue out. No spitting, except in athletics, where drinking water then spitting some is part of the hydration process. (Remember that boys do tend to spit more than girls—not only is it modeled, but it's also a male biological-territorial marker.)

**Environmental Manners.**    The kinder years are a good time to teach the boy what is appropriate in his intimate environment. For instance, adult areas and kid areas are sometimes separate. If we are having a get-together, it's appropriate at times for the kids to have their own space in the basement. If our kids have not gotten enough of our love and attention generally, this separation will be harder to enforce because they will constantly invade our adult area in hopes of getting attention. Perhaps in your house one of the couches is okay to climb on but another not. This rule needs to be enforced. Rules about environmental distinctions and boundaries are good for teaching the boy his own boundaries.

Environmental manners also include demands. Verbalizations like "I'm sitting there!" need to be redirected to "May I sit there?" The boy will make many, many mistakes, regressing often—but still we must patiently redirect him.

Also included is the rule that children walk their guests to the door, as do adults. It is very appropriate for a five-year-old to walk a guest to the door. Teaching manners in the home—the boy's most intimate first environment—encourages later good manners in nature (e.g., "Don't litter," or "Carry out of the campsite what you brought in"), the workplace, and other environments.

### Pick Your Battles

Throughout the moral training of our kinder boys, and of boys in later stages of life, it is important to develop an internal hierarchy—we have to pick our battles. Certain morals and manners are imperative: a boy doesn't hit his friend or family member except in appropriate play;

vicious backtalk is not allowed, nor hurtful comments toward others. Certain manners are less imperative: he walks a friend to the door every time, he wears to school the clothes his parents pick out for him. *In order to nurture the boy well, we must pick our battles, know which rules are core rules and which morals are core morals, and allow the boy some independence on those that are not core.* If I have a plan for my son's daily clothing, I am probably too controlling and will suffer a son who backtalks more than he would were I less authoritarian about the little things. I am also robbing him of the opportunity to become responsible for certain aspects of his life.

### The Question of Lying

Kinder boys will generally not lie in the sense adults do—look us right in the face and maliciously send us off course or try to harm another's character. But they will experiment with lesser versions of lying. It is common for a kinder boy to answer "No" when asked a question you know should be answered "Yes," or vice versa. At this stage, we do well to assure them that telling the truth is the most important thing, and will not always lead to absolute punishment. And we must help them tell the truth. "Now, son, I asked you if you took that hammer off the workbench. You're giving me a look like you're thinking about lying. You don't want to do that, do you? Tell me the truth and you won't get in trouble." Generally the boy will come through with the truth. We will deal more specifically with chronic lying in chapter 7.

### The Question of Stealing

A mom told me about her son, Lindsay, just five years old. Mother and son went into Starbucks one day. Lindsay asked if he could have some candy, pointing to a wrapped chocolate. Mom said, "No, we're not getting candy now." While she was over at the pickup counter, getting her coffee, he pocketed the candy, hid it all the way home, then took it to his room and began eating it. She walked in to tell him to get ready for dinner and surprised him. Once she confronted him, he told the truth. She made Lindsay get back in the car with her and they took the candy back.

In most cases, an appropriate response to stealing involves the primary action Lindsay's mother engaged in: making the boy take it back. A step-by-step response would include

1. Reprimand: "Son, this is very wrong, it's shameful, it's not something we do." Your child's self-esteem is not harmed by this truth.

2. Reach out: Call the store and brief them so that you make sure they will act in an adult way in helping you train your child. You do not want them to respond to your child with: "Oh, that's okay, you can have it."

3. Restitution: Take your child back to the place of offense and make him apologize, return the stolen item, and make other restitution if necessary (e.g., pay for it if he has eaten it). If restitution comes out of your pocket because your son is too young to have money of his own, then you require restitutive activity—perhaps increased chores, which we will discuss in a moment—by which he pays you back.

4. Extract a promise: Following the act of apology and restitution, talk with the boy continues, and the boy must be compelled to apologize to you, as the parent, as well as to promise not to act in that way again.

Throughout this process, it is important for you to gauge whether your child truly understands what he has done wrong. If need be, get your partner or other extended family member involved in coteaching your boy.

### Helping Him Channel Aggression

Some boys can be quite aggressive during the kinder years. We wonder how to guide that aggression within moral limits. We also wonder what kind of aggressive play is normal and what is over the line. Let's explore these topics.

**Guide Aggressive Play and Fantasy.**   A mother told me about overhearing her son say to another during a cops-and-robbers game in the backyard: "I'm going to kill you." Moms often wonder whether it is okay to allow boys to play with toy guns. What, indeed, do we say to a boy who threatens to kill another? Why would we let our kids play with weapons of destruction, even if they are plastic toys?

While obsessive aggression play can indicate problems in a boy, the vast majority of aggressive play runs off steam and provides kids with game plots in which they learn honor, commitment, and courage. Much of it challenges boys to hone their physical skills. It provides fantasy landscapes for natural aggression so that boys will rely less on being aggressive inappropriately in non-play social environments.

While it is appropriate to say, "It scares me when you tell Brandon you want to kill him," and while it's important to talk to your son about where he got the impulse to say that, it is also important, in most cases, to be serene about his "threat." While it is appropriate not to overwhelm him with toy guns and to keep him from modeling violence from gun-oriented media, it is natural for his testosterone-male-brain-driven system to make even twigs into weapons, so we don't want to overreact either.

One thing we know quite clearly about male fantasy and aggression play is that there is no proof for the notion that if a five-year-old gets involved in *normal* male fantasy play he will become violent. His violence later in life generally comes from traumas he suffers and other genetic and environmental causes, not from boyhood fantasy play.

**Be Aware of *Real* Aggression Problems.**   In the kinder years, a lot about your boy's personality will clarify itself. Is he shy? You'll get a good sense by the time he is six years old. Is he a "leader"? Between home and school, you and his teachers will see the answer.

You probably also will be able to see where he is on the "aggression scale." Every parent intuits whether his son is more toward the bully end or the victim end, with most kids in between. A good book for help in this area is *Taming the Dragon in Your Child,* by Meg Eastman and Sydney Craft Rozen.

If your boy is still hitting you when he throws tantrums, or screaming, "I hate you, you're stupid!" or hitting other kids a lot, or pushing and shoving more than is appropriate for male play, now is the time to make sure he becomes gentler. Use the two kinder years to socialize him heavily in controlling his aggression. If you don't do it now, you are *significantly more likely* to have a harder-to-control adolescent male on your hands.

Keep a journal of how many times he does something inappropriately aggressive. After one to two weeks of journaling, you should have a sense of what he's doing and whether you need to increase his discipline. You may need more help than you're getting from the boy's other parent in teaching him appropriate behavior.

If need be, get professional consultation, perhaps with a school counselor or a therapist who knows about boy biology and boy culture. Because inappropriate aggression tends to show up more clearly as the boy moves toward early adolescence, we will explore bullies and bullying in more depth in the next chapters.

## A HEALTHY MORAL AND EMOTIONAL ENVIRONMENT

What is a good environment for creating a well-disciplined, morally competent young boy? Here are some key things to look at in your home and child-care environments.

### Being Wise Parents and Authorities

As children grow older, parents and caregivers are supposed to grow wiser, too. Here are some ways in which your kinder son may, without verbalizing it, need your wise character.

The boy learns so much by modeling and imitating, and so much when, in a moment of confusion, he can trust that if he is like Mom, Dad, or another caregiver, he'll be doing right. When the authority says, "Be like me," the child's internal voice wants to reply, "Okay, I'm just like you, and that's why I feel good about myself."

"Clean up like I do. Watch, son."

"Talk quietly like I'm talking."

"Run like I do."

"Believe as I do."

Confident, trustworthy authorities make confident, trustworthy kids.

**Develop Parenting Teams.**   In the old days, there was a lot of extended family around to mentor and enjoy kinder kids. Nowadays, the boy's environment often doesn't include all this caregiving personnel. Yet it can if Mom joins co-ops and checks out with other moms what is normal, and if Dad joins up with his brothers and their kids to play soccer, and vice versa. These are parenting teams that form spontaneously. People "hook up" with one another and raise their children together. If you are raising a kinder boy without some kind of parenting team in place, you are not getting the full support you and your children need.

**Provide Order, Missions, and a Defined Environment.**   Once I watched a savvy grandpa with his extended family at a buffet restaurant. His six-year-old grandson sat next to him, eating happily; then, every few minutes, Grandpa gave the boy a task.

"Can you get a fork for Grandma?"

"Get me some more pop, would you, son?"

Each time, the little boy jumped up to do it, and came back proudly with the task done. He garnered words of praise from Grandma, and a silent nod of thanks from Grandpa, which he seemed to enjoy equally. Mainly what he got was the fun of mission and the sense of accomplishment.

A mom once described to me how she brought order to her son's chaotic life.

*One night he pulled his socks off and just threw them on the couch, then ran off to play. I saw in a split second how that disorder was not necessary—he was old enough to create his own order. I called him back. "Take your socks to the hamper and put them in there, please." He did it, then went back to playing. For the next few weeks, I insisted that he put things in their place—toys, silverware, books he'd knocked off a shelf. Initially, he didn't like the change, but gradually he got it. A couple months went by, and our house was a more orderly place. His whole life just worked better. He had gotten old enough to take that responsibility.*

**Teach Him His Own Address and Phone Number.** One little way I can measure how connected a family is to each member is whether the kindergartner knows his own address and phone number. Children should be taught them as toddlers, of course, but they may forget them. A wise parent makes sure the child absolutely knows them by the time he is five years old. By age five, the boy's brain will be capable of remembering these essential elements of his safe environment.

**Provide Children with an Environment Where Kids Must Listen and Cooperate.** The family unit is the foundation of the boy's development, and he must be taught to listen to what he is told, and then cooperate. A lot of permissiveness in this area is not good for little boys. They really need to be directed toward good listening and cooperating skills. Even if we have to spend part of every day for a few months gently compelling the boy to listen, repeat what we've instructed, and fulfill the instruction cooperatively, we will be rewarded for our patience with a good son.

## Preparing for School

Josh was a bright, smiling five-and-a-half-year-old whose parents weren't sure if he was ready for first grade in the coming fall, or if he would be better off in a second year of kindergarten. His parents got advice from many people, then finally decided to put him in first grade. He had trouble keeping up with the other kids; he had problems socially; he cried when he came home. His parents wondered if he was in a phase of some kind. About ten weeks into the school year, his mother said to his father, "We've made the wrong decision. He shouldn't be in first grade."

His father agreed, but now worried that Josh would suffer an even greater self-esteem crisis if removed. Josh's parents, teachers, and support system came together again and decided that there was definitely risk, but it had to be done—he was to return to kindergarten.

He did return, and once more flourished. One of the most troubling things I heard as I engaged with this family in this process was the mother's comment "I just feel like there is such a pressure to get him started in school. I don't know where it comes from, but we just didn't want him to be behind."

There is a huge pressure. *While most boys may be ready for first grade by the legal age, some boys will not. Your son may be one of these.* The boy who isn't ready feels depressed in the early school situation and becomes "trouble" in that class. He also has a greater likelihood of failing in the later school years, and a greater likelihood of getting involved in uncontrolled and immoral behavior. A long-range study begun in 1961 in the Chicago area followed first-graders through high school. This research was led by psychiatrist Sheppard Kellam, who found that school problems in a child's early years were associated with problems in adolescence.

"Almost fifty percent of the males rated as moderately or severely underachieving in first grade reported a high level of depressed symptoms ten years later," according to Dr. Kellam. He found that females were not similarly affected. His team concluded that "it appears to be an important difference for males compared to females in the meaning of failure to master first grade learning tasks."

The fragility of the male brain reappears as boys start their journey through school. Where earlier studies showed that boys who don't attach well to their mothers in infancy end up with lower intellectual abilities than similarly detached girls, now we find that boys who do poorly in school end up later with psychological and moral difficulties more frequently than girls.

**Hold the Boy Back Until He Is Six and a Half, if Needed.** Louise Bates Ames of the Gesell Institute, a leader in child studies in New Haven, Connecticut, argues that, based on their studies, boys ought to be around six and a half before they enter first grade. While your intuition as parents and caregivers carries the most power in any decision about school entrance, and while your son might do just fine entering school before six to six and a half years old, the Gesell study matches my own experience with many boys. We have found that the "maturity gap" is a definite problem for boys, and that it does not recede. Many of these boys who keep falling behind throughout the second, third, and fourth grades began their problems when they entered first grade too early.

In a survey of 450 middle school students in Virginia, school and social performance was assessed based on the age the children entered kindergarten. Younger children (whose birthdays fell between September and December) experienced more failures in middle school, and had lower test scores even in the fourth to sixth grades. More than 44 percent of these early entry boys had to receive some form of remedial help during the kindergarten to middle school years. That is a huge amount—nearly half. And when the researchers looked at which children failed a grade, three times as many of the early entries failed than the normal entries.

One of the greatest gifts we can give our boys is a long, hard look at when they are ready to enter school. Again, not all boys will need to be held back until six and a half. Some will be gifted kids who *need* accelerated learning. But many will benefit from a later start. Part of the reason lies in the brain.

**Be Aware of Brain Functioning and Early School Issues.**   In many ways, the young boy's brain matures more slowly and matures differently than the young girl's.

The *cyngulate gyrus,* which controls some aspects of emotional development, the *prefrontal lobes,* which control certain aspects of intellectual development, and the *corpus callosum,* which allows cross talk between brain hemispheres, are different in males and females. Because of structural and functional distinctions in the brain, a male tends to be more oriented toward "external space"—the geography of what is outside of him—and a female tends to orient more toward "internal space"—the geography of what is inside of her. Males tend to test out better at understanding the contours of external space—geography, depth perception, direction—and, physically, to gravitate toward the greater use of external space to show happiness and distress. Watch boys and girls enter a room. You're more likely to see the boys use the room by running around in it, moving their hands along the walls, jumping up and down in it more. You are also more likely to see the boy in a room of toys gravitate toward the blocks and trucks and weapons and other spatial toys, and the girl more likely to create verbal relationships with her objects—dolls, houses, accessories.

These differences heavily impact our kinder kids. The classroom, especially in the first grade, is set up more verbally than spatially. It's not a large open space; it's a closed one. It's one in which verbal skills—being able to use words—are more important than being able to jump around. It's one that encourages the child to read as early as possible, something the male brain is generally less well formatted to do than the female. In fact, it is not unusual for males to gain their advanced verbal skills six months to a year later than females.

Not only is the classroom environment often difficult for many developing male brains, but when difficulties emerge, little boys are more likely than little girls to act out their distress, their sense of failure, and their boredom. Sometimes their self-esteem drops in ways that make them "discipline problems."

Males also express their emotions by using more space—hitting walls or other objects or people; bumping into others and things; "blowing off steam" by running around, throwing things, playing competitive games. In all this use of space, the verbal component is lessened—the very component that generally lowers the risk for discipline or moral problems.

Many of our little boys not only fail to fit in the classroom at the age we pressure them to enter it, but also will act out against their distress in ways that compound the problem. They'll upset students and teachers and then parents when all they really want is approval.

Fortunately for Josh, his parents and school did what was best for him. If you have a boy in a similar situation, don't be afraid to hold him back.

### Chores and Allowance

The chores we require of a boy and the allowance we give him do not always overlap, but sometimes they can, so let's deal with these together.

**Chores.**   Chores build self-esteem, responsibility, and, ultimately, moral competency. The kinder years are a time when chores can become complex and when carefulness and follow-through should be well established.

If your son is supposed to clear and clean the table every night (a very good chore for a five-year-old), he should be led in clearing the dishes to the sink, not to a scatter of far counters; he should completely clear the table; he should wring the sponge out and then wipe the table, keeping the crumbs in his little hand (as much as he can); then he should set the chairs back in order. The full job is his. He may need help with aspects of it, but it is nonetheless *his* job.

By age five, he should fold some of his own clothes and be a "helper" with snow shoveling or raking or other indoor and outdoor tasks. By age five, the boy can get himself dressed and tie his own shoes, generally speaking. He can also clean his room two to three times per week (with some help from parents or older siblings or friends who have come over and messed it up with him). It will be a few years yet—if ever!—before the "cleaned" room will match our standards, but nonetheless he will do his best if we insist.

**Allowance.**  By five years old, your son should start getting a set and ritualized allowance. Every family has to decide what is appropriate, and compensate with each generation for inflation. Neale S. Godfrey has penned a number of wonderful books to assist us in deciding on how to handle allowance. *Money Doesn't Grow on Trees* and *A Penny Saved* are two my family has used.

There are some key rules to allowance giving.

1. Teach why it's given and what money means in your family.

2. Make sure the boy divides his allowance into separate caches. Here is a suggestion:

   1/4  for immediate use

   1/4  for short-term savings—to buy a small toy once enough money accumulates

   1/4  for long-term savings—generally for college

   1/4  for charity

3. Don't give allowance as a reward for doing chores or homework. Those things have to be their own reward. Sometimes you will reward good works with money, but generally not the chores the boy knows are his responsibility.

4. Use allowance giving as a teaching tool about financial responsibility, prosperity, gratitude, and other lessons.

5. Be consistent in giving—withhold it as a punishment when appropriate.

6. Let it increase appropriately as the boy grows older. *A Penny Saved* gives a good grid for increasing allowance throughout a child's growth.

7. Handle money together as a family—talk about it together, go out to spend it together as an important part of family life.

### Discarding Cultural Stereotypes

Recently a young couple with a five-year-old wrote me about their son's love of dolls. "He prefers 'girl' things to 'boy' things. He feels like a lot of the other boys are scary, or too rough."

Many boys go through a time of thinking other guys are too rough. Many boys go through a time of preferring dolls to weapons. Some boys just never take to rough-and-tumble play, and grow into adolescents who despise the pecking orders and hierarchies boys gravitate toward. *There is nothing wrong with these boys.* If a boy wants to play with dolls and with other girls, he is following his internal rhythms and feelings and ought to be supported.

If your son cannot socialize well with other boys over a period of one or more years, then it is time to be concerned. But if he's playing with dolls, let him enjoy them. The kinder years are not years to "force" him into cultural stereotypes of what is "male" or "masculine." The culture, and the boy's internal male drives, will take him in the direction of the masculine as it needs to, without our having to shut down the play he likes for the play we think he should like.

### Media Use

Video games damage the attention spans of millions of kinder and older boys. I hope you'll consider limiting computer use to supervised educational games and no unsupervised Internet access. Consider, also,

very limited television use, such as Disney videos and a few kids' programs a week. One hour of television a day, or one and a half hours if a
movie is being watched, is appropriate. Any more than that probably indicates the kinder boy is not reading, playing, or relating enough to living, breathing family members and friends.

As we've discussed earlier, one of the greatest moral and discipline
challenges we face in raising boys is posed by media stimulation. A five-
or six-year-old is *our* child, and a certain territoriality about him in the
face of the media is appropriate. Just because a poster of *Halloween:
H$_2$O* exists does not mean he is allowed to put it up in his room. We
need not allow *anything* in his room we don't feel is valuable to him as
a growing boy. If he wants it up, we explain to him how unworthy and
disturbing we find it, then we don't have to say much more about it.

Some language that is useful in justifying our actions to our kinder
boys might include

"People are getting hurt in that, and it's mean."

"We wouldn't even watch something like that—why should you?"

"Because I said so."

Sometimes adults will decide it's just not worth the hassle to try to
get our kid to bed one night, so we'll let him stay up and watch an adult
sitcom or cop show with us. A little of this won't hurt, but as a general
rule it should not be allowed. *Nearly all programming in the evening is
inappropriate for a six-year-old.*

For the most part, whatever media he takes in should teach a moral
lesson. If he watches something like *Batman* or *Star Wars* and can't talk
at all about moral issues—who was bad and good, why the good had to
fight the bad, who was helped and who was hurt—then he is too young
to watch it. Generally for a six-year-old, I would avoid the *Batman* and
other video cartoons; the *Batman* movies are much too violent. *Star
Wars* movies might be okay, because they will appear much more like
kid fantasy-aggression play. But it's okay only if it doesn't bring nightmares and if the boy can articulate its themes and characters. The boy's

kinder years are the time for you to start talking to him about the shows and commercials he watches, what he is learning from them.

### The Rituals of Life

Not enough can be said about the importance of rituals and routines throughout a child's boyhood in developing his sense of discipline and morality.

In the morning, for instance, the boy needs a routine for getting ready for school. He can now dress himself, eat the breakfast put in front of him, brush his teeth, make his bed, get his shoes on, and so on. If the boy won't get dressed, often the threat to close his door till he does will cure him. He generally will not want to be cut off from family activities in the morning.

In some families, the children watch television in the morning as a part of their ritual. It would be better for the boy to fulfill chores and play.

In the evening, bedtime rituals remain equally important. Twenty minutes to a half hour is an appropriate length of time for tucking the boy in, lying down with him, chatting with him, or reading to him. The independence and self-esteem he builds by accomplishing his morning and evening rituals serve his self-confidence in other parts of life.

**Service Work and Charity.**   Service and charity are important ritual activities. If you haven't begun a family service project already, the boy's kinder years are a great time for you to do so. Perhaps you can volunteer at a homeless shelter once a month. Perhaps you can make trips to a nursing home every two weeks. Or perhaps some opportunity for extra service exists in your family—for instance, you have a dying relative and you see him or her every week and take gifts. It's very important to start the boy at this time in his life with a conscious and even ritual sense of service and charity.

**One Toy In, One Toy Out.**   By the time the boy is five years old, it is important to institute a ritual by which for every new toy the boy gets, an old toy goes to someone in need. When my children get a toy or another valued item, they go through the ritual of giving a similar item to

Goodwill or another agency. A mother of three sons taught me this family ritual. It is a very useful way to inspire a sense of charity, to control materialism, and to help boys articulate the worth of toys and "things." The toy they give away ought to be one that's in good shape—not one that they would throw out anyway. Charity is a process that demands respect for the recipient.

## PHILIP'S STORY

Philip was a six-year-old full of energy and athleticism. His parents decided to put him on a soccer team. Its practices and games were held in an indoor soccer complex at the southern edge of town. Usually, Philip's mother took him to soccer, and the drive was pleasant, full of chatter and good cheer. Then, when they got to the complex, Philip would seem to get antsy, jumpy. By the time practice had begun, he would get hard to handle, a little obstinate; he wouldn't listen. Instead, he'd create disturbances. He would yell out, he would run around, he would even crash into other kids inappropriately. In his mother's words, "He became a discipline problem. He just did bad things. His coach and I didn't know what was going on."

One day, Philip's mother spoke with his teacher. "Is he having trouble with team sports, do you think? He hasn't had trouble with other kinds of group things. Could he be having trouble with authority? No matter the time-outs or reprimands or lost privileges, he just keeps doing these things at soccer."

Philip's teacher had an insight. She had raised sons and remembered those indoor soccer complexes. She also had noticed over the kindergarten year that Philip spoke more loudly than most of the other kids. His parents and family knew he was pretty loud, too. The teacher asked, "Have you had Philip's ears tested? Do you think he might have a hearing problem?" What if a lot of the areas where he needed discipline had to do with his hearing, and with his caregivers and environments not understanding what was going on?

Philip did get his hearing tested as soon as there was an opening at the pediatrician's. Sure enough, it turned out he had very sensitive ears, much more sensitive than average. The pediatrician explained what the teacher had intuited: "The indoor soccer stadium is the wrong place for him—it's too loud—he is also probably ioud because he hears others as being loud, so he imitates."

Philip's parents took him out of indoor soccer and provided him with lots of outdoor play and, when outdoor soccer started, an outdoor team. They explained to him about his ears, and thus he and they felt a lot better when they had to correct him for being too loud. He understood now that it was because of a personal *strength, not a moral weakness,* that he was being corrected. It was because he had a special gift, not because he was "just being a loud kid." When Philip stopped playing the indoor soccer, most of his "bad" behavior ended.

Philip was truly lucky to have such vigilant caregivers. Isn't it true, so often, with our young boys that we don't really know the hidden reasons for their behavior when in fact there might be hidden reasons that have nothing to do with the boy's character? Many times, much of what we consider "bad" about him is really his reaction to something in his environment. He reacts in the very loud, physical, disruptive way that Philips all over the world react, until someone notices that there is a problem in the boy's environment or nurturing system.

# Part Three

## NURTURING THE MIDDLE YEARS OF A BOY'S DEVELOPMENT

The Age of Convention
(Seven to Twelve Years Old)

# SIX

# The Between Years

NURTURING BOYS OF SEVEN AND EIGHT

There is a wonderful story from East Africa about a king and queen of a large oceanside kingdom who require their people to bring them gifts every day—fish, inland crops, animals from the hunt, talismans, and amusing stories of life at home and abroad. These gifts are no substitute for taxes. The people pay taxes as well. Every day at least twenty members of the community bring gifts, and they walk away feeling blessed but just a little poorer. This tradition goes on for generations, with only a few grumblings among the people.

One day, however, an eight-year-old boy feels that he has awakened from a strange slumber and must make a new, freer life for himself and his people. He tells his mother and father that the leaders' requests should not be honored. The parents are mortified and tell him to leave well enough alone. The community is happy, prosperous, and safe. The gifts are a small sacrifice. The boy calms his parents with feigned agreement, but when it is his turn to take a gift, he rebels—he walks up to the king and queen and says, "I have nothing for you today, not even myself. You are taking from the people but not giving. I will not be a part of it. If you must, banish me."

The king and queen say, "We'll do no such thing. In fact, we've wondered for a long time, as our fathers and mothers did, why no one has stood as you are standing and asked for a reckoning of the tradition."

Surprised by their lack of rancor, the boy went on. "Then you will no longer force your people to bring you these gifts every day?"

"We will not," the leaders agreed. "Go and tell the people you have confronted us in this way and now no one needs bring us a gift."

The boy, feeling quite good about himself, took the message to the people. He was loved, admired, and lauded a hero. Each individual family felt richer, their coffers more full. Each one had to work just a little less hard. They all had more time on their hands. It felt good.

But then something began to happen to the community. Here and there a bit of poverty emerged. This family, then that family, had not enough to eat one day. There were fewer beautiful things in the community, and fewer celebrations. Fewer children were being conceived. People saw less of their leaders than they wanted, and less of one another than they needed. After a few months, no one was happy anymore with the boy, and they shunned his family.

The boy and his mother and father went to the king and queen apologetically. The boy himself could see that he had done something wrong. He got down on his knees and asked the leaders to explain what he had done wrong.

The king said, "My son, where do you think those gifts go when they are brought to us?"

The boy did not know.

"Why, they go to people in need. Did your house not receive a talisman nine months before your birth?"

The boy looked to his parents, who confirmed that they had been unable to conceive for years, but one morning a talisman appeared at their door. Nine months later, the boy was born.

"We take each gift and distribute it as needed," the queen said. "In this we are not thieves of the wealth but we are like water that moves each gift around the ocean bed.

"Go and tell the people this."

The boy and his parents told what they had learned, and life returned to normal. The people worked hard again, planting and tending their crops, exploring the far seas, making the crafts of their hands, and bringing the best of each to the king and queen, who made of each gift a new gift in return. The people returned to the loving dictatorship they lived in, knowing now that without it in the center of their freedom, they would not live happy lives.

This story represents hidden elements of the growing minds and hearts of "between years" boys. I call the years of seven and eight the "between years" because the boy is between childhood and adolescence—little rebellions emerge, but he still wants the safety of our dictatorship. He's in second and third grade during this time, still a very innocent child, but he knows that he's "getting older" and is "not just a kid anymore." He's moving toward nine years old, which is the beginning of male adolescence for most of our sons. He experiences new awakenings, constant and charged with fervor, in which he realizes that he, at seven and eight, has some new powers and he strives to exercise them, while hoping that his caregivers will maintain their authority and give him direction.

In the African tale, the boy does not really know how the world works and has to suffer in order to learn. He has to make mistakes, and he even has to feel moments of exile from his community. He wants to understand the workings of his world, and he'll make waves to do so, but he does not want the loving, safe dictatorship at home to fall apart. The boy is in between lives and worlds. He is beginning the second major developmental episode of his life.

## YOUR SON'S SECOND DEVELOPMENTAL EPISODE: AN OVERVIEW

The boy's brain has developed through his infancy and the early years. Now his brain will develop through his middle childhood and early adolescence.

### His Intellectual Development

The more social interaction the boy has—with parents, teachers, peers, groups, and educational tools—the more he learns. Where he was a complete sponge in the first developmental episode of his life, by about the time he is in second grade, he becomes more of a *discerning* sponge. He picks and chooses more. Yet he remains very dependent on his caregivers to help set goals, objectives, and limits.

The more intense the stimulant in his life, the more easily he'll absorb it. The less intense, the less he'll attend to it. Part of how he discerns what to think about is by choosing between "boring" stimulants and "exciting" ones.

As we observe his media use, we notice his search for intense stimulants, too. By about the time he enters third or fourth grade, a boy often can begin to be obsessively absorbed in television, video games, and movies. The fast-moving images and intense special effects come into his mind more quickly and intensely than other educational or life experiences.

The boy is thinking more "cosmically" now—asking questions (even if he never speaks them) about nature, God, space, the earth. He might get very interested in science fiction or other kinds of "cosmic" entertainment. He probably will be very interested in how things work, how they're made. His brain isn't capable of full abstraction yet—this comes in adolescence—but it is beginning to understand the basic underpinnings and undercurrents of the universe.

### His Emotional Development

In his emotional life, the boy seeks both relationship and solitude, enthusiastic displays of affection and calm self-possession. As he progresses through the second developmental episode, he's adding thought to his feelings quite a bit more, so his feelings often take more time to make themselves known.

And yet he will not want to overrely on his reasoning powers when matters of the heart require him to give and receive unconditional love. He often will let you know in no uncertain terms what he's feeling.

This boy really wants hugs, kisses, praise, handshakes, admiration, respect, attention, challenge, and all other loving interactions that help him feel safe. He begins to be clear on what "happy" looks like in others' lives. If he has the social opportunity and the safety of a protected life, he will discover how to make himself a happy boy. The search for happiness is one of his primary objectives. He's not experimenting too much yet with the moroseness of the middle teen, or the angst of the late teen and early adult. He may upset the kingdom for a few hours at a time, but he'll want to find stability again quickly.

This developmental episode often coincides with family tragedies—deaths of grandparents, divorces, other kinds of sicknesses and losses. Depending on their inherent personality structures, some boys are capable of putting on severe emotional armor in the face of a tragedy, but they need immense help working emotions through.

By about age nine or ten, many boys will begin to channel primary feelings like pain, grief, fear, and sadness into anger. They will talk less about what they're feeling, and cry less, but they may hide out in rooms more, bash the joystick around, kick furniture, yell, pick fights, or brood. Some boys also will begin to fear being out of control—small phobias and panic attacks are not unusual for boys in the second developmental episode. They may feel life spiraling away from them, becoming too complicated. They will perhaps insist they can't finish a lesson or play the soccer game or go to Grandma's house.

Simultaneously, many boys will now start to delay reactions to feelings or completely miss the fact that they are feeling something at all. Every year they grow older, their brain system becomes more "male" in many of the structural and functional ways we've already discussed. Thus, by the time your boy becomes an adolescent, you might notice that he acts more and more like a "little man" who doesn't talk as much about feelings.

Also, by age eleven or twelve, boys will probably begin to experience their psychological separation from their mothers (and from their fathers, too). They will begin to pull away from Mom, verbally and physically. Throughout the second developmental episode, we sense that this separation is going on and we prepare for it, even when we're not conscious of doing so.

### His Biggest Task

The boy's biggest task is to learn the ways of his social situation—at home, at school, on the street, on the playground, in church, and wherever he is taken. He has a keen sense of justice—he asks himself, "Have I been treated fairly? Have I treated another person fairly?" He wants to be shown what the compassionate act would be ("Son, you'd be a hero to your little sister if you'd just let her cuddle with you to fall asleep tonight") and what the honorable act would be ("Son, your friend Marty does bad things, and you know he can hurt himself—it's up to you to tell us if he does something really bad so we can help him"). He wants to do what it takes to belong—not as a slave but as a hardy member of human society.

He knows that he is a boy, not a girl; thus, some of his moral development and search for belonging will occur in boy-specific ways. For instance, whereas a girl might be very concerned with the social rules of verbal interactions among people at a parents' party, the boy may be more concerned with the social rules of a hierarchical enterprise, like a soccer game or good-guys/bad-guys game in the backyard. During the second developmental episode, boy culture and girl culture (while sharing immense overlap) do divide up—boys on the playground learn more about society through spatial activities, girls more through verbal activities.

### He Is in the Age of Convention

The boy is very interested in the way people act and interact. He is often very sensitive about how he fits, and he can break down in tears when he thinks he has done wrong or done badly.

Whereas in the first six years of life, "Do what you're told!" was of primary value, and while the boy still needs the comfort and safety of obedience, now he is more involved in making his own comparisons between our instructions and the codes of the outer society. Much of our best teaching occurs as we verbally aid him in comparing what we expect and what other parents expect, how we are similar and different from the world he is discovering, and what freedom we think and he thinks he can handle. We come to rely, in the years when he is about seven to twelve, on showing the boy how to make the right choices for himself. If we are successful, his adolescence—indeed, his life—will go much more smoothly.

## DEVELOPMENTAL MILESTONES

The second developmental episode of your son's life begins when he is seven to eight years old. Let's focus on that specific development now.

### His Intellectual Development

The boy's intelligence is developing at a very fast pace, which is a blessing but also can be the cause of some problems.

**Attention Span Problems.**   It is normal for many boys to develop problems with attention spans during these years. We discover that discipline problems in schools and at home are caused, to a great extent, by the boy acting out his frustration at *not* being able to focus on activities that he and the society know are important for him. Males find themselves in a paradoxical and fragile situation in regard to attention span.

The male brain system is a "lateralizing" system. It is what we call a "task-focused" brain. The brain is set up to focus intellectual neural activity on the area needed to accomplish a specific task, and to deplete blood flow and neural activity from areas of the brain not specifically necessary to the task. All brains, of course, do this, but the female brain does it less than the male—the female brain keeps a number of centers going at once with more agility than the male.

Thus sometimes you'll notice that males get more overtly frustrated than females when they're working on computers and are interrupted. They get more "zoned out" in front of the TV for longer hours. People will joke: "Guys seem to be able to do only one thing at a time." The male brain, while not this limited, is nonetheless formatted in this direction, probably because for 99 percent of our human development, the male brain had been used, primarily, for the very focused activity of hunting.

While young males have always experienced their own forms of attention span problems, they did not seem to experience them as frequently as they do now. We have nearly 3,000,000 boys on Ritalin, the primary medical treatment for attention span problems like ADD and ADHD. Many of these boys are just little Huck Finns, normal boys whose emotions the culture wants to suppress with medicine—but many do actually have attention span problems. Why so many attention problems in the last few decades among our males?

Specialists think what is happening is this: Our media intake, activities orientation, lack of reflection and prayer time, and chaotic physical environments (e.g., busy city environments, where ADD and ADHD are more common) are overstimulating the male brain in ways it's not set up to handle. It is becoming *normal* for young boys to be overstimulated. A hundred years ago, boys had more reflection time and, of course, no visual media intake. Now, our boys' lives are less supervised and more hyperstimulated. Neurologists often call our present child environment "hypermediated" because it includes so much media input and other distractions.

If you are noticing problems with your son's attention span abilities, diagnosis is important, as well as a concerted effort to *de*stimulate his day. Turn off the radios, music, TV, video games, computers. The overstimulation is locking his brain down, or "freezing" it. Because of its normal proclivity to cut off other neural activity in order to focus on one task, the male brain does not have as many internal resources for dealing with new stimulants. More easily than the female brain, it will freeze, and normal brain functioning will be overridden.

Not only is destimulation important, but so is patient training in activities that build the attention span: reading, doing specific chores, helping to cook a meal. If your son likes music, involve him in music lessons—in which his brain has to actively participate—rather than letting him listen passively to music on a Walkman. Activities like these require the boy to build up, even rebuild, his ability to focus his attention on tasks.

### His Emotional Development

The boy in the between years is becoming aware that he has certain strengths and certain weaknesses, certain abilities and certain lacks. He may become strangely afraid, at times, of playing soccer or taking music lessons or being criticized. He will need lots of encouragement to "take the first step." Once he takes the first step, he may find a new home for himself in the activity, and his courage may grow. But he might need lots of help getting over his fear of failing, of being "found out."

**Giving Him Lots of Hugs and Kisses.**   One day at the grocery store, I saw a tall, heavily bearded man dressed in cowboy boots, jeans, and a flannel hunting shirt step out of an old Chevy pickup with dual gun racks in the back window. The license plate read "Elkhuntr." His eight-year-old son jumped out, too, on the driver's side, into his father's arm. The father gave him a hug and said, "Love ya, son," and they walked hand in hand into the grocery store. What a gift!

**Helping Him Name Feelings.**   Often boys of seven and eight need help to "name" their emotions and to develop emotive language. If we ask a girl and a boy how it felt to be rejected by a friend, both may say, "Sad." But many times when we ask the boy to explain his feelings in more depth, he freezes up.

Even to this day, many experts insist that boys freeze more than girls mainly because we've socialized males away from their feelings. Yet even in southern Italy, where the males are often very "emotive," they still identify their internal feelings with less conversational depth—less variety of words, fewer multilayered emotional responses, less self-disclosure—than females. Much of what your boy experiences is based on how his brain works and then on how the society interacts with his developing brain.

It is crucial for males at this age to develop themselves emotionally through two primary kinds of assistance from you.

1. Task-directed emotional development: The boy needs you to direct his emotions toward care of others, empathic activities, service activities. "Why don't you go right over there and help

Mrs. Peterson by giving her a hug, son? Doesn't it look like she needs one?"

2. Filling in the words for him: The boy is often asking by use of his silence, "How should I be feeling about that?" You respond suggestively, if necessary: "Doesn't that feel sad to see that?" or mad, or happy, etc.

It is often normal for males to need "emotional direction." In some cases they will lose the opportunity to know themselves unless you say something like, "Son, you look confused. In your situation, I would be feeling very scared right now. Are you scared?"

### His Moral Development

The boy's conscience—his inherent sense of right and wrong—has been developing throughout the first six years of life. Now the boy quite consciously *feels* the inner pain of lying, cheating, or stealing. He doesn't feel it every time, but he feels it often. And especially when he's caught doing something wrong by an authority he loves or trusts, he knows his own mistake. He may try to rationalize or escape punishment, but he does know. His understanding is beginning to move beyond "I better do right so I don't get punished" to "When I don't do right I feel bad." The boy does not yet have a fully developed conscience, but it's in there, beginning to shine through.

**Look for Moral Fragility in the Boy.**   These are watershed years in which we often can begin to measure how our boy is going to "turn out" morally. The Justice Department launched a major research study regarding youth offenders and discovered that *the average violent juvenile criminal starts getting into trouble at seven years old.*

The American Medical Association's Archives of Pediatrics and Adolescent Medicine recently reported a study from Case Western Reserve University which found that children who are exposed to violence and who inappropriately display anger in their early years are more likely to commit violent acts later. One of the ways to monitor their potential for later violent acts is to watch how they interact with peers when they are seven or eight. Do they bully, for instance? Also, according to the study, we need to watch carefully how they interact with adults at this age. Do they constantly get angry with adults?

Without realizing it, we lose many of our sons to their emotional and moral fragility in these between years. While the loss may not show up until adolescence, it begins now.

Does your son have uncontrollable episodes of aggression? Does he yell at you every day? Is he a problem in school? *Now is the time to make his moral situation the highest developmental priority.* Everything we do in these years to teach our boys self-control, compassion, honor—everything we do to protect their family bonds—is a necessity, not a luxury. If you are having a clear problem with your son's anger or violent behavior, later sections of this chapter will help you.

As we have said before, just because a behavior is within the normal range (see page 170) does not mean it does not require discipline.

## DISCIPLINE TECHNIQUES

Many useful discipline techniques have been covered already and will still apply to your seven- or eight-year-old. I hope you'll refer back to the Discipline Techniques sections in previous chapters.

### Being a Strong Authority

A mother wrote: "My household never functioned much like a democracy. I always said it was a dictatorship and I was the dictator. I did listen, and sometimes I rethought the way I thought about some things. But usually, good, bad, or indifferent, it is or was my way, and I'm happy to say that with the help of God I didn't do too badly."

Bravo! Let's all support this kind of authority.

### Creating Discipline in Your Verbal Interactions

You carry a lot of discipline in your verbal and nonverbal cues with your son. Here are some things to be clear on.

## The Range of Normal

It's normal for the boy to verbalize more and use his body less to express himself than he did a year or two ago; yet he will still hit inappropriately once in a while.

It's normal for the boy to watch you and others closely for how to act in the social world.

It's normal for the boy to experiment with backtalk and other verbalizations of independence. ("Did you finish making your bed?" "Maybe.")

It's normal for the boy to take things personally that seem very small to us as adults.

It's normal for the boy to conceal some of his feelings.

It's normal for the boy to act very dependent on parents for approval, and to become immensely needy at times.

It's normal for the boy to become very clearly his "own person"—very neat if that is who he is, very sloppy if that is who he is. His personality is crystallizing now.

**Practice Certainty.**   It is good to be certain about most things you ask for. The boy needs you to

- *know* very clearly how you expect him to behave in nearly all social situations;
- *tell* him exactly what you want him to do, patiently and repetitively, if necessary; and
- *follow through* to make sure he does what is needed and expected in a timely manner.

**Be Immediate with Your Firmness.**   If your son spits in an inappropriate way, you immediately and firmly say, "No spitting!" If your son backtalks, there is an immediate response. The boy in these years of life is spreading his wings a bit more than in the last two, but he still needs the firm ground of obedience. The "tougher" the kid—more spirited, headstrong, and bent on playing power games with you—the more you need to be patient but tough. He needs you to act with authority so that he respects your authority. Your son may get no second chances for a few days. If he keeps doing things he knows are wrong, he is given one warning; then he suffers the logical consequence.

Exceptions come when the boy's toughness is caused by some form of abandonment, abuse, or neglect on the part of the authority. In that case, the toughness is the boy's defense mechanism, and breaking through it will require not intransigence on the offending parent's part, but new forms of love and affection that rebuild trust in the boy. You will need to spend more time with the boy, do more things with him, help him regain his trust in authorities and in you.

**Handling Sarcasm.**   In these between years, boys often begin the verbal experimentations with personal power that will, for some, be dominant in later years.

"Son, did you clean up your room?"

"Not exactly."

"Son, I asked you to finish your chores."

"Whatever."

Sarcasm to authorities, jesting, and one-upping in games with friends all are normal developmental attempts at a personal sense of strength and authority. The parent and other caregivers must hold the standard for what is acceptable behavior. If "Whatever" feels rude to the parent, she should forbid the verbal behavior. Overreaction is not necessary, however, since the behavior is developmentally normal.

**Handling the Boy's New Sense of Negotiation.**   It is normal for boys in the between years to start negotiating with us about a lot of things. "If I do my chores, can Frank come over?" "If I finish my dinner, can I have *two* pieces of candy?" "If I'm really good all week, can I go to Grandpa's for the weekend?" The boy is learning about the marketplace that life is; he's learning how to measure up and perform well; he's learning what his duty is and how completely we'll compel him to fulfill it. Even in exacting punishments, it's good to involve the boy: "You were told to finish those chores and did not do them in the appropriate time. What privilege should you lose?" He negotiates a solution to his bad behavior with you. Simultaneously, it's useful to help him learn more sophisticated negotiation techniques: "When you came to me with that idea, son, if you had said _____, now *that* would probably have swayed me, but since you said and did _____, I said no."

**"But Timmy Gets to Do It. Why Can't I?"**    Timmy gets a gerbil, but our son doesn't. Timmy gets to watch all the TV he wants, but our son doesn't. Timmy gets to backtalk his parents, but our son doesn't. Children in the between years start carefully comparing their lives with other children's lives, their homes with other children's, their schools with other children's. "I'm bored at school, Mom. I want to be home-schooled like Mike. He only has to go to school till one and then he has no homework." This verbalization of comparisons with other kids is quite normal, and good for socialization. It is an opportunity to teach our children why we do things as we do, and what's good about what we do. By making constant social comparisons, the boy is measuring himself and his people to see what his own and their strengths are. Our discussions with him will benefit by being about what he has and what we think is important in life.

"You already have a dog. That's enough responsibility for our family."

"You are a really good reader, which is what we value. Television is just less important to us."

"We respect you, and we expect you to respect us."

"School is a better place for you than home—you're a kid who likes to be with other people a lot."

Each comparison the boy makes is an opportunity for us to teach him more about his positive qualities, and our own as a family.

### Handling Sibling Rivalry

Seven- and eight-year-old boys can engage in a great deal of sibling rivalry, whether siblings are older or younger. It can become physically aggressive in worrisome ways—wrestling and pushing matches where a child gets a little bit hurt; verbal aggressions that hurt a child's feelings; excessive competition at games and activities, which leaves the younger sibling feeling like a failure.

It is important to note that *most sibling rivalry activity is normal.* Yet each family needs to develop appropriate boundaries. A mom recently told me: "I have two boys who just fight, fight, fight with each other. Sometimes it's just wrestling and fun stuff like that, but other times it gets pretty harsh. It's hard to know when to intervene."

I think the most important thing to remember is that *the home is meant to be the safest place available to your child.* Sheila, a teacher of twenty-three years and a mother of four grown sons, wrote me a letter about a number of issues, including sibling rivalry. I hope you'll find her words as clear and moving as I do.

*In my home, fighting was never okay. Hitting was never sanctioned. I never allowed my sons to hit each other. If there was a fight, the older one was responsible. I would discipline a younger boy for bothering an older one, but the older ones were never allowed to even fight back.*

*I also stopped mean talk and teasing between the boys. I was very firm about that. **I talked in terms of home being the place where you were safe***—that the rest of the world was hard enough to deal with, at home you didn't have to keep your guard up.*

*The result of these policies (which included parents—Don and I had to treat the home as a safe place, too) is that my sons are all good friends now. They were required to treat each other with respect from a young age and so they now feel deep respect for each other.*

*When we invested in a bassoon for George, there was no feeling of resentment on the part of his brothers. George said he thought that was because they all know that I would do the same thing for them, if it was needed.*

*Emphasis mine.

*When I look back I'm very proud that years of working hard to help them be fair to each other have really paid off.*

Sheila's rule may seem too strict to some parents, but I think it is a good starting point: Wrestling, aggressive play, rough-and-tumble play are fine, but no hitting to hurt, no rageful verbal jabs, no sibling rivalry that upsets the safety of the home. There will be a little—a home is a small space to put all that energy in without there being eruptions—but immediately, safety has to be returned to the home.

If you find it impossible to make sure there's little or no violent fighting, it is at least essential to make sure your children shake hands after the fight and regain their respect and affection for each other. They are siblings, after all—over the span of years, siblings must be loyal to each other.

### Praise and Criticism

The boy is coming of age now, and we should look carefully at how we praise him. We still want to praise more than we criticize, but we don't want to praise every little thing. And we want to mix more criticism in with the praise. The boy does not mind our helping him modify himself to fit social convention. He wants to know what's "wrong" so he can fix it and increase the respect he gets from us and the larger world.

If the boy is supposed to do the dishes every night, he does them whether he's praised or not. A few times a month, spontaneously, we praise him, but we don't feel obligated to praise him each time. If, however, we're giving him a new task—doing the pots and pans, too—we should praise him a number of times just as he's getting going.

If the boy is doing poorly at daily tasks, we need to critique him patiently and concretely, to tell him exactly what he is doing wrong and, if possible, model (show him) how to do it correctly.

If we notice that our son feels weak in a certain area—in math or writing, in soccer or basketball, in making friends—we need to praise him and encourage him constantly. Yet, still, it won't hurt him to be critiqued. "One of the reasons you have trouble making friends, son, is you wait for them to call you. Why don't you call Sammy? I'll help you." It is essential to remember that criticism builds as much self-esteem as praise. Both must be practiced carefully and appropriately.

In offering criticism, it is often very helpful with boys of this age for you to contextualize the critique in your own childhood: "When I was a kid, I didn't make friends well either—I was shy, like you. What I did was . . ." When the boy knows he is a creature of inheritance, he has a larger context in which to see himself. And he has access to more information and more reason to ask questions. If a parent criticizes without practicing good self-disclosure, the son can feel alone.

## MORAL TEACHING

Moral teaching and training in these years stands on the ground you already laid in previous years. Much of what we discussed in previous chapters continues to apply here.

### Building Spiritual Life

"God has a plan for you," we might say to our seven-year-old son.
"Grandma died so she could be closer to God."
"Grandpa died because he had finished his jobs in this life."

These are answers to the big questions—questions about life, death, honor, happiness, God, values—and our between boys need them to be clear. Some boys will flourish by beginning their somewhat lonely journey toward their own spiritual path during these years, but most boys are not ready for that loneliness and need us to provide the big answers.

**Leave a Few of the Big Questions Open.**   The between years is a time also of expanding intellect and spiritual competency, so our answers can become more complex than they were previously, and we can throw some questions back at the boy. "I'm not sure why all those people had to die in that hurricane, son. Why don't you pray?" Or: "Maybe it's one of those mysteries I can't solve, but you, as you grow older, will understand." Spiritual mystery is becoming a strong part of the boy's life and needs to be encouraged.

## Rules to Live By

Here are some rules to live by that I hope you'll find useful when giving your son a summary of what you expect of him.

1.  A between boy may not talk back to a parent except in games and jest.

2.  A between boy will do his chores every day, with some reminders by parents, but not many.

3.  A between boy will treat adults with respect and will practice good manners.

4.  A between boy will participate in family rituals and extended family activities.

5.  A between boy is not just a little boy anymore—he has to earn some of his privileges with good behavior.

6.  A parent will treat a between boy with respect, especially respecting the new ideas he's forming about who he is.

7.  A parent is still the authority in the between boy's life, and nothing will change that.

Now is the time to rely more heavily on your spiritual community, however it is formed. Increase your son's attendance at church or other programs.

### Teaching Good Manners

Manners are morals. This is a good dictum to teach boys of this age, and of course to remind ourselves. "Our friends are still eating, so you may not be excused. It's polite to be with our friends at the table."

"No, you may not go watch a movie in the basement while your friend plays alone in your room."

"You will say you're sorry and shake hands."

Boys become more independent from us during these years, so your household will gain by deciding which are "primary" manners and which are "secondary" manners and insisting on the primary ones.

No cursing at each other, no angry hitting of living beings, no yelling while someone is driving the car, no leaving friends alone at your house—these might be matters of primary importance to you, and you give swift punishments if they are not upheld.

Putting the toilet seat down, or forgetting to ask to be excused from the table, or interrupting once in a while—these might be secondary manners to you, and you might treat them accordingly.

### Beginning a Service Activity as a Family

If you did not do so during his kinder years, it is now important to develop a service activity you all will engage in every month. Perhaps it's picking up litter as part of a county program, or feeding the homeless at a shelter. It will include volunteering in some way. It will bring immense rewards as your children and you bond, work together, help others, and develop the life of compassion together.

### The Question of Lying

A dad recently wrote me about his son, age eight, who is basically a good kid but was going through a phase of lying a lot: "He says he's done things he hasn't, and insists he hasn't done things he has. He took a bath the other day and peed in the bathwater, then when I came in and saw the yellow, he looked me in the face and bald-face lied to me about it: 'I didn't pee in the tub, Dad, no way.' He just looks me and his mother in the eye and lies. What is going on here?"

Further in the letter, the dad revealed that the family was going through a particularly traumatic time. His son was acting out the trauma.

It's common for kids to go through phases of experimenting with lying, but chronic lying generally means something is wrong in the family. If your son is a chronic liar, it's best first to wonder if there is some tension in the boy's life or family system that is compelling him to unconsciously seek negative attention by lying.

- Is the child getting enough positive attention in his life from his caregivers?
- Is the child going through a normal testing or parent-child separation phase, and using lying as his method of asserting his independence?
- Has there been an event in the boy's life that he perceives as deeply unfair or unjust—is he lying to strike back?
- Is the child trying to prove he's *tough* for some reason—is there other bravado or posturing behavior showing up elsewhere, for instance, at school?
- Is the child diverting family attention to himself in hopes of stopping a tragedy? Sometimes children will start lying or otherwise seeking negative attention when their parents are fighting and the child is scared a divorce or other trauma will occur in the home.
- Has the child been abused—physically, sexually, or psychologically? Chronic lying or other immoral behavior and the attendant negative attention may be his way of punishing himself for his perceived faults.

Solving a chronic lying problem begins with trying to understand the possible causes, then giving more positive attention and moral training, and redressing an injustice.

Here are some other key elements to curing the problems.

1. Parents need to be sure the child understands that he *is* lying. A conversation about his lying might happen at a "safe time," like just before bed, when the child is feeling open.

2. Parents need to condemn the child's action—"You lied, and that is wrong"—for a period of time before starting to criticize the child's character—"You are a bad boy." Generally, surgically criticizing the action over a period of a few weeks, combined

with fixing the problem that has caused the lying behavior, will take care of things.

3. A certain amount of ignoring can sometimes help. Not every lie needs to be attacked by the parent when dealing with a chronic lying phase.

4. Only as a last resort is it useful to say, "Son, I can't trust you anymore," and really mean it. The long-term consequences of a child really believing his parents don't trust him include very untrustworthy behavior as adolescence approaches. Preferable language would be: "I can't trust you, but I want that to change. I hope after a while you will prove you are trustworthy again."

## Helping Him Channel Aggression

Your son or another boy he knows may be struggling with his own aggression right now. Aggression is certainly a moral issue, and boys want a great deal of training in how to handle it.

**Play Aggression: Activities and Toys.** A mother of two boys, seven and five, told me about walking through a toy store with her children. Her seven-year-old asked if he could buy a plastic sword. Mother and son calculated his allowance and determined he had enough. The boy took the sword off the shelf, and the mother and sons stood in the checkout line. Behind them was another mother, who bent down to the boy and asked, "Why would you want to play with a toy that can hurt people?" The boy didn't have any words, but his mother said quickly, "Because it's fun!" She became very agitated by what she called "the prejudice some people have against boys and the way they play."

It is very normal for many boys in these years to engage, for hours at a time, in aggression activities. We've dealt with these in more detail in earlier chapters and will continue to better understand them in later chapters. It is important that boys find outlets for their aggression so that they can continue to learn to regulate it. These are also good years to teach boys more about their own aggression—where it comes from, what it should be used for later in life (e.g., for helping people). Boys at seven and eight are getting smart enough to be taught the morality of aggression: "When you play the game where you're Predator and your two friends are Superman and Batman, do you notice how you don't just hit each other, you're really after something, like a prize, or to help someone, or to win the kingdom?" Adding "lessons" to aggression play is now very appropriate.

**Finding the Line Between Aggression and Violence.** In an Oregon school district, an eight-year-old boy was suspended from elementary school for repeatedly singing a violent version of the *Barney* theme. He changed the original lyrics—"I love you, you love me, we're a happy family"—to "I hate you, you hate me, let's kill . . . " (and he filled in the names of classmates). One of the girls whom he had threatened to kill in the song complained, and the boy was taken to the counselor. Soon after this incident, he sang it again, and he was suspended.

There were arguments on both sides about whether the suspension was right. The boy's mother exacted harsh punishments at home, so she argued the school did not need to. The school, which is located near a high school in Oregon in which an adolescent boy shot and killed his classmates, felt compelled to exact a swift and powerful punishment.

The boy's behavior needed a strong punishment, in my view, because it crossed the line from aggression play into a repeated threat of violence. It was an action *repeated* by the boy even after he had been shown appropriate behavior.

Especially because the inappropriate behavior occurred so close to a traumatized community, it was difficult for the school administrators to do other than they did. While many boys are unnecessarily pathologized for what is normal boyish aggression play, this boy's *repeated* behavior required immediate discipline.

Boys in the between years truly are caught between a lot of internal impulses. One second they want to yell and scream from frustration, the next second they are concentrating on a game. One second they like someone, another second they feel utterly rejected. This is a very impulsive time, and our task in large part is to help them manage impulses.

The line between aggression and violence is drawn for them, quite often, by only the slightest impulse. Teaching the boy in Oregon which impulses are violent and which are healthy aggression was the moral duty of his caregivers. Hate talk is never acceptable, nor is kill talk, except in appropriate games. If kill talk occurs in a Batman game—"I'm going to kill you, Joker!"—it is a normal part of fantasy play and does not cause discomfort.

Outside the appropriate purview of the game, the caregivers must forcibly return the boy to a position of compassion.

## A HEALTHY MORAL AND EMOTIONAL ENVIRONMENT

Perhaps your seven-year-old son is now having more say about his immediate environment. You used to put posters up on his walls; now he picks them. You wallpapered his room when he was little; now he may not like the wallpaper. About little things like this, we need not intervene too much (unless the posters don't fit our values). But when we say "environment," we don't mean just these physical things. Our young son's environment is a multidimensional world of activities, places, expectations.

### The Family Environment

Many boys around seven or eight will begin needing "alone time" with each parent—time when they can work on their bond with Mom without Dad and the other siblings around, and time with Dad in the same way (also, at times, similar opportunities with grandparents). These between years are good years to instigate the policy of one alone-time opportunity per week.

It is possible that now or in the next year or two you will notice a pull in your boy to have specific alone time with *male* role models—Dad, grandfathers, uncles, older brothers. It is important to protect and savor these times. During some of these times, son and dad might play physical or board games together—boys of seven, eight, and even older need the dad to let them win some of these games! A young boy who can playfully beat his father at running or at Monopoly sometimes will grow up more self-confident.

**Be Aware of Father Hunger.**  Researchers at the University of Pennsylvania and Princeton University recently completed a study in which they confirmed that the likelihood of a male ending up in prison can be measured by the time he is seven years old. The studies confirmed that the single most important factor in determining if a male will end up incarcerated later in life is not race, income, parent education, or urban residence, but whether or not he has a father in the home. Just when they need Dad to help them understand social convention and moral life, often Dad is missing. If your family is facing this circumstance, it is crucial to develop a plan for the next couple of years by which you help the boy retain a father bond or find a similar bond with other elder men so that he doesn't lose his trust of his father, of men, and then of himself as a male. (Handling divorce, single parenting, and stepparenting will be covered in more depth in the next chapter.) M. Gary Neuman's *Helping Your Kids Cope with Divorce* is a very valuable resource if you are going through a separation or family breakup.

**Monitor Addiction to Activity.**  It is normal during these years for both parents and children to find themselves "addicted" to activities—karate on Tuesdays and Thursdays; basketball on Mondays, Wednesdays, and Fridays; soccer on Saturdays. The boy craves activities through which he learns about himself and the world—physically, mentally, socially, and spiritually. Parents feel guilty if they don't take every opportunity to fill the boy's craving.

Yet this "activity addiction" in the boy is also an "action addiction." He may be learning a lot but without appropriate reflection time, reading time, imagination time, prayer time. His life is out of balance.

The seven- or eight-year-old is looking for our guidance not only into activities but also into self-reflection and balance. He knows, unconsciously, that self-regulation of his own personal energy and power requires having a varied life. He needs to work hard, but he needs to think and reflect, too.

If we as parents are work and activity addicted, he has modeled it from us. Our whole family may want to adjust its constant hunger for action. One sport, one musical activity, and *maybe* one other extracurricular activity is all that is necessary, or perhaps healthy, for the boy and his family.

**The Family Conference.** If you have not already, you might want to develop the institution of the "family conference." Through it, many things will occur, not the least of which is the growth of your son's sense of safety in talking to you about your discipline techniques.

A family conference is a time held sacred by the family for discussing *anything* of importance to *anyone* in the family. It is run by the parents, but it can be "called" by any member of the family.

In the family conference, we might discover that our son has been bullied, or that punishment we provided this morning felt unfair to him. While we are the dictators in the home, we may very well end up saying, "Son, you're right. I was unfair. I'm sorry." We may also end up showing him that we were right and he is mistaken, and thus have an additional opportunity to continue the discipline in conversation.

**Dealing with a Death in the Family.** Our children desperately need us to talk to them about death from as early as they can understand it. They need to know that death is a part of life, and an important part of each family's history. In the first six or so years of life, they tend to apprehend things like death through imagination, so they need us to help them visualize angels and other helpers. These images help them feel safe. As they move into the second developmental episode of their lives, this method still may work, and the discussion can become more sophisticated.

While a beloved person is sick, our children need us to bring them near the sick one, hold his/her hand, talk honestly, feel the presence of one who is dying but who still breathes with life. Our children need us both to grieve and to continue to endure in hope.

Once the person is dead, as much as possible, our children need to have a role in the ceremony of the dead—in the funeral, the wake, the sitting *shiva,* and so on. Even if their role is small, they need to be included. When they themselves seem lost in emotions, they need us to lift them up.

Throughout the period following the death, it is essential that we inspire our children to continue their spiritual conversation with the beloved—to talk to Grandpa in their prayers, to get advice from Grandma. Photographs are important; memories are important. When your children are young, it is useful to teach them to get moral advice from the dead elder who was a good moral role model. "When you can't decide what to do in a situation, son, and we're not around, maybe you can pray to God and talk to Grandpa about what he would do."

If the child has lost his own parent to death, all of what I've said needs even more attention. We can expect this child to experience extreme emotions and to require immense support from the surviving parent and the whole extended family.

In no cases, because our child is a boy, should we assume that somehow he is strong enough to handle these deaths on his own. There is ample evidence, as I've noted earlier, that in many ways boys are actually more fragile than girls when it comes to handling certain traumas.

### The School Environment

In the previous chapter, we looked at how difficult the early school years can be for little boys. We talked about making sure your son is mature enough for elementary school.

As your son engages now in second or third grade, vigilance about the character and quality of his schooling—and his individual fit in that school—needs to be just as severe. Our boys need "boy-friendly" classrooms, and while many educators naturally create them, some educational systems do not. The teachers in these unfriendly classrooms don't understand youthful male energy or the way many males learn. Statistics show that boys get lower grades than girls on average, are labeled "learning disabled" three times more often than girls, and are medicated for learning problems about eight times more often than girls. Unfortunately, the boys themselves usually express their boredom, confusion, or other learning disabilities by acting out in ways that make them discipline problems and lead to negative labels.

Currently, most teachers leave M.Ed. programs and teacher certification programs without being comprehensively educated in the differences between male and female brain systems, hormonal systems, and acculturation. They seek to create classrooms for elementary-age children that are androgynous. These efforts often work, but when they do not, the child most likely to fail is the boy. Ninety percent of elementary teachers are women, many of whom were not brought up with brothers or have not raised sons. They do their best given how little teachers in general are valued. Yet your son can end up in a classroom in which this teacher, unconsciously, expects all second-graders to act and speak like a verbal-emotive seven- or eight-year-old girl for whom putting pen to paper is somewhat easier and for whom fidgeting is not as much an issue.

If you have any suspicion that your son is in a classroom that is unfriendly to his development, you have the right to approach the teacher and, if you get no help from her, to go to the administration in the school.

A wonderful program to help kids who show signs of problems in school is the Big Brothers and Big Sisters school-based mentoring program. Check with your local Big Brothers and Big Sisters agency.

**Insist on School Activities That Enhance Moral and Discipline Development.** For a time, our culture experimented with the idea that we could separate academic education and character building. This experiment is waning as we realize that, developmentally, our children's brain systems do not separate these two. While our public schools remain, by legal necessity, places of separation between church and state, they do not need to be places of separation between moral learning and academic success. Many schools are closing this gap.

Some schools now use multigenerational classrooms: For instance, the first, second, and third grades all are in one room. Thus, the older kids (the third-graders) help the younger—at the year's beginning, each third- grader is assigned a first-grader to mentor. Multiyear classrooms are very useful for teaching all children responsibility. They provide younger children with role models, and they provide older children with roles.

Ann Gross's third-grade students at Mary E. Roberts Elementary in Moorestown, New Jersey, developed a "Ten Ways to Tolerance" bulletin board. The ten ways they brainstormed and posted were as follows.

1. Talk to people who annoy you.
2. Don't think your opinion is always better.
3. Accept apologies.
4. Apologize to each other.
5. Don't "get back" at people.
6. Don't judge people by their beliefs.
7. Think before acting or speaking.
8. Get to know people before judging them.
9. Respect other people's opinions.
10. Think about people's feelings.

These sorts of school and classroom attentions to moral life are essential for your between years boys. These schoolboys need their attention focused on how to behave, and they need to be part of the process of brainstorming their own rules for behavior. They need to generate ethical concepts in groups, for they are becoming very social beings for whom morality is an interactive phenomenon.

If your son goes to a school or classroom that is empty of moral or character development innovations, you might seek another school or do what you can to volunteer or to become an activist in your school district. A very fine source for wisdom, inspiration, and practical advice is Thomas Lickona's *Educating for Character.*

**Insist on Classroom Discipline.** Lowell School is a school in Washington, D.C. Teachers there told me about an incident like so many we find in schools all over the country. The third-grade classroom was an active place in which learning went on quite well. However, there were three "alpha" students—very high functioning and, in this case, all males—who competed with one another to be the best and fastest at their lessons. This natural competition would have been okay except that the boys were gradually losing their self-discipline: Not only were they chatting, fidgeting, and looking over shoulders, but also they were turning in sloppy work because they were in such a hurry to "be the best."

Their teachers had to intervene, to "knock them down a peg" by giving them bad marks and reports on these lessons, and by asking them to articulate exactly what they were doing wrong. The boys didn't like getting bad marks, and quickly improved. They were separated for a time in different parts of the classroom, and they were compelled to monitor their own behavior better.

The intervention was useful not only for the boys but for the whole class. In these years, your boys learn many of the social conventions by watching how the alphas are handled by the supreme alpha—the teacher. Strong, caring discipline is essential in a classroom of second- and third-graders.

**Doing Homework with Your Son.**   Boys in these years often are getting homework—about an hour or more a night. Parents often think there are only two good ways to help the son get his homework done: Either stay clear of him and make him do it on his own, or hover over him and help him continually. I would suggest taking the middle ground.

- When he asks for help, provide it by brainstorming and pointing him toward resources—dictionaries, encyclopedias, and yourself. He can feel free to ask you specific questions about specific problems.

- When he seems terribly stumped, give him a jump start by answering one or two questions or problems on his homework sheet with him.

- Employ the question format more than the answer format. In other words, "What does this mean?" is better than "Son, that word means . . ."

## Chores and Allowance

A good environment for a between years boy is one with reasonable and definite chores in it, and an increase in allowance and its responsibilities.

**Chores.** Doing household chores together builds family bonds. Folding the clothes together is a chance to talk about things while working together. All chores bond the boy to his home and hearth.

If your seven- or eight-year-old son is resistant to chores, it's useful to look at whether you have a definite group of chores for him. Often the young boy needs to know what is expected of him, and he may do them less well if they are arbitrarily altered or removed. Also it can help to leave the boy alone to do many of his chores—he feels a little more independent this way.

I suggest sets of morning, afternoon, and nighttime chores, then sets of weekend chores. Many of the weekend chores could be done together as a family, and some of the daily chores could be as well. Certainly, by the time the boy is seven, he can take out the garbage, clear and set the table, do some of the dishes (on a schedule that fairly employs all the siblings throughout the week); he can unload the dishwasher, help with the laundry in some way, and do some housecleaning. He can clean his room as necessary, or once every few days as a rule.

**Allowance.** We have discussed allowance in earlier chapters. Now is the time to increase allowance as appropriate, *and make sure some of the allowance is tithed to causes or charities the boy cares about.* It is good to help him articulate why he cares about a particular charity.

## Media Use

Although you may have been able to keep a younger boy away from most media, by the time your son is eight, it is very difficult for you to prevent the media from becoming a powerful part of his life. So much culture and convention is based on what the media proffers—through what kids are wearing, what they're talking about, what kinds of behavior they exhibit. Furthermore, using media can be a healthy way for your son to explore the world.

**Television Use.**   The single most important thing parents of seven- and eight-year-olds can do is preview the programming their children are watching. You may need to watch the shows beforehand or with the boy. You may need to call around within your family and friendship network to learn what the shows are about, and hear from adults who have actually seen them.

A good resource for learning more about appropriate child-viewing guidelines is

TV Parental Guidelines
P.O. Box 14097
Washington, D.C. 20004
www.tvguidelines.org

While this group provides good guidelines, I believe that *all TV rating systems are probably not as protective as you may want to be for kids of this age.*

If misused, television is morally and emotionally dangerous; if well used, it's a blessing. One family TV night per week is, for instance, a wonderful way to increase family bonds. When commercials come on, parents can teach boys about the media and how it works.

We can say, "What do they want us to buy, son?"

"A car."

"How are they trying to get us to buy it?"

"I don't know."

"By pretending we can fly if we're in it. Can you really fly in a car?"

"No."

"Good, son. Always be smarter than the TV."

Here are some guidelines for healthy viewing.

- Except for a family TV night (or another special occasion), one hour of TV per day is appropriate for seven- and eight-year-olds.

- When friends are over to play, TV is generally to be considered unnecessary. Simultaneously, if the weather permits outdoor play, TV is unnecessary.

- If TV use is clearly becoming an alternative to parental involvement in the boy's life, then it is dangerous to the family system. "Turn the TV off, son, your father's home!" is a very appropriate refrain to sing in a home of close family bonds. TV is best considered one of the least important things in the boy's life.

- TV use for educational purposes (e.g., a *National Geographic* special) is an exception to the one-hour rule. However, if this exception is occurring every day, the boy is spending too much time in front of the screen.

- A reasonable time watching sports programming is also an exception. Often, a seven- or eight-year-old will not sit for the whole game anyway.

- TV in a child's room is to be avoided.

**Video Games.**   I opened up Sony PlayStation's "Cardinal Syn" game to see what it was like. It is advertised as a game in which to find "torture, mutilation, rivers of blood, bestial howls, and living death chambers." In its story, the Clans of the Bloodland are fighting for control. A prophet offers the Book of Knowledge, which brings peace, until the prophet leaves and the people begin fighting again. Many fighters show different kinds of prowess as the game unfolds.

In the between years, and for the next few years, many boys can become very interested in games like these. They fit the very spatial male brain, and they fit the inherent desire in the male psyche to test the self in aggressive arenas. Objects move through space in aggression activity and bring a sense of order, disorder, and delight. Young girls (and females in general) gravitate toward these games less often.

Even though the male's brain is attracted to these games, they can be dangerous to the boy's brain development, and thus his emotional and moral development.

- The games affect the aggression centers of the brain, like the amygdala, increasing male aggression.

- The games represent social conventions that teach violent solutions as opposed to more varied moral responses to social stresses.

- The games are addictive—stimulus addiction is now a major problem among our males.

- The games rely on "fixated eye movement," a trancelike state that TV relies on. Think of fixated eye movement as akin to an altered mind state caused by mild drug use. Seeing it that way inspires us to be more vigilant about protecting our children from it.

- The games deemphasize verbal responses and overemphasize spatial responses—i.e., manipulating the joystick or the buttons on the Game Boy rather than using words—at the very time when the male brain desperately needs to increase verbal-emotive responses.

- The games desensitize the boy to *real* pain, stunting rather than building compassion.

- The games destimulate the kind of neural activity that attention span development requires.

A half hour of Game Boy a day is probably not a big deal, but much more should be looked at carefully. I generally advocate no video games or Game Boys for boys until they are nine years old. In centuries past, young boys gravitated, like our boys do in video games, toward heroic stories. They sought to learn through their storytellers their own heroic potential. The difference, in the past, was that real people told the stories. The whole village or religious group or extended family helped the boy understand the story through verbalization, allowing the boy to create a deepened imaginative response—emotional, moral, and spiritual. Most of the visual stories our boys come into contact with now are spatial stimulants only—they just don't help the boy's brain develop in the way his brain needs to develop at seven or eight years old.

**Movies.**   I often find myself in arguments with dads about what kinds of movies boys ought to be watching. One father of a teenager I've known since toddlerhood said to me recently, "But Mike, you know that I took T.J. to whatever movie he wanted to see. After the divorce, this was one of our best ways of being together—we both liked movies. He saw some terribly violent stuff, but look at him, he's doing great." The divorce occurred when T.J. was seven, and the father and son did see many movies together, and T.J. is a fine young man—on sports teams, getting good grades, holding down a part-time job, and nice to be around.

The thing that moved me the most, however, in my conversation with T.J.'s father was his statement—after all the rationalizing was over—that "well, if I had it to do over, I wouldn't take him to those movies. I guess I did it for me, not him. I did it because I wanted to be the dad he'd love who gave him anything. Now, as we talk, I realize I didn't protect him well enough like a dad should."

Allowing seven- and eight-year-olds (and any child not yet thirteen) to see most PG-13 movies is inappropriate. Allowing them to see any R-rated movies is, as a rule, inappropriate—even if older siblings are watching them on video and our young boy begs.

**Computer Use.**   Your sons may be using the computer and the Internet for research, to download materials for schoolwork, and to search out interesting Web sites—for instance, about science projects. If supervised, this computer use is good. If your son has not yet begun using the computer for these purposes and is not using it much more than a few minutes at school, *he will not suffer socially or economically later in life.* The computer is yours to decide about. If your son is spending more than one to two hours in front of an entertainment screen—the TV, video games, and movies—another hour or two in front of the computer is not healthy for him.

## The Rituals of Life

A great-grandmother, married fifty-seven years, said to me, "You've got to give boys lots of adventure when they're young so they'll want to stay around after you marry them." I asked her to flesh this statement out, and she told me that of her seven children, twenty-three grandchildren, and eight great-grandchildren, about 80 percent are boys! She knows a lot about them, she said, and she noticed that the ones who had been brought up with "the most love and attention, the most respect for their parents, and the most room to roam and become little heroes" had made the best husbands.

As we got to talking, she said that she always made sure her boys had lots of little "rituals" in which they could find adventure—going to the family farm every weekend to visit her parents was one; going out for a treat once a week was another. "The boys need lots of little roads to find their adventures," she said. Sometimes an adventure is just the wind in the trees, or playing heroes with friends, or fixing a car with Dad, or running errands with Mom. Each of these was presented to the boy or was discovered by the boy to be something pleasant and also a little bit heroic, something on which the society, in some small way, depended.

**Create Rituals for Thinking Out the Big Questions.** Boys gain by developing rituals through which to learn life's big lessons. A reading ritual is one of these—perhaps reading every night the stories and books that have something of value to teach. If your son likes writing, encourage him to keep a journal in which he writes not only daily events but carries on conversations with God, with an imaginary you, or with an imaginary teacher. You might also challenge your son to write a fable every month in which the characters learn some worthwhile rule.

Should your son have no proclivity toward writing and little toward reading, you may want to make sure to set aside time for moral conversation—the dinner table, before bed, while en route somewhere, or when you're at the park. These boys are hungry for more moral conversation than they get in just an hour at Sunday school.

**Honor Bedtime Rituals.** Seven- and eight-year-old boys are still very ripe for bedtime rituals. Some will still want you to lie down with them, cuddle, talk, listen. These rituals remain essential and need our encouragement. Now is a good time to listen to the boy's day, and then to tell a story of our own day or perhaps of something from our own childhood, and also to talk about moral or other intriguing issues that have presented themselves to the boy and to us, whether at his school or on the news. This is also a time to pray together and to facilitate the boy's prayer life, if these are appropriate in your home. An 8:00 P.M. bedtime is still appropriate (except as we've noted in earlier chapters, with boys who just can't get to sleep at this time), now with half an hour added for reading and ritual, so that bedtime is now final at 8:30.

## EVAN'S STORY

This story came to me via e-mail, and was titled "The Fence."

There was a boy of eight named Evan, who had a bad temper. His father gave him a bag of nails and told him that every time he lost his temper, he should hammer a nail in the back fence.

The first day, the boy drove thirty-seven nails into the fence!

The second day, twenty-eight.

The third day, nineteen.

The fourth day, fifteen.

Gradually, it dwindled down, for Evan began to discover that it was easier to hold his temper than to drive those nails into the fence.

Finally, the day came when Evan didn't lose his temper at all. He told his father about it, and the father suggested that he now pull out one nail for each day that he was able to hold his temper. The days passed, and the young boy fulfilled this plan.

And finally, the day came when he was able to tell his father that all the nails were gone from the fence. The father took his son's hand, and they went to look.

"You've done well, son," he said, "but look at the holes in the fence. The fence will never be the same."

The son saw that it was true, and a small tear came to his eye.

The father continued to hold his hand and said, "When you say things in anger, they leave a scar, just like these scars. You can put a knife in a person and draw it out and then say you're sorry a hundred times, but the wound and the scar will always be there."

The son understood the lesson, and he and his father held each other. Walking away from the fence, holding his father's hand, Evan decided to live his life differently from that day forward.

# SEVEN

# Pre-Adolescence

## NURTURING BOYS OF NINE AND TEN

Here is a Hawaiian fable.

After a long hard day, a mother was walking along the beach, taking a moment before she had to get back to her work and her family. She saw a figure far ahead who kept bending over and tossing something in the water, then walking forward, bending over, doing it again—like a cripple, perhaps, with spasms, or like an awkward dancer.

When the mother finally caught up to the figure, she saw it was not a cripple or a dancer but her ten-year-old son. He was picking objects up from the shoreline and throwing them into the water, one by one.

"My son," she called to him, "what are you doing?"

"I'm throwing starfish into the ocean," he replied.

Indeed she could see now that he was picking up all the starfish that commonly washed onto shore, and throwing each one back into the water. Her son knew she walked here a great deal, but he had never come before. She felt stirrings of strange and new feelings about him, as he seemed a little older, for the moment, than the son she knew back home.

"And why are you throwing them out there?" she asked as he continued his task.

"The tide's going out," he replied. "If I don't throw them out now, they'll die." Then he looked at his mother. "You walk here a lot. Don't you throw them in, too, so they won't die?"

His mother said honestly, "No, I suppose I don't. There are so many miles of beach and so many starfish. We aren't going to make much of a difference." As the mother and son occupied one parcel of the shore, they could see countless starfish along the water.

The son looked up at her, holding a starfish in his hand. "Mother," he said, "it makes a big difference to this one." And he threw it into the water, rescuing yet another.

With a tear of joy in her eye, the mother gazed for a moment at her wonderful son, then bent down just as he had been doing, picked up a starfish, and threw it in the water. Together, without another word, the mother and son threw starfish in the water until the sun set.

This story reminds us of how close we are with our pre-adolescent sons of nine and ten, and yet how they are becoming their own people. Where we always led them, now just a little, we notice them leading us. We notice a brightness of moral intelligence in them, and a widening of compassion. We notice that they are becoming more adult—the boy in this story had not come onto his mother's stretch of beach until now; he is joining her in the adult world, even if just a little. Now we can feel very proud of our son's moral and emotional development, and proud of all we've done with him. It is also a time of rapid internal growth. Perhaps on a symbolic level, each starfish is a part of the boy that he is now becoming aware of. Filled with hope, he tosses each part of himself into the larger ocean, wondering what will become of each, and hoping each will find a home in the larger world.

## DEVELOPMENTAL MILESTONES

For some boys, adolescence can begin when they are between nine and ten years old. Some boys are already looking toward adulthood with the voraciousness of an adolescent. We generally call the years of nine and ten "pre-adolescence," however, because most boys are *not* yet adolescents—they're merely on the cusp. "I'm not a little kid anymore!" is a heartfelt statement for them.

### His Leap in Moral Development

When your son was little, in his early stages of development, he tended to experience morality as a matter of *obedience* or *instrumentality*. He knew he shouldn't do wrong things because he was told not to. He decided what was fair based on bartering so that his own needs were met—he gave what he had to in order to be able to take.

As he became seven and eight, he checked out the social conventions and tried to adhere to them—conventions laid out mainly by parents and their representatives in schools, churches, and other institutions.

Now your son's moral intelligence is gaining even more variety and depth. He can think out options more. He senses that his family container is actually not an absolute, but an essential part of a larger social container. And as much as he's mindful of the family's rules, he's also trying to learn the rules of the larger group—he tries to match rules in his head; he tries to get not only the love of a few caregivers by his moral "goodness" but also the attention of other groups and authorities. He expands his apprehension of suitable life models beyond close authorities—hence media and other role models start to take on more importance to his growing mind.

He will begin to notice the impossibility of satisfying everyone— that being a "good boy" to Mom might be the opposite of being a "good boy" to some high-risk peers. So he has to choose between Mom and peers. This choice making continues through adolescence, pulling him in many directions. The Catholic Jesuits have a saying: "Give me your child for the first seven years of his life, and you can have him for the rest." Since the foundation for character development is laid in the first years of life, that's when we want to do that work. If we've done it, we can trust that later he'll do the right things. This concept should give us great relief as our sons reach pre-adolescence and move forward. If we have raised them to high standards of self-discipline and moral development before now, we can trust that they will *generally* navigate the new choice making with honor and integrity.

Beyond the pre-adolescent's attention to larger social rules and choices, his moral intelligence is also developing a candid exploration of people's *intentions.* His brain has developed so that he can think out, with some depth, *why* Dad, Mom, Joe, the president, or even he himself has taken a particular action. Not all the time, but now at least some of the time, he is asking himself: What did that person mean when he did such and such? What was he thinking? Pre-adolescence is when this search for intentionality—for the meaning of the action—begins in earnest. It is beautiful to watch. We now can talk to the boy, at least some of the time, about how intentions affect our judgments of others, and of ourselves.

As we nurture boys in pre-adolescence (and beyond), we can use our knowledge of the boy's leap in moral intelligence. I find that this pre-adolescent time period is underused by schools and homes. It is a time when we should *increase* character exploration, moral dialogue, and spiritual depth in a boy's life, for now the boy can truly begin to understand *meaning.*

Before focusing on appropriate discipline techniques for your pre-adolescent son, you might want to review what behavior is within the range of normal for him on page 200.

## DISCIPLINE TECHNIQUES

Most of the discipline techniques you've set up will continue to work in your son's pre-adolescence. Your pre-adolescent son very much *wants* to be well disciplined. When he is not, many of the reasons that applied two years ago apply now—he needs attention, he is being given too much leeway with rules, he wants the safety of strong authority. You may also notice him acting in undisciplined ways because something

## The Range of Normal

It's normal for the boy to engage in little pulls toward independence—small experiments with backtalk, or "forgetting" to follow an instruction, or even a hint of disdain for the parents' way of doing things. These often will be couched in humor or sarcasm.

It's normal for the boy to develop one or more strong academic or athletic focuses.

It's normal for him to have or be seeking one best friend.

It's normal for the boy to be a little curious about sex (this curiosity may be enhanced if he has older male siblings or has been sexualized early by media or another influence).

It's normal for the boy at nine or ten to start channeling primary feelings—like fear, pain, shame, and guilt—through anger, thus letting us know he's hurting or scared by these feelings.

It's normal for the boy to experiment with cheating at board games or other activities.

It's normal for the boy to begin having a "public" and "private" life—he hugs Mom at home but sometimes he wants to be a "free agent" in public, acting as if she's not a huge authority over him.

It's normal for the boy to develop distinct interests in other peers' lives, habits, and acquisitions.

It's normal for the boy to begin to notice in startling ways how imperfect his parents really are.

It's normal for the boy to become immensely moral—even surprising us with his truth-telling—yet simultaneously he may start experimenting with boundaries (perhaps trying a cigarette with some older boys).

If a divorce has occurred in the boy's life (many do during these years), it's normal for the boy to become very lonely and begin acting out in ways that grow naturally from trauma: excessive backtalk, anger or rages, high-risk behavior, drops in school or athletic performance, lying, and cheating.

> It's normal for the boy to look toward manhood but still be very much a
> boy. It's even normal for some boys still to wet the bed once in a while at
> nine.
>
> It's normal for the boy to become very conscious of how he re-
> ceives respect, and to feel humiliated easily but to cover up those feel-
> ings.

that has happened in school or elsewhere is bothering him, and he is
not able to call it to his own or your attention without becoming obnox-
ious or unruly. His undisciplined actions—his excessive testing or acting out—are a plea for help in understanding "What's wrong with me?
Why do I feel bad right now?"

### Providing Reasonable Consequences

For all pre-adolescent undisciplined behavior, reasonable consequences are appropriate punishments. Boys this age can be sent to
their rooms, told to "go sit over there and think about it," and given
other forms of more mature "time-out." They certainly still can lose
privileges. While more sophisticated versions of earlier discipline techniques all can be applied to pre-adolescents, in most cases, the boy will
need to suffer some sort of reasonable and natural consequence as a
part of the discipline. Sometimes the consequence will be obvious:
"You didn't clean up from dinner as you're supposed to, and you ignored my requests. You'll receive no ice cream and you'll get in bed a
half hour early." Sometimes the consequence is delayed and less obviously connected to the act: "I told you three times to clean your room
and you did not. You won't have a friend over like you wanted next
Saturday."

Sometimes the consequence must be severe: "You cheated today,
and then instead of taking responsibility you got mad at Brandon and
got him in trouble. I know you want to go to the hockey game this Friday night, but now you will not. You'll use that time to think about what
you did, and write Brandon an apology note."

Now is a good time for you to increase how often you let your son pick his own punishment. If he picks one you consider too lax, you are the ultimate authority who can add to his choice. However, his act of choosing empowers him morally in any case.

### Creating Discipline in Your Verbal Interactions

Throughout the boy's life, how we talk to him means a great deal to his development of self-discipline. In pre-adolescence, boys become very observant (even if they never reveal it) of how we speak to them.

**Ask Rather Than Interrogate.**   Certainly there will be times when you need to interrogate your son. But most of the time, calm queries, repeated as needed, can elicit the responses we want. Remaining calm is something to focus on throughout your son's pre-adolescence and adolescence, as circumstances between you and him can become gradually more frustrating.

Especially when trying to elicit truthful responses from your son about deep emotions, concrete queries are generally best. "Is something bothering you, son?" has a tenderness the boy needs. "Can I help you, son?" "Have I or has someone hurt you?" Often we will need to verbally help our pre-adolescent boys "discover" their hidden pain by verbally filling in blanks. The boy simply may not know what he's feeling.

**Praise and Criticism.**   A pre-adolescent boy gains the bulk of his self-esteem through one-on-one attention with those he loves, by feeling an important part of two or three major social groups in his life—extended family, clan, clique, or friends—and by receiving a balance of praise and criticism.

Some parents, educators, and caregivers lean more toward being judgmental, others toward praising. Your son still needs a higher ratio of praise to criticism.

Based on developmental studies, I have devised a developmental scale for praise and criticism which I hope you'll adapt to fit your discipline system as you verbally correct your son's bad behavior and reward his good actions.

## Ratio of Compliments to Corrections

| | |
|---|---|
| From Birth to Six Months: | 10 to 0 |
| From Seven Months to Eighteen Months: | 10 to 1 |
| During Toddler Years: | 8 to 1 |
| During Kinder Years: | 7 to 1 |
| From Seven Years to Eight Years: | 7 to 1 |
| From Nine Years to Ten Years: | 7 to 1 |
| From Eleven Years to Twelve Years: | 6 to 1 |
| From Puberty Onward: | 5 to 1 |

## Dealing with Backtalk

A mother recently wrote, "When is it appropriate to ignore backtalk? My son is a good kid but sometimes gets into asking backtalk kinds of questions. Like, I'll say, 'Alex, please take the garbage out,' and he'll say, 'Why?' or, 'It's not my turn, it's Timothy's,' or, 'What a waste of my time.' Do I ignore some of these?"

It often is appropriate to ignore backtalk and just keep going on with the instruction or command. Ignoring backtalk actually shows strong authority.

"Alex, please take out the garbage."

"Why?"

"I've put it by the back door for you."

When the child uses questions or sibling comparisons as backtalk, he is not crossing the line into disrespect that you need to correct. If, however, he crosses the line, you must not ignore it.

"Alex, please take out the garbage."

"You do it, Mom, I'm busy."

Now the child needs a reminder of who the authority is—a consequence, a loss of privilege, a stern lecture, a discussion of why he's being rude, a time-out.

Sometimes backtalk is a way many boys assert independence and authority and save face. If the boy is nine, ten, or older, much of the backtalk may be of this kind:

"Tory, please clean up your room."

"It's my room, and I don't want to."

"I asked you to clean it up. Begin within five minutes, or you will lose the use of the television for tonight."

"Yeah, right. I'll watch TV if I want."

My personal preference is to confront this attitude: Tell the boy his behavior is inappropriate, and take away the television privilege. I believe that children should show respect for their parents even when they don't like what their parents are saying or asking for. Perhaps the conversation would go this way:

"Tory, when I asked you to pick up your room, I treated you with respect, and I expect you to treat me with respect."

"Well, respect would be letting me clean up the room when I want to."

"No, son, that will only come when you have your own house. As long as you live here, you have the right to be treated with respect but not the right to refuse to do logical and important chores. This is not a conversation we're going to have again today without a severe consequence to you. Do you understand?"

"I guess." Then he stomps out of the living room and goes toward his room to clean it up. (His last bit of belligerence is a face-saving technique and can be ignored.)

In general, when dealing with backtalk, serenity, patience, and clear authority can be successfully augmented with surgical doses of guilt. "Son, when you go through the day treating me like one of your young friends, disrespecting me, and trying to get me in fights with you, I feel sad about our lives, about what your dad and I have given you." There is nothing wrong with using guilt at certain times, not only for backtalk and belligerence but for other behavior in your son that you're not proud of. Deep down, your son wants you to be happy with him and proud of him. If you're not, he needs to know it.

### Disciplining the Hard-to-Handle Boy

A Texas police officer, forty-seven, described her experience years earlier as a fourth-grade teacher. Suki was twenty-eight years old when she encountered "this very hard boy" from the projects. He was pre-scribed Ritalin, but Suki didn't require him to take it. "I kept him very busy instead," she told me. "I didn't believe in medicating these guys." The boy's special-ed teacher did make her give it to him one hour before he was going to special-ed classes. Suki told me that though the boy backtalked, fidgeted, and often upset class, she could see he had a good heart. She did what we all know is best for a hard-to-handle boy: She in-creased, rather than decreased, her attention to him. She stayed late to give him one-on-one attention.

Despite all efforts, one day he got upset and kicked Suki in the thigh. In an instinctual reaction, she kicked him back (physically, at ten, he was a big kid, already nearly as tall as she). "I'm telling you," Suki re-counted, "you should have seen his face. He was amazed!" He also got angry, telling her he would hit her. She told him she'd hit him back. They stared at each other, furious. Neither ended up striking again. Each backed off and calmed down. "And you know what," Suki recalled happily, "things got better for him after that. He blossomed. The school psychiatrist read me the riot act when he heard. I got in trouble for what happened. 'Talk!' the psychiatrist said. 'Talk to the kid, don't strike!' Now, basically, I agreed with him, and I knew what I did was wrong in its way, but I also said to him, 'Sometimes a mule won't plow straight without a swat on the behind.' I'm not sure there's just *one* way to get to kids—talking to them. Maybe that works most of the time. But with some of these boys, they need to know who to respect. Then they plow straight."

If you are dealing with a hard-to-handle boy, at home or in another environment, it is worth considering that *once in a while* you may have to do something unconventional, and perhaps physical, to help the boy see whom to respect. When he becomes hard-to-handle, he is doing so in large part so that the trustable authorities in his life will show the kind of strength he needs to see in order to respect them; once he re-spects them, he will follow them anywhere. Earning a boy's respect gen-erally requires patience and one-on-one attention; sometimes it needs the punctuation mark of unconventional action.

If you tend to be a calm person who does things for others a lot, unconventional for you might be to yell and refuse to do anything for the boy.

If you tend to be a person who already verbalizes a great deal, unconventional for you might be to become silent for a few hours or days.

Most often, with troubled pre-adolescents, intervention by police or other social authorities is not necessary—but if it becomes so, we must not be afraid to pursue it.

And most often, the way to get through to the hard-to-handle boy is to keep working on holding his trust. He often becomes "cured" because we work through his problems with him and never give up. The few months of trouble come to a cathartic moment, perhaps, in which our trust for each other is reestablished. One mother, who previously never hit her son, told me that when he was ten she slapped him. He was being immensely rude and refused to look at her or listen to her. The slap startled, even scared, both mother and son. It "woke us up," she said. Mother and son talked about the behavior that caused it—the son admitted he had the slap coming. Neither he nor she wanted it to happen again—they both realized they preferred their calmer relationship.

### Attention Deficit Hyperactive Disorder

More and more boys are being diagnosed with ADHD and ADD, as we began to discuss in the previous chapter. Your son may be one of these. Many boys also are being diagnosed with learning disabilities because of behavioral and discipline problems.

As we've previously discussed, the male brain is in some ways a more fragile brain system—less adaptable than the female; boys are three times more likely than girls to suffer learning disabilities, and seven times more likely to suffer ADHD and other attention-span/hyperactive disorders; and classrooms often are set up contrary to male energy and learning styles. Furthermore, our boys are more likely than our girls to suffer *and appear to suffer* these kinds of problems not only because of social and environmental confusions about how to treat males but also because the male brain secretes smaller amounts of certain chemicals, like serotonin, which naturally calm a brain system down.

*Yet while many boys do suffer an actual ADHD or ADD brain disorder, I estimate that nearly two-thirds do not.* Most boys diagnosed as having the brain disorder actually suffer attention and impulse problems that grow from overstimulation in their environments, emotional disturbances in family systems, lack of enough attention from caregivers, and school classrooms and teaching techniques that are not boy-friendly.

If your son's teacher says he has ADHD or ADD, do not stop there. Get an objective, professional diagnosis from a psychiatrist or psychologist who is trained specifically in the disorder and who is aware of the fact that these disorders are almost completely a "cultural," American phenomenon (remember, 90 percent of the Ritalin used in the world is used in America).

A teacher or professional pushing you into immediate Ritalin use who cannot prove to you that your son actually has an internal brain problem may, with all the best intentions, be taking the easy way out with your son. No matter the source of your son's condition, the Ritalin will probably improve his behavior—but so would more love and attention, a better classroom, less media stimulation, and better emotional development.

I've listed resources at the back of this book to help you decide if your son really has a disability or brain disorder, or if he is being labeled and unfairly forced into that diagnosis and its attendant medication.

If, however, your son does actually suffer ADD or ADHD, he will benefit from proper medication, and your life will become easier as he becomes far easier to discipline.

## MORAL TEACHING

Moral teaching of pre-adolescents can be challenging but also very fun. Some of the activities through which moral training occurs, and some of the topics, can bring up wonderful memories of growing up ourselves and can help us refocus on important topics and concerns. Moral

## Rules to Live By

Here are ideal rules for a child to live by in pre-adolescence. When he does not follow them, our punishment is reasonable, consistent, and swift. And the boy is always encouraged, in some way, to redeem himself.

1. A pre-adolescent should call home to tell his parents what he's doing and where he is. It is not appropriate for parents to be unaware— at any time—of a nine- or ten-year-old's location.

2. A pre-adolescent should speak in respectful tones to parents and all elders. Sarcasm is allowed only if joking and jesting is shared between the adult and child.

3. A pre-adolescent should avoid excessive whining. Whining is not a good success strategy for any human being. Sometimes adults think that if they cut off a boy's whining they are cutting off his "feelings." Most often, however, whining in pre-adolescence is not caused by pain, grief, fear, or any other deeply held feeling.

4. A pre-adolescent should articulate a grievance in appropriate ways. Boys of this age need to develop their ability to articulate feelings using language that fits social convention.

5. A pre-adolescent should protect the feelings of others when possible. This means that if little sister still believes in Santa Claus, the older brother should help her in that pleasure rather than trash it.

6. A pre-adolescent should eat what adults eat (for the most part), act in adult social situations as the adults act, be adaptable to the flow of the family's life, and not be too picky about getting his own way.

7. A pre-adolescent should consider chores and other activities that help the family to be as important as sport or recreation.

8. In social situations away from the home, a pre-adolescent should behave according to the standards of responsibility taught in the home. If an R movie is being watched at a friend's house, it is reasonable to expect our pre-adolescent son to call home and ask permission to watch it, or to go and do another activity.

teaching during this time is best carried out in ways that help us to bond more with our growing child.

Because the child is at an age when a number of moral issues arise, you will find this section on moral teaching longer than some of the previous ones.

### Moral Training in Supervised Groups

As he has been growing, he has sought out group activities, and you have provided them—in extended families, in schools, in churches. Yet now it is developmentally appropriate for even more moral training to occur in church groups, service clubs, the Cub Scouts (and then the Boy Scouts), and other groups that help your son grow in compassion through supervised peer experience. Should you choose to get involved yourself as a supervisor or mentor, you might have some real fun training the boys.

The newest Boy Scout handbook makes its organization's moral intentions very clear. The handbook not only talks about everything from chivalry to Internet warnings but reminds the young reader of the Scout oath and the twelve laws: "A Scout is trustworthy, loyal, helpful, friendly, courteous, kind, obedient, cheerful, thrifty, brave, clean and reverent." Cub Scouts and then Boy Scouts provide other very valuable resources for a boy's ethical develoment. Their "Ethics in Action" and "Ethical Controversies" curricula compel kids and adults together to brainstorm ethical solutions to life problems.

While in every group experience a lot depends on the leader, and while at times any group experience can go sour, the vast majority of Scout, church, and other similar experiences help guide the pre-adolescent in helpful ways.

Some parents of boys who are having troubles in academic or social areas may find it useful to enroll their sons in more structured schools. Many boys, once put in a new, somewhat rigorous peer environment in which ethics is emphasized (most boys' schools, and private and independent schools, emphasize ethics training to a greater degree than many other schools do), show improvement and find a new lease on education and themselves.

Now is also a time to think about introducing a fatherless pre-adolescent boy to a group of some kind *and* to a one-on-one male mentor, such as one provided by Big Brothers and Big Sisters.

### Sports and Athletics

Often we think of sports and athletics merely as physical exercise. Sometimes we think of them as opportunities for kids to socialize. We certainly acknowledge that they teach competition and how to win. All these are valuable contributions, but none alone captures the *whole* experience. Put together, they create in the boy an important experience of *moral development.*

*Sports and athletics are one of the clearest, most important supervised community activities through which our children are trained in morality.* Children learn decency, fairness, responsibility, compassion, honor, and every other moral competency through the intense experience of becoming part of a team, working together, competing, making friends, dealing with conflict, accepting criticism, succeeding, failing—and all the while they gain skills and agility through which to control their own bodies.

Some people ruin sports experiences for kids. These include bullies, bad coaches, and overzealous parents. Each of us, as a community member, will be more inspired to deal with these negative influences if we realize that they jeopardize not just the "sports" experience but also this opportunity for moral instruction. *The Cheers and the Tears,* by Shane Murphy, and *Why Good Coaches Quit,* by John Anderson and Rick Aberman, are both very fine resources for anyone who is trying to understand and improve a child's sports experience.

Some boys do not take well to team sports and instead are more attracted to music, drama, or other arts. Hopefully we will guide these children toward their own supervised group and individual activities—in church, in school, in Boy Scouts, and in other clubs—and give them the same moral development opportunities that sports give them.

It is generally not useful to force a pre-adolescent to participate in a sport, but it is good to give him many options and see if he'll choose at least one that keeps him in constant contact with a healthy team experience.

### What to Do If Your Son Is Being Bullied

If he has not already, your son may experience bullying in the pre-adolescent years. It's fair to say that sometime in his life, your son, like all boys, will do so.

One of the most important questions a parent can help a child answer is "When do I fight back?" If your son is being bullied, what do you tell him to do about it?

There is no single thing to teach a boy about surviving in the difficult world of growing up. We must teach all the options.

- When appropriate, turn the other cheek.
- When appropriate, hit back.
- Being bullied is not "your fault."
- Develop physical confidence through athletics or martial arts so that you are less likely to be a victim of a bully.
- As quickly as possible, get other adults and peers involved to form a "personal team" by which to face an aggressor.

When he does this latter, your son may be accused of being a tattle-tale, which can really sting him, so if adults get involved they need to tread carefully. I find, however, that boys in this age group really want help. *Thus it is important to teach boys to talk to a trusted elder when they are being bullied.* During the first ten or so years of a boy's life, he generally does not want to face a bully alone. Later in adolescence, it is more normal for him to wish to do so.

Here are things you as the parent can do.

- If a boy is being bullied a lot, find out why. In animal interactions, bullying males often pick the weakness in a victim male very wisely. Sadly, bullies have good intuition about flaws in others, and they attack those flaws. While your son needs a lot of help in stopping the bully's actions, he also may need subtle help in fixing the part of his own behavior or character that is flawed. If he is whiny or constantly plays the victim role or insists that he is physically incapable of playing games everyone else plays, he may need extra help from you in "growing beyond" these traits.

- Keep communication lines open constantly with your son or any bullied boy.
- Being bullied is very humiliating and cuts into the heart of a boy's self-esteem. Keep him talking about his feelings and/or working these feelings through.

### When Your Son Is the Bully

A mom recently wrote, "Charles is always so angry. He has become the class bully, and he's only in fourth grade. He was suspended from school because he took his shirt off, rubbed it on the guinea pig in the classroom, then shoved it in the face of a boy who he knew was allergic to guinea pigs. The boy had to go to the hospital. I was so scared and ashamed. What should I do about my son?"

One of the hardest moments in life is when we realize that our own child is hurtful and dangerous. When we realize our son is a bully, we need to look at (and often get professional help for) these key elements.

1. Does he suffer a brain disorder or conduct disorder that medication can help?
2. Are his parents getting a divorce, or is he acting out to get the attention of an emotionally disengaged parent?
3. Is he modeling the behavior from his father, mother, or other role model?
4. Is he or has he been physically, sexually, or psychologically abused or substantially humiliated?
5. Is he choosing a bullying style (perhaps because of his physical strength) by which to make up for deeply felt insecurity and instability?
6. Is he being stimulated by far too much violent media imagery?
7. Are the discipline systems in his home and school inadequate?

Generally, we will intuit the source of the bullying by answering these questions and can immediately enlist the help of professionals and our extended families. If your son feels guilty about his bullying, or if you can bring him to feel guilty, he is on the right track. If he feels no shame, guilt, or sadness at all, it is essential you get constant help until he does.

*Before It's Too Late,* by Stanton Samenow, is a very valuable resource for dealing with bullying and violent behavior in your child. The Johnson Institute's "No-Bullying" curriculum (800-231-5165) is very useful to schools, as is the video *Set Straight On Bullies* (National School Safety Center, 805-373-9977).

### Sexual Morality

We will spend greater time on this topic in the next chapter, on pre-puberty. Here in pre-adolescence, the boy is beginning to understand sexuality. He's "sexualizing" himself and being sexualized by his culture. Some boys by now might want to look at *Playboy* or even peek at an older sister naked. It's pretty innocent stuff, but it is a beginning.

As appropriate for his development, explanations of birds and bees needs to begin or continue. A book called *Beyond the Birds and the Bees,* by Beverly Engel, is a wonderful aid. Your conversation with your boy need not be unpleasant—hopefully it will be a beautiful moment in family life. And it will continue in more depth in pre-puberty.

### Teaching the Art of Thoughtfulness

The pre-adolescent boy is ripe for training in the art of thoughtfulness. Boys are seeing how they affect others, and the effects of time, disease, pain, joy, and life on everyone. They want the "social strokes" they receive for doing something nice for someone, especially an elder, a teacher, or a parent. They are very sensitive to the feelings of others but may not jump at the opportunity to be thoughtful and help out. However, should we direct them toward thoughtfulness and help them focus in that direction, they will flourish. "It means so much to Grandpa when you help him fix his car," we might say. We might have to encourage our son to help Grandpa, and even facilitate the timing. There's an old Russian saying: "Give him a fish, he'll eat for a day. Teach him to fish, he'll eat for a lifetime." It applies to self-confidence and skill building, of course, but I think it applies also to teaching thoughtfulness. We can do things for our sons, do things for Grandpa, do things for everyone, but at some point we have to fully make sure our son is doing them. As he gets used to helping out, he will help out for a lifetime.

### Expanding the Moral Dialogue at Home

Your boy's pre-adolescence is a time for you to begin a ritual of moral debates and moral puzzles with your son. At the dinner table, for instance, you might lay out a scenario and ask the boy what is "right" and why. While driving on a long trip, you might present a moral dilemma and have the son resolve it.

Your son might come home and present a moral puzzle: "Billy lied to me. He said he would play with me at recess, then he played with Tim. He does that a lot." Here is an opportunity to help your son decide Billy's intentions, or ask Billy what his intentions are, and to give meaning to the word "lie."

Both the spontaneous and planned teaching of "moral literacy" are very important as the boy's mind now expands to include intentionality in moral judgment. In previous cultures, Bible stories were told and questions raised, or legends told and points of view argued. Your pre-adolescent son will probably enjoy having these debates in whatever way fits your family's everyday life. Some of your stories can come from TV and movies.

As the boy gets more and more articulate about moral thinking during adolescence, this tradition that you set now will become one through which you can help him solve moral puzzles in his own life during the complex adolescent years.

## A HEALTHY MORAL AND EMOTIONAL ENVIRONMENT

At the core of a healthy environment for your pre-adolescent are the values; the love your son receives; and the structure, limitations, opportunities, and discipline in family and caregiving groups. To support your efforts to help your pre-adolescent son develop, you might want to pay special attention to these aspects of his life.

### Spiritual Development

God is very much a parent's ally at this stage, and again, please substitute for "God" whatever word for divinity applies in your life. The sense of God is beginning to change in the boy, however. Just as he no longer believes in Santa Claus, his mind is developing enough for him to think comments like "God knows when you lie" or "God needs you to be very helpful today" are "little kid" kinds of comments. He's ready now for a deeper vision. God remains an invisible authority in his life, but he is also able to see God as a much more complex force.

If your family attends religious services, your son's attendance should not be optional. Church activities need to be part of the fabric of the family's culture.

### Honor Obedience

Sometimes as a pre-adolescent begins pulling away from parents and other authorities, adults will assume the boy is ready to be very independent. He isn't. He's just testing the power of the authority to handle his own baby steps in adolescent drive. He feels safest if he knows the rules, is compelled to follow them, and is guided by the family discipline system and an environment of good limits and healthy structure.

### Chores and Allowance

Pre-adolescence is not a time for laxness of responsibility at home. By now a boy can probably mow the lawn, mop, sweep, and do nearly anything required (within his own size and height limitations) by his parents. He can hold to a family chores schedule. Gradually, we find ourselves directing very active boys toward more outdoor chores than indoor. Doing chores and working with and for the family are two of the primary ways a pre-adolescent confirms the lessons in fairness he has learned. He helps, and so he gets help. This is fairness at its best.

Allowance shouldn't be given as payment for chores. Chores and the maturity they bestow are their own reward.

### Don't Leave Him Home Alone

A home environment in which the boy finds himself alone for extended periods is usually not a safe one for him. Nine- and ten-year-olds are generally too young to be left alone in the house for more than a very brief time. Among "latchkey kids," the most crime, substance abuse, and teen pregnancy occur between three and six in the afternoon—more than after dark or late at night. Supervision and parent/adult involvement are crucial until the boy is much older, when he probably will spend more of the latchkey hours with coaches, mentors, and peers.

Baby-sitters for the pre-adolescent remain appropriate. All the way through the boy's middle adolescence, you should make sure that an adult or older sibling is home when your son comes home, although the pre-adolescent boy should take on most of the responsibilities for his own needs while the baby-sitter is around—the baby-sitter is available mainly to provide safety and supervision.

A mom recently told me about her nine-year-old son's comment to a new baby-sitter. The mother was telling the baby-sitter the routine to be followed for baths and bedtime for her boy and two younger girls. The son interrupted her, taking over the explanation of the routine in great detail. When the boy finished, the baby-sitter said, "Well, you have a very clear routine, don't you?" The son replied, "We like it that way. We know what to expect." This is music to any mother's ears. The routines in the home had gone on for so long that the child had come to enjoy their safety, their very "routineness."

### Don't Overdo Privacy

Privacy needs can increase during a boy's pre-adolescence, both for parents and children. How do we handle these changes?

Privacy is a privilege that parents give a pre-adolescent boy; it is not a right that pre-adolescents take. The boy might say, "Mom, could you knock before you come in my room?" This statement is normal for many boys to make and a useful step toward independence. While he is playing a certain game, or while a friend is over, perhaps we do knock. But the knocking is not something he ultimately controls. If we don't feel it appropriate to knock at other times, we tell him why. A pre-adolescent's room is not off-limits to parents.

When children want privacy, parents expect it, too. "From now on, son, you have to knock to come into our room. Okay?"

It helps us at times to realize that most of our ancestors and their children had no privacy. Privacy in a home is a new phenomenon. Only the very wealthy ever had it on a consistent basis.

*We should never allow our son of any age to put a lock on his door.* To allow this kind of privacy indicates a distortion of trust. We must ask what we have done to lose our child's trust and/or what the child has done to lose ours. Exceptions to this rule generally fit into three categories.

- We have lost authority with and are even perhaps afraid of a troubled adolescent.
- An adult child is returning home to live and requests complete privacy.
- You have a blended family in which trust between siblings and stepparents and children may not have been established yet.

### Protect Your Precious Moments

A home that builds precious memories is a healthy environment for your boy. Sometimes you have to work hard to have and hold these moments and their memories.

The boy is getting bigger physically, but he's just as hungry for precious moments with Mom, Dad, and other beloved caregivers. He may still want you to lie down at night with him and chat. Throwing a ball with you might be a precious moment, or taking a walk with just him and the dog. Strong bonds make moral children. Protect these bonds in your home and other family environments as if they are the lifeblood of the boy's development.

### When Parents Divorce

"We have to give our kids a fighting chance, not just when things are going well, but also when they're going badly." These were the words of Gayle, a mother of five sons and three daughters, who was going through a divorce. Eleanor Roosevelt said, "Character develops in people who face the challenges of life head-on." If it is the fate of your family to go through a divorce, this divorce will become one of those character-developing experiences Roosevelt talked about. And you and all your support systems must do everything necessary to give your kids a fighting chance. Since many divorces occur when our kids are pre-adolescents, let's discuss it here.

Judith Wallenstein, a longtime researcher of marriage and break-ups, completed a twenty-five-year study that tracked children whose parents divorced. She found that even when the children were middle-aged, their parents' divorce was still one of the most, if not *the* most, life-defining events in their lives. She found also that most of the children suffered profound trauma, and many did not fully recover. Her studies of divorce have been corroborated by other researchers. A divorce is like a war in the child's home, and it can affect the child like war trauma. Statistics corroborate the moral impact of divorce on children. Boys whose parents have divorced are *five times more likely to commit crime than boys whose parents have not.* Thus if a divorce occurs, parents, clan, church, and school communities must come immediately to the aid of the child.

Simultaneously, I will never forget the mother of two sons, a lawyer by profession, who wrote, "I divorced my husband because the moral lives of my boys were at stake. He was a domineering man who wouldn't allow me to be an equal emotional and moral authority. Once we broke up, I could fully guide my boys." Her sons are now in their late twenties and doing very well. In her case, as in many others, the boys turned out very well. Yet she, like every divorced parent, knew to give her boys constant, vigilant love.

With proper support, children can come out of their parents' divorce with character and strength. Your son may go through a phase of acting out and scaring you at some point after the divorce. It is his way of punishing you, testing you, and condemning himself for his perceived part in creating the breakup. Your son may go to extremes of emotional neediness or stoicism.

If possible, do not divorce with the idea that now you have the right to condemn the other parent. Your son needs you to forgive the other parent as quickly as possible and immediately develop a working relationship with your ex-spouse.

If possible, provide a safety net for your children by increasing contact during the divorce and afterward with extended family members and others who can create mentorial and healthy peer relationships with your children.

Talk to your child as much as possible about why the divorce occurred, and *take full responsibility for your part in it.* Be honest also about the flaws you saw in your partner, the reasons you left that person, and your openness to your son's creating whatever relationship he can with that person.

In talking to your child, make sure he understands that the divorce was not his fault.

If your son is nearing the second decade of his life and wants to live with his dad, consider that option a worthy one. E. M. Hetherington studied how children perform under various custody arrangements and discovered that custodial mothers have more trouble controlling their children than custodial fathers, and boys have statistically fewer behavior problems in the custody of Dad than of Mom. These studies may not apply to you—the father in your case may have abandoned his children or may be dangerous, you may be a better disciplinarian than he, and so on. On the other hand, if a boy is having behavior problems, his father might provide the best environment for him for a given time.

**Stepparenting.**   A stepparent is a "parenting partner" in most cases. Generally, a new spouse is not a "parent" unless he or she adopts the children or raises the children from their infancy. This parenting-partner role is a difficult one. He or she must ultimately bow to the needs of the biological parent when it comes to parenting. Should the biological father be completely unavailable, and should the mother support the stepfather adopting the children (and if a bond forms between the stepfather and stepchildren), then the stepparent can become the father. The same goes for a stepmother and a biological father.

In any case, it is important the new spouse try to become friends with the ex-spouse and keep him or her in the loop (should this person be interested and available).

The stepparent also should work as hard as possible to bond appropriately with the stepchildren, *but give the process at least a year or more* and be as patient as possible with backtalk, acting out, and children's anger and depression.

The stepparent might insist that the family find a mentor—an extended family member or counseling professional—who can help them through the chaos.

The stepparent also can be vigilant about watching children's indicators of distress.

1. Falling grades
2. Difficulties in athletics and sports where success existed previously
3. Noncommunication and isolation of the stepchild
4. Abnormal and destructive rages
5. Other high-risk behavior

Sometimes the stepparent earns the trust of the new and blended family by his or her vigilance. Always it is earned by ongoing expressions of patience and love.

As soon as possible, it is essential that the biological parent and stepparent decide on a common discipline system. Maintaining consistency in a new and blended family is crucial.

## Media Use

Even though his thinking is becoming more sophisticated, your son still needs protection from unhealthy media influences, especially those that sexualize him too early and those that provide visual stimulants of gratuitous violence. These images "imprint" on the brain—they leave "neural impressions" on the brain—that then can stimulate and direct his behavior. Many of his behaviors that are not appropriate during pre-adolescence—early sexual experiences or violent tendencies—are encouraged and in some cases caused by the neural impressions he gained from watching adult programs.

The pre-adolescent years are confusing for children and their parents because the media becomes so large a part of a boy's cultural life. Even if we restrict programming at home—using rules, v-chips, rating systems—our son can still go to friends' houses and partake. We feel badly when our son is bonding with other children who are going to an R movie on a Saturday afternoon, but we don't want him to be left out.

Yet the boy is a child, and if we do make exceptions to our media rules, it is important that we not make too many. What standards can we use to decide which movies, TV shows, and video games are appropriate?

**Video Games.**   Video games should never become a large part of a boy's life, *especially if the boy is showing any signs of being socially, academically, or athletically behind, or if he has attention span problems of any kind.* As we've already seen, video games exacerbate problems in male neurology by focusing the male on spatial distractions that don't commit the brain to sophisticated neural growth.

**Total Visual Stimulation in a Day.**   Total visual media use in a day (as always, with exceptions for special occasions) ought to be no more than two hours. Content of TV programming should mainly be comprised of family shows—almost all prime-time television is adult-oriented and inappropriate. Even some kids' programming may be too advanced for your son. As we've discussed in the previous chapter, *a TV in any child's bedroom is not good for the child—it keeps him from socializing, getting exercise, being with the family.* No private, unsupervised Internet access is advisable—there's too much danger of the boy seeing things he shouldn't. Computer use can skyrocket during these years and into early adolescence, but it ought to be monitored by the adults so the boy does not spend more than two or so hours per day with all computer and visual media combined. Sometimes the Internet will be a good source for homework assignments, so this time increases because of educational requirements. Even that shouldn't happen every day. Books, audiotapes, and doing homework with Mom and Dad the old-fashioned way should never totally give way to visual aids. Perhaps in your home you have a ten-year-old Bill Gates who likes to spend hours a day on his computer, inventing new software. In a case like this you might make an exception, but even then you will want to watch for negative by-products of excessive computer use—for instance, lack of socialization, lack of variety in intellectual and emotional skills, irritability, and other mood swings.

If my suggestions seem too strict, I hope you'll modify them to fit your intuitions. One good thing to remember: However much media your son engages in, it should never be a substitute for physical work-outs, karate, swim team, and other hands-on activity. Pre-adolescents need constant physical activity through which to learn use and control of their own bodies.

**Three Key Standards.**   Visual media, like all else, must be held to certain developmental standards. Here are the three key standards I hope you'll use to build rules about visual media in your son's life.

- Caregivers should not encourage a growing boy to attach too much of his development to a machine.

- Caregivers should not let the vulnerable and growing child's brain see images it cannot comprehend, if at all possible.

- Caregivers should not let a boy see images he cannot or should not experience with his own body and soul at this time in his life.

These standards require us to make sure that the boy is not stimulated by violent stories whose moral and emotional values cannot be comprehended, and that he is not stimulated by sexual stories depicting acts he cannot (or should not), with his own body, put into action.

Before letting a nine-year-old see *Terminator 2*, we ask if he can comprehend, perhaps with our help, the moral outcome of the violence. If he can, we then ask ourselves if he can comprehend how the individual acts of violence harmed each victim. If he can articulate, to some real extent, the moral and visual content of the film, then we might let him watch. Most, if not all, boys of nine will not be able to do so. It is a rare nine-year-old boy who should see even *Saving Private Ryan*, in which violence is not gratuitous but essential to the film's point.

**The Biology of Pop Culture.** People often forget that "pop culture"— the media, the movies, TV commercials, music—is linked to a child's development biologically as much as socially.

Biologically, what much of pop culture and media are doing to male development can be simplified in this way: Pop culture inspires the explosion of testosterone (and the attendant brain changes of puberty) as early as possible. To a significant degree, human neuroendocrinological systems respond to external stimulants to regulate hormonal flows. In other words, while a male's testosterone surges based on his preset genetic pattern, it surges also in response to external stimuli (e.g., when kids compete in games and when they view sexual imagery). As we allow children to watch imagery appropriate to adult or even middle/late adolescent thought and experience, we catalyze their adolescent neuroendocrinological system earlier than it should be engaged. We make little boys into biological adolescents who still have little boys' minds. This biological problem is perhaps one of the hardest to document in our child raising and yet is one of the most destructive in American family life. It continues our general cultural motion toward creating males who are ill-disciplined, confused, lonely, and immoral.

**Moral Abandonment of the Boy.** To a great extent, when we forget the biology of pop culture and do not apply key standards to the pre-adolescent boy's media use, we begin a kind of moral abandonment of the boy. We set him up to morally fail.

Unregulated sexual imagery can induce a boy to do what his body is not ready to do (e.g., he will sexually grab or harass a girl, he will make lewd comments, he will begin the adolescent process of trying to find a sexual mate earlier than our society needs him to). The adult world will call him immoral for these things, as it should, but without taking responsibility for the fact that the adult world taught him these things.

Similarly, when he is stimulated toward verbal aggression and physical violence by his neurological acquisition of violent models in the media, we will call his actions immoral. He will do as he sees on *T2* or *Scream* and get in trouble for it. We have set him up to fail by not supervising the initial stimulants of his pre-adolescent impulses.

So while we might, during his pre-adolescence, increase the amount of visual media stimulants we allow our son (letting him go to more sophisticated movies, letting him play a little more on his Game Boy, giving him a little more computer time), we must always remember that he is a child whose mind and body can easily get out of sync with each other if he is allowed stimulants that confuse his developmental process. (The same goes for monitoring his music, too. While typically benign, some pop music sexualizes and violates the developing pre-adolescent mind severely.) We are moral caregivers to the boy all through his development, and we must do our duty to protect our child.

### The Rituals of Life: The First Rite of Passage

At age ten, the boy enters a new decade of his life. He opens the door to his adolescence, the time when he must begin to become a man. This doorway into new spiritual, social, and psychological mandates is one the boy feels but cannot describe. Yet his behavior and hidden thoughts will mirror the existence of the door—his tiny pleas for independence, his sexual curiosities, his gaze at the world of grown men. The passage to manhood is so complex that societies have always made sure that boys can't turn away from the door nor walk through it without understanding what they are getting into. Thus societies have provided boys with rites of passage.

Our society has perhaps the *least* well defined rites of passage of any on earth. We actually encourage our youngsters *not* to grow up in the deepest and most necessary ways. Then, when they reach the age of maturity (between eighteen and twenty-one), we thrust manhood upon males who are still psychologically and spiritually boys. We don't wish for the Good Son to be unprepared, so I will suggest a series of rites-of-passage experiences in these "Rituals of Life" sections. The first occurs around his tenth year.

The family and extended family ought to organize themselves around the boy's budding adolescence. Everyone can decide how each will help this boy become a man. The family and clan thus treat the boy's adolescence as a "second birth." Men—fathers, male mentors, male relatives—must increase their participation in the boy's life.

The rite of passage itself involves a gathering of his family and clan in a celebration of the coming of manhood. This celebration could take place at his tenth-birthday party or at another specially created afternoon or evening event. Perhaps he is given inspiring gifts. He might sit in the center of the circle of friends (this rite does not have to be over-ritualized) and receive one comment from each elder about what strengths they see in him and what visions they have for him. He might be told by his family and clan what the "mission" of the family has been—to help others, to take care of the land, to lead communities—and begin to see himself in that mission. His parents will give him new freedoms and new responsibilities as of this date, and articulate these to him. (If you are a single parent, still angry at a former spouse, now might be a good time to reach out in a healing way toward the other parent so that he or she at least is present at this rite.) Perhaps the boy will be permitted to alter somewhat his physical appearance. One family told me about how much their boy wanted a pierced ear like his dad. On his tenth birthday they let him get his ear pierced.

This rite is the first of four, and the boy will gather energy over the next years as he anticipates the second rite, which occurs at age thirteen or fourteen. Over these few years he will go with parents to more adult occasions. For instance, my wife and I recently went to see Jane Goodall speak, and seated beside us were a mother and her ten-year-old boy, who was dressed in a suit and tie. He fidgeted a little during the lecture, but he acted very "grown up." This was obviously a high and new occasion for him—one he was proud of.

At the end of his first rite of passage, as at the end of all rites, the boy might be given some type of badge of honor to inspire him over the years—a family heirloom, perhaps. As a colleague of mine who leads Boy Scout camps put it: Boys adore badges.

## LESTER'S HOPE: DO EACH OF YOUR ACTIONS AS A GIFT TO SOME LIVING THING

Recently I received a letter in a plain white envelope with no return address. My address was written in a very shaky hand. I assumed it was written by either a child or an elderly person with some palsy. I opened it and discovered, from its brief contents, that it was written by a man in his eighties. He had been a pilot in the European theater, he said, after a tough upbringing on a farm in Iowa. He had returned to farming but then gotten into farm equipment sales. His life had brought him one daughter and three sons, sixteen grandchildren, and three great-grandchildren. His wife had been dead for twenty years, and he himself was now dying of cancer. He was writing me, he explained, because "I can tell from your books that you are a man of honor, and I thought you might like this poem I wrote to my ten-year-old grandson who was having some trouble."

I cannot fully thank the man for the poem because he only signed his letter "Very truly yours, Lester." But I hope that its publication here will be thanks to him, for his poem is a beautiful description of the pre-adolescent boy in his life.

### Brandon, Your Life Is a Gift

*What is the reason for my life today?*
*Why am I alive today?*
*Why do I have the honor of breathing today,*
*of smelling the spices in the kitchen,*
*of touching the hand of a friend,*
*of working for the good of the world?*
*I have asked that question every day of my life.*
*Now I know the answer, but it took me over eighty years.*
*My life is a gift, and Brandon, your life is a gift.*

*Do each of your actions as a gift to some living thing.*
*Live with the discipline and courage of a man.*
*Live every day like this and you will know,*
*at my age, you've become happy.*
      *We are all with you, son.*

# EIGHT

# Pre-Puberty

## NURTURING BOYS OF ELEVEN AND TWELVE

Jack was eleven, a fifth-grader, who returned home from school one day feeling very low. His good friend Peter was playing basketball with some of his older brother's friends and wouldn't let Jack join in. For days, Peter had been acting this way. At twelve, he was taller than Jack by about eight inches, more physically mature. Jack finally listed all of what Peter was doing—not only rejecting him but also taking things from him and bullying him.

"He pushed me against the locker," Jack told his mother.

"He took my pencil and broke it." Jack described Peter's show-off behavior, grabbing the pencil and putting it between his middle finger and ring and index, then smashing his hand down on his knee till the pencil broke in two.

"He doesn't like me anymore. I want to get him back." When his mom, Janine, asked him what he should do, Jack said, "I want to punch him in the face."

Janine told me that this was the first time she had seen so much seething anger in her son. Janine had been raised with three brothers and was not afraid of her son's angry impulse to hit. Her own moral values, however, prompted her to help him find another way to deal with his anger. "Would that be the right thing to do?" Janine asked.

"I guess not," Jack replied, sullen.

"Have you tried to talk to Peter?" Janine asked.

"He's just being an asshole. He won't talk to me."

"Do you know why?"

"No. He just pushes me and stuff. He won't tell me why. I just want to know what's going on."

"If he won't talk to you, what are you going to do?"

Silence.

"Can you just ignore him for a few days, or a week, and see what happens?"

"I don't know. I guess." After continued conversation, Jack was convinced he should ignore his friend.

A few days later, Peter pushed him, but Jack walked away. "I just frowned at him and walked away," Jack reported to Janine, his face wearing one mask of triumph but also another of sadness. There were a few other verbal incidents with Peter in which Jack walked away again. One time, Peter came up to Jack and asked him why he walked away. Jack told him he didn't like being a punching bag. Later that day, Peter came up to him and apologized for his behavior.

"Mom, Peter and I are friends again," Jack reported that night.

Like so many boys in the pre-puberty years (and continuing, with increasing ferocity, through adolescence), Jack and Peter wanted respect. Each in their own way tried to understand what respect is, how to ensure it, how to behave in pursuit of it. Peter tried the tack of rejecting smaller or younger kids in favor of older alpha males. Jack was stunned, at first, by his friend's behavior, certainly not consciously understanding or being able to articulate Peter's developmental moment. He felt not only the anger and pain of emotional rejection but the severe feeling of being disrespected. He wanted to regain his respectable posture through an aggressive act. With his mother's help, he found another way, practiced that way, and ended up regaining not only his self-respect but also his friend.

Jack's comment "I just want to know what's going on" is one that boys in pre-puberty articulate through actions and words. They study, read, observe, ask questions, and hope to learn "what's going on." They are like detectives discovering their own powers of rationality and wit and how to understand their place in the world.

Their self-esteem takes a very large hit as their minds expand, starting at around ten, and they notice that the universe is huge and somewhat indifferent to their needs. Even though they can't talk much about it, these boys are often overwhelmed by society and its expectations. This developmental step is accompanied by vulnerability and fragility, which shows up in a boy's immense sensitivity to being disrespected. In pre-puberty, puberty, and into middle adolescence, boys very often see that new knowledge is the antidote to lowered self-respect and so plot their course toward constant learning.

## DEVELOPMENTAL MILESTONES

At eleven and twelve, boys are moving toward puberty. We will assume puberty begins at thirteen and is more than half fulfilled by fourteen because it usually occurs during this time. However, the start of puberty before or after is also within the range of normal. Puberty is when a boy experiences his largest growth spurt—he grows nearly as tall as he will be in adulthood, and also accumulates muscle mass and body weight that will approximate his adult average. He develops secondary sex characteristics—increased size of testicles and penis and amount of body hair, and sexual cycles. He experiences also the bulk of his adolescent development of adult brain capacity and functioning, especially in areas of abstraction and emotional response.

Because the boy is not in puberty yet but his brain is moving through changes that set up the massive personal transformation, he is in a somewhat confused and confusing state.

### His Brain Development

So many clues to your son's behavior lie directly in brain development, so let's take a look at what's happening in his head. The boy's brain is now changing quickly, and yet parts of it are not changing as fast as others. Thus the boy's thinking and impulses can appear sense-less. For instance, neural activity in parts of the brain that handle memory is increasing unevenly. The boy can now remember things he never could before (for instance, mathematical equations), but he can't seem to remember what you told him to do an hour ago. Sometimes parents don't realize this discrepancy and think their son is rebelling against them when he just doesn't remember! This memory gap is a neurological piece of the boyhood puzzle, and the boy requires patience, repetition, and a well-structured life.

His understanding of emotional responses, as well as up-and-down moods, has a lot to do with brain development (to say nothing of hormones, which we'll cover more completely in the next chapter). But again we see unevenness: While many parts of his brain, especially the one that handles abstract intellect, are developing rapidly, the prefrontal cortex—the part of the brain that uses rationality to calm instinctive re-actions—is developing less rapidly. It is one of the last parts of the male brain to develop fully. So while the brain is moving toward "knowing what's going on" in society, mathematics, human relations, literature, moral systems, and anything else it can find to think about, it is not quite yet developing the strong ability to temper aggressive impulses. Blood flow that will, in ten years, go to the prefrontal cortex is now going to the amygdala, which governs gut reactions like aggression. An adolescent is not as mature as an adult in some very clear, neurological ways.

Just because the pre-pubescent boy's brain is developing in a confus-ing way does not mean we are powerless to help it develop toward bal-ance. We can actually help the boy develop parts of the brain, like the prefrontal cortex, by encouraging him to discuss and understand his own and others' emotional reactions. It is almost an equation in brain science that the more you get a child to focus on a certain kind of activity, the more his brain (within its genetic and biological limits) will develop neural activity to accommodate the focus. Thus, while in general boys in pre-puberty and beyond may not talk as much about feelings as girls, they can be brought to their full potential by our constant inducement.

### His Verbal Development

One mom of an eleven-year-old said to me, "What's with this boy? He used to be so laid back and sweet. Now he won't talk, or suddenly he wants to talk about everything at once." No matter how verbal or non-verbal the son, every parent should expect some changes in his production of and use of words.

Some boys will develop a nearly adult sense of humor. One grandmother told me about how her eleven- and eight-year-old grandsons behaved at breakfast. The two boys were having one of those argumentative mornings—who showered first, who used the toilet first, who ate the first pancake. All of it became an argument. Grandma thought she would give a moral lesson in the middle of their argument over the first pancake. "I think if Jesus were here today, he'd say, 'Let my brother have the first pancake; I myself will wait.'" Almost immediately, the eleven-year-old said to his younger brother, "Okay, Ben, you can be Jesus."

Boys are gaining verbal skills at this age—especially if they are genetically verbally inclined. They are inviting us to be more verbal with them and more complex in our talk and thinking. They also use words to pretend performance and prowess. You might tell your boy something and hear a quick "I know, Mom!" Quite often, he doesn't know at all. He is simply fulfilling his imperative to look important by using verbal skills.

### He Still Learns by Imitation

While in his early years he was quite the imitator, doing whatever Mom or Dad or another kid or a TV character did—a mimic of the world around him—your son is still quite an imitator, but in a more sophisticated way. One sophistication is his ability to delay imitation. He sees something on a TV program or in the home or school that he consciously or unconsciously wants to copy, but he waits a few days to do it. He knows the social rules now and that he has to find the right time and place.

Simultaneously, research tells us that by the time they are in sixth grade, kids can pretty well understand what others think of them. As they alter their behavior to fit what they think others want, they now imitate both what others do and what they believe others expect. Thus now is a time for parents to add new challenges and to work hard to be good role models. Remember that the boy cares deeply about what each role model does and thinks. Do not abandon a boy to young adulthood—he is not ready yet.

### His Moral Development

Pre-pubescent boys generally have a "law-and-order" orientation in moral thinking. The boy wants to discover the core or hidden rules of each social order, whether the peer group or his family, and follow these. He wants law, and he wants order. He feels morally sound when he commits himself to the rules. At the same time, he starts to look carefully at what he thinks are not core rules. "Don't hit people" might be a core rule, but somehow it doesn't apply when he's alone with a friend and just wants to spar, wrestle, and even get physically mad.

Though his moral thinking still adheres to law and order, it is not unusual for a pre-pubescent boy to decide, a little bit here and there, that a parent's core rules and his own might be different. Thus the boy starts chipping away at what we parents think are core rules. "But Mom, when you said I couldn't watch TV until I did my homework tonight, I thought you meant I just had to have a plan for doing my homework." "No, son, I meant no TV until homework, and you know it." "Well, you know, I'll get it done, Mom." Our definition and his will differ—or he'll try to rationalize differences even when he knows better.

One of the reasons he may be asking questions, looking for modifications, and even trying to get rid of certain rules is that he thinks he's smart enough now to figure out which of the rules are essential. He might play some games with the rules he thinks are not essential (like cursing rules, for instance, or bedtime rules), compelling us to alter them a little. He might also raise our ire as he tries to mess with rules we think should remain sacrosanct.

Some pre-pubescent boys will overmoralize their own actions. One mom told me about her eleven-year-old who hadn't been physically sick in a couple of years. He became very ill with the flu and told his mom, "I'm being punished for everything I've done wrong." The boy is morally very sensitive right now—open to moral suggestion and so open to his own moral assessments of himself and others. He may think something is a moral issue that may not be.

## DISCIPLINE TECHNIQUES

Discipline techniques that worked well in pre-adolescence should still work for boys in pre-puberty—especially the imposition of natural and reasonable consequences.

Your son may now push envelopes and boundaries more than he did last year, so you may need to pick your battles more carefully. You will certainly be able to give longer, more complex explanations. Accountability is very important with boys this age, and we must always guide the boy to take responsibility for his actions. And of course, the behavior of his role models is crucial in helping him develop self-discipline.

### Stopping Rudeness

Discipline of pre-pubescent boys can be confusing because of the normal pulls to independence boys are feeling and often acting on by chipping away at previous rules. Most often we see these actions in verbal rule-breaking: an increase in cursing, in backtalk, in dissing a parent in public. *While patience and serenity are good parental responses, they can be overdone.* If a boy is being rude to a parent, the parent must address that, especially if he's being rude in public.

"Son, that was very rude, and I felt put down and disrespected. I don't recall saying things like that to you."

"You may not say it, Mom, but you treat me like a kid."

"Then point out to me next time I treat you like a kid and you don't like it, but you can't talk to me like that in public again. The next time it happens, there will be a significant consequence."

Boys do not actually want to be rude to their parents. Only if they've experienced a sense of ongoing injustice do they opt for true disrespect.

## The Range of Normal

Given the mental, emotional, and social complexities of pre-puberty, most of what the boy does is "normal" (though very often will need discipline). Since by twelve or so years old all human beings reach a point of diminishing influence by their closest caregivers, we must assume and hope that the parenting plan we've used up to these years has created a Good Son, a boy who will act out now (if he acts out at all) mainly in ways that fit within the range of normal. Should we have neglected his discipline and moral development, or should there have been a trauma in his life, he will more likely—during pre-puberty, puberty, and adolescence—exist at the high-risk end of the range of normal and become morally at-risk in the human community.

It's normal for the boy to want lots of new challenges—to start playing a new musical instrument or to take a long trip to learn lots of new things.

It's normal for the boy to question a lot as he *applies his own powers of reason and rationality* to things he used to take for granted, as well as things he used to accept just because a parent said them.

It's normal for the boy to be better at time management now, at personal organization, at planning.

It's normal for the boy to falter and go askew, to take on more than he can handle, and to need permission to curtail something or let it go.

It's normal for the boy to feel deep, inarticulable impulses of fear—fear of not belonging, fear of being disliked, fear of being left out.

It's normal for the boy to want to talk about his fear, and it's normal for him to get angry when you try to talk to him about it.

It's normal for the boy to be hungry for leadership and opportunity to prove himself—he's coming to understand now how high everyone's expectations are, and he needs leaders as he seeks to meet them.

It's normal for the boy to go through a phase of laziness.

It's normal for the boy to feel humiliated by peers. It is painful to watch and help him work through, but a certain amount of peer one-upping and humiliation is normal.

It's normal for the boy to seek one or two very strong, loving authorities in his life. If he does not have one or more of these people who are "always there for him," it is normal for him to become very insecure and to act out.

It's normal for the boy to still cry sometimes, and also normal for him to cry less now.

It's normal for the boy to talk about how he's feeling, but also to want to hit a punching bag instead.

If you have been unjust, then right the injustice. If you have not, point that out. Either way, stop the rudeness before it becomes too large a portion of your conversation with your adolescent son.

Once in a while, a pre-pubescent boy will become so withdrawn that a parent's only conversations with him are his rude confrontations. If this interaction is happening in your family, seek immediate help from within your extended family and from professionals.

### Grounding the Boy

If you have not yet used this discipline technique, now is a good time to begin. Grounding him will become a valuable discipline technique to use throughout his adolescence.

Trudy, forty-one, told me about her two sons, Jim Jr., eleven, and Jeremy, eight. Jim Jr. had a friend over, and during their time together, the friend left his watch. No one could find it. The next day, Jim Jr. found it in his coat pocket and took it to school and wore it as if it were his own. When he came home he threw his coat on his bed and Jeremy rummaged through, finding the watch. Trudy came in, saw Jeremy with the watch, and confronted the boy. Perhaps in a moment of confused loyalty toward his older brother, Jeremy "admitted" to having taken the watch while Jim Jr. looked on. Jeremy got in trouble for lying and for stealing. His punishments were severe, but he accepted them all. Jim Jr. not only let his younger brother get in this kind of trouble, but he even said, "You should have told the truth, Jeremy," as if he were a parent.

A few hours later, Jeremy felt the weight of the punishments and told what really happened. Trudy confronted Jim Jr., who himself confessed. "It was the first time that I realized how cruel my own son could really be," Trudy said to me. "He not only watched his little brother get in trouble for nothing, but he pretended to be so righteous all the while. Jeremy was in tears, and Jim Jr. just made his brother suffer more."

Trudy took all punishments off Jeremy and *grounded* Jim Jr. For one week, Jim Jr. was not allowed to play with friends, watch television or movies, or call any peer. He had to do double chores. Jim Jr. was instructed to take the week to understand how mean he had been, how unsympathetic, that he had lied (even if only by omission) in not confessing in the first place, and that while he hadn't stolen the watch, he had nonetheless lied to others about it being his. He deserved to be grounded.

To me, the word "grounding" is appropriate not only because it implies that a child is required to stay on a particular ground but because it means "getting grounded in what's right." Because of his sibling rivalry or his moral experimentation, Jim Jr. was not grounded in true self-discipline. "Grounding" brought him back to himself.

In general, expectations of our son's behavior should be reasonable but high. An adolescent boy does better when his caregivers err on the side of demanding more from him rather than less. If your son is failing to meet a number of clear expectations, he has probably suffered some trauma or has been given too much unrestricted and irresponsible liberty in his upbringing. If you are in this situation, his pre-pubescent years are the time to rein him in, to get a great deal of help, especially from males who are strong authorities and well respected by the boy. Now is the time to make sure he has success in school, athletics, and the arts; a Big Brother; a Boy Scout troop; a healthy group of kids to be around; and a spiritual community (we will discuss some of these in more detail in a moment). On page 239 is a list of Rules to Live By for boys in pre-puberty. I hope you will use it to help form your own list. You may want to post your list or give it to your boy.

## MORAL TEACHING

Father John Sanders, Headmaster of St. Augustine's School, a boys' high school in San Diego, said recently: "Every boy is called to be holy." As I listened to him discuss this idea, I recalled the implication of the Hebrew word for holy, *kodesh,* which involves *separateness.* One who is holy is in some ways separate from the masses because he is directly focused on his search for ultimate purpose. Just as every boy is called to be holy, every boy is called to find his own version of holiness—in pre-puberty and then further in adolescence. While the boy generally remains well connected to his family's and community's sense of what is moral, he is also searching for his own sense of what these things mean. Now is a good time for us to listen to the boy's self-expressions of spiritual growth and to reward them with conversation and aid; to spend more time in nature with the boy and in church youth activities; and to show the boy how holiness transpires in a conversation, a piece of music, a poem, a good deed.

### Sexual Morality

We will cover more details in subsequent chapters, but it is essential that we begin at home, school, and even within spiritual communities a high-quality discussion of sexual matters with our pre-pubescent son. Sexual morality is becoming of immense importance to the boy and to his community. The boy has probably entered a time of having crushes on girls.

Without reservation, now is the time to teach abstinence to males. Boys of this age should not go much beyond looking at pictures of girls, maybe making a plea to a real girl to show him something, and some sexual touching of the self and even other males. The boy may be masturbating with increasing frequency now, and that is absolutely normal.

## Rules to Live By

1. A pre-pubescent boy should do chores according to a posted schedule without your nagging.

2. A pre-pubescent boy should practice cleanliness in family areas (living room, etc.), and clean up after himself.

3. A pre-pubescent boy should clean his room at least once a week.

4. A pre-pubescent boy should not whine for things, but find other verbal ways to ask for what he wants.

5. A pre-pubescent boy should help out around the house when asked, and often when not asked, even if the helping does not involve posted chores and even if it keeps him from entertainment and other pleasures.

6. A pre-pubescent boy should initiate much of his own homework responsibilities.

7. A pre-pubescent boy should bathe and practice basic hygiene.

8. A pre-pubescent boy should make his own lunch for school when appropriate, make sandwiches for himself and friends he has over, and eat a reasonably healthy diet.

9. A pre-pubescent boy should go to bed on time, probably between 9:00 and 9:30 on a school night.

10. A pre-pubescent boy should speak respectfully to elders, to teachers, to parents.

11. A pre-pubescent boy should accept punishments parents and other authorities impose, as well as prepare and plan punishments with the authorities.

12. A pre-pubescent boy can, by age twelve, stay home alone for a few hours at a time—but if we allow it very frequently, we can consider the boy at risk of being "unsupervised."

13. A pre-pubescent boy should follow family and school rules pretty uniformly, but if one feels very wrong to him, he should begin a process of redress by using words and developing a moral argument, not through violence or other unreasonable means.

Some boys will also become entranced by sexual fantasies—likewise, very normal.

At this time we should teach the boy the sacredness of human sexuality. Mothers should be open about sexual issues—letting the boy know how it is to be female, and making sure the boy shows women a high level of respect. Mothers need to react to talk that is disrespectful, and react strongly. Often boys will try out "funny" sex-related talk, and the mother (and other caregiver) must remind him that it's not funny if it hurts someone.

Now is also a time for fathers and other men to take a special interest in teaching the boy healthy lessons about sex, sexuality, and respect for women.

Here are some issues to cover with a pre-pubescent boy.

- There is a very special time for intercourse, and that time occurs much later in life—only after months, perhaps years, of getting to know someone. Intercourse occurs after one has made a significant commitment of honor and responsibility to that person.

- A boy and man have to be immensely respectful of a female's sexuality. A girl's growing body and sexuality may be difficult for her, and she does not need harassment.

- What a boy hears from peers about sex is incomplete. It is the job of parents and other elders to teach boys everything they need to know about sex.

- Media sexual imagery is often *not* a model to follow. For every program of sexual content our pre-pubescent sees, we must make sure we have provided him an equal share of discussion about consequences.

In pre-pubescence, most boys can handle age-appropriate and repeated lessons on not only sexual mechanics but also hormones, the male brain, male fantasy, what promiscuity is—everything. I've written a book for boys aged ten to fifteen called *From Boy to Man: All About Adolescence and You,* which you can hand directly to your son. It is short and illustrated and can help him and you deal with sexual and male issues in a boy-friendly way.

### Teaching Honesty and Loyalty

A sixth-grader knows what it means to be honest and to be loyal. He wants greater and greater challenges from his caregivers and environment in practicing these. He will find it difficult to tell on a friend, so he must be taught when it's appropriate and when it's not. As puberty approaches, stakes get higher and behavior grows more dangerous and complicated. The boy needs to know your bottom-line standards for honesty and loyalty, and he needs them to be realistic. You know you have succeeded with this boy when he comes home to you at twelve years old and says, "My friends are doing things I don't like. I'm not going to do that with them."

### Teaching Toughness and Tenderness

A boy needs clear "tenderness" training in pre-puberty. He's beginning to toughen up, and toughness always needs to be balanced by tenderness. He needs to be shown how not to make people suffer and how to help those who are suffering. Perhaps he needs to visit sick people, homeless shelters, nursing homes so that he experiences and must even minister to people who are suffering and need his empathy. Now is not a time to "protect" our son from seeing real death, decay, pain, and grief. It is a time to engage him in helping injured animals. So much tenderness is taught here.

By the same token, some boys will not be toughening up very well at all. They may be late bloomers in terms of both socialization and hormones. They may be more "sensitive." If your son is obviously having trouble in his social sphere—if he is lonely, without friends, afraid of athletics—he should spend more time with a kind but tough grandpa, coach, or teacher. He does not need to be clubbed on the head with toughness, but he may need a little more help from his environmental influences in developing personal armor.

Telling our own stories of having felt overly sensitive is a very important tool. "You take things personally, like I did when I was your age. Here's what I had to learn to do." We cannot "save" our very vulnerable son from all pain, but we can help him learn to process it. The more close and trusted adults and peers we help our son find, the better. One of my markers for whether a very sensitive pre-pubescent will "make it" is whether he has a best friend. If he has a close, best friend and a relatively stable, loving family, he's generally okay.

### Guiding the Boy's Moral and Spiritual Quest

The pre-pubescent boy wants to find missions in life, and may develop an overarching urge to start seeing life as a quest.

Pre-pubescent boys like being part of huge groups of people or huge schools for short periods of time, but generally they prefer to have a small group of friends and to know that this subgroup supports them. We see this imperative acted out in their cliquishness during these years. Everyone in the little clique is generally after some sort of unspoken subtext or goal—often it's just "to be cool."

We want more for our son than for him to recognize only "being cool" as his quest, so we must ask, "What quest is my son living? What mission? What sense of vision is he developing?"

Now is the time to think about these things and begin dialogue about them, continuing with even more fervor over the next few years. Perhaps athletics is the center of your son's quest for a time. Does he participate only to win, or is he after something else, too? Help him notice the quest he is living, and manage and even expand it. Perhaps you are very involved in social-justice concerns and he is following you into these. Talk to him about the quest you are making. Similarly, patriotism can become a quest for a family and its children.

"I want to know what's going on!" the pre-pubescent boy cries. And: "I want respect!" These dual imperatives are based on and succeed by a boy's development of himself as a hero on a quest.

### Teaching Proper Consumption

Every family containing pre-pubescent children is challenged with consumerism. Kids want lots of things, or are pushed to want them by peers and media. This urge began early in the boy's life, of course, but often it is not until the boy starts to be more independent during pre-puberty, at around eleven or twelve, that he becomes a major consumer. He buys his own CDs, games, candy, books, even some clothes.

Moral training and good discipline are about helping the boy learn impulse control; they're about helping him moderate his life of consumption. What we use and consume are not just "economic" issues but issues also of morality and of soul.

With your son's help, you may want to create a weekly grid of what he buys and what he earns. Teach him the perils of overconsumption; show him the lack of discipline implied in just walking into a store and buying whatever he wants. Compel him to attach meaning to each purchase. And teach him to enjoy most the things he earns because he worked hard rather than just because he's got a few dollars to burn.

As parents, you should buy him only a few requested items. He can use his allowance to buy much of what he wants. We still buy his necessary clothes, shoes, etc., but he can buy "fun stuff" and any clothes we don't feel are necessary. We want to avoid bonding him with designer items. One or two of these might be rewards for good action, but buying him lots of these just pushes him to a peer-group materialism that negatively affects his development of humility, self-discipline, and healthy individuality.

In this developmental time, what others do is of such proportion to him that he sometimes has difficulty separating himself from the mass of convention. For the most part, being a creature of convention is a good thing—the boy learns what society and culture are and how to exist successfully in them. On the other hand, his foundation is not the society and culture, it is himself and his close, loved ones. In the end, he himself, the family that loves him, and the community he serves are his bedrock. His moral sense and self-discipline within his body, family, and community are his ultimate path to success. Excessive consumerism and materialism pull him outside of this path.

## A HEALTHY MORAL AND
## EMOTIONAL ENVIRONMENT

Your son may be taking increased charge of certain matters in his environment now. Perhaps he is planning his own calendar a little more. He may want to arrange his room a certain way. He may be making judgments of his parents' environment, finding it passé. He may become very focused on his own clothing and how it helps him fit in. He can become very much a "clique" person, hanging out with a subculture of kids who themselves have picked out a certain place or environment—under the freeway bridge, or at the bleachers, or in science lab.

### Handling Peer Pressure

If the boy is falling into a crowd of friends that leads him into smoking, doing drugs, drinking alcohol, stealing, or being sexually promiscuous—beyond the minor "experimenting" that is normal for a boy—parents have the absolute right to end these bad influences. "You can no longer spend time with David," we say, and we explain why. If possible, we show our concern by trying to get help for David in the school, and by offering his parents help.

While it is within the range of normal for a fifteen-year-old to dye his hair and do other things we might consider "wild"—e.g., ear piercing and other body alterations for the sake of shocking parents and others—it is not normal for pre-pubescents. It is generally brought on by the influence of peers, often older ones. We have the right to monitor this activity closely and disallow those we consider unhealthy. We can explain why we've disallowed it, and we can remind our son that "Because Dan does it" isn't a good enough reason for our son to do it.

This is a time to teach our son *personal standards* for behavior. While "You don't have to be like the other kids; just be yourself" is hard for him at twelve to accept—the pull of peers is strong and his pull to individuality less strong—we must begin teaching it. If our son is well bonded to us, we can be successful by saying, "In our family, twelve-year-olds don't do that kind of thing. We have other standards of behavior, and here's what they are." In this case, "being himself" will mean being not like unruly peers but rather like a well-behaved boy.

Sometimes, no matter our efforts, our son will get in with the wrong crowd, and we will not have the authority to extricate him. Often this situation follows a divorce and a loss of bonds or parental authority in a boy's life. In this situation, it is essential we get help from extended family members, schools, community members, and professionals. If we are losing authority in the life of our pre-pubescent son, his adolescence more likely will be a place of high risk for him and for us.

### Be Very Involved in the Boy's Life

Our pre-pubescent sons are desperate for admiration and respect. They need us to be present at their accomplishments. One mother of three sons, all of whom played football, told me: "I decided to go to every game. If my son could get flattened, I was going to be there." Her vigilance led her to be there for her sons, to congratulate each one, admire them, and show them respect. A dad told me that he went to every one of his son's violin recitals and every concert, and even had to take a pay cut to do so. Grandparents and others who care need to populate recitals, ball games, and other outings with the boy. The whole extended family needs to form a clan environment of admiration for the pre-pubescent boy.

### Changing Roles of Family Members

The pre-pubescent boy's basic sense of his place in the family will change. Yet, simultaneously, the boy wants it all to stay as it has been—comfortable, close, not too demanding. The boy wants to be around Mom and Dad, and when he doesn't, he still wants to know he is beloved by them and other close caregivers. Your son wants to be more independent but doesn't really want to suffer the full consequences and responsibilities of independence. He's in limbo—his hormones have not yet propelled him toward independence, but his brain is expanding so much that he cannot live comfortably without making gains in independent thought and action.

**A Mother's Concerns.**   When our boys turn eleven or twelve, moms may find themselves worrying about whether they're losing their sons' affections or, conversely, whether they're turning their sons into "mama's boys." If the son at eleven or twelve is constantly bad-mouthing his mother or is pulling away completely, a mother needs to get help in understanding why and in re-bonding with the boy. If the son is still completely compliant in the way a seven- or eight-year-old would be, afraid to leave his mother's side, she should also get help. We will look at each extreme of adolescent mother-son bonding, but first let's say something about how the culture pressures mothers of adolescent boys.

Most pre-pubescent sons are neither mama's boys nor are they unbonded with mothers. So much of the confusion and pain mothers go through regarding bonding are pushed on them by a culture that is confused about how to handle adolescence in general. When cultures are confused about child development, they impose huge pressures on mothers. Mothers in our culture are pressed not to be too smothering, yet also not to let go of their son. Mothers often feel they have to be "perfect"—if not, the boy will turn out to be an insensitive, irresponsible man, or they'll crush his growing independence and he'll be unable to function well in society.

It is essential for mothers, and for all who care about them, to join in lifting this burden of perfection off the mother of an adolescent boy. Mothers generally need much more support from our culture, and less harsh criticism.

In ancient cultures, there was a planned separation of boys from mothers—the men took over a lot of the parenting of the boys once the boys hit pre-puberty—and thus mothers and the whole community knew more about and planned out much more a mother's relationship with her adolescent son. In our culture, little is planned, and mothers and sons find themselves confused about their relationships with each other.

We will deal in more detail with mother-son separation in the next chapter. In pre-puberty, standards of bonding and attachment are pretty clear. The mother-son bond is going appropriately if

- the boy generally respects his mom's authority;
- the mother has an open line of communication with the boy;
- the mother allows the son some new freedoms and provides him new responsibilities with every growing year of adolescence;
- the son is not responsible for the mother's emotional or mental state of mind;
- the mother is becoming less responsible for the son's minute, everyday needs;
- mother and son share moments of affection—both in talk and in hugs;
- the mother shows respect for the son's father and males in general;
- the son shows respect for girls and women; and
- the mother allows the son to have his own ways of feeling, doing, and being (as long as they don't go against the moral standards of the household).

Of course, divorce affects all of these behaviors. If divorce is occurring or has occurred in your home, it can deepen the already normal role changes between pre-pubescent children and their parents. We have looked at divorce in the previous chapter and will continue to weave the theme of divorce throughout the rest of this parenting plan.

Whether a divorce has occurred or not, I find that the three areas of mother-son interaction to highlight most distinctly in our present culture are

- whether respect is being shown by the son to the mother;
- whether the mother is making the son her emotional crutch; and
- whether the mother is allowing the son his own *emotional* life but still holding him to high *moral* standards.

If a son is not showing his mother respect, the mother-son bond is in crisis—likewise if the mother is making the son into "her little man."

No matter her issues with men, her son must never be required to fulfill her. And finally, many mothers focus so much on their fears about their son's changing emotional style—he cries less now, talks less, and so on—they forget that his emotional style is his own to develop but that his moral life is still in great part hers to assure.

**The Increased Need for Fathers and Males.**    At some point in a boy's pre-adolescence or pre-puberty, the family will notice the boy's increased attention to masculinity and the father. Many fathers work away from their children, opt away, or are forced away from their sons, and "good fathering" becomes nearly impossible for them. Many men grow up feeling emotionally abandoned by their own dads, and these men, in therapy, recall the absence of their fathers during their own pre-puberty.

For about two hundred years (especially since the Industrial Revolution), the activity of fathering has been increasingly stymied by economic necessities. Fathers have often moved away from the one-on-one care of their early-adolescent sons. This unavailability can be devastating for certain boys, so let us spend a moment here making some suggestions.

- If the father has been gone a lot in the earlier years of the boy's life, it is time now that he begin his journey back. If he has not been an active parent, it is time now for him to become one. We want that bond to be strong by the time the boy's puberty hits, so that the full burden of parenting a pubescent boy does not fall on the mother. As with all my comments about the father, should he be unavailable, the presence of a grandfather or other caregiving male, or coaches, teachers, and Big Brothers is essential.
- The boy may need increased alone time with the father or a male mentor—such as one-on-one outings.
- He may need the father to help guide him toward additional male mentors (mothers can guide him too, of course).
- He will need the father and other men to begin the long process of challenging him in personal success and teaching him the rules of life from the male point of view.

- He will need to be able to talk about values, ethics, and choices with the father.

- He will need the father to engage him in dialogue about masculine stereotypes the father feels are not useful to a developing man.

In all of these activities, the father is teaching him how to be a man in the world, and teaching him the "male mode of feeling." This phrase stands for something undefinable—something boys learn from men through osmosis, through contact, through the revelations that occur when boys follow older men around.

While the boy needs his dad to help him see through masculine stereotypes, he needs his mom to engage him in this dialogue, too. He does not see his bond with his mother and father as an "either/or." He sees both parents as essential. So we adjust to his changes more like sand moving slowly in the desert than like a sudden storm.

Intermediate activities and systems are an important part of the boy's changing mother-son and father-son bonds. School, church, and activities like Boy Scouts are intermediate, second-family activities to which the boy can turn for love and structure as he challenges the boy-parent frameworks. Sports also serve part of this function. Pre-pubescent and pubescent boys with no intermediate structures (and also without a father) are the most likely population to join gangs.

### Supporting Single Mothers

Jarelle became a single mother when her oldest son was eleven. She began a support group for single mothers and asked each mother when she entered the group to write about her experience and share what she needed. Jarelle shared with me some of these women's wisdom about raising sons alone. All of what follows is paraphrased from the words of the single mothers.

- Fight even the small stuff when it comes to disrespecting Mom. Mom is Mom; she's the boy's lifeline, to a great extent, and he ought not be cruel to her.

- Yes, it's great to value your son's new independence, but don't let him get away too often with "I don't need you anymore," at least not till he really doesn't.
- The boys should contribute to the family as early as they are able. This action gives them positive pride and helps the family.
- Form an alliance with the boys; make them take pride in protecting the family.
- Make sure you have a plan for the boy and that he's part of making up the plan—he needs a plan for his life.
- Don't show just your anger when he does something wrong; show your fear. If you were scared by something he did, show how scared you were. Boys don't like to see their mothers scared unless their mothers really have lost them.
- Use older siblings as mentors for younger siblings.
- Every church and other religious institution should form mentor programs to help single moms. In these programs, a church member, well established in the community, helps the less financially and socially fortunate single mother.
- If things go too far with a boy, get help from others and have an intervention to get him to realize the danger of the smoking, drinking, drug addiction, or other behavior.
- Don't try to do it all alone. Rely on the dad and remain friends with him if you can, and rely on any others—form lots of adult bonds and get help through them.

A great deal of what the single mothers advised and asked for pertains wonderfully to any parent in any situation. A great deal of it pertains to single fathers, too.

### Supporting Single Fathers

More and more men are becoming single fathers, and many single fathers, as well as single mothers, are emerging into their new role in their son's pre-adolescence and pre-puberty as divorces occur toward the end of the child's first decade of life.

Jeff is a single father of two boys, twelve and fourteen. While the mother is somewhat involved in the boys' lives, she lives three thousand miles away and can't do a lot with them. Jeff has found support in a men's group that he and another single father formed, with the help of a local YMCA.

"Becoming a single father has completely changed my life," Jeff said. "I used to be a 'father,' bringing in the paycheck, but now I can see I wasn't much of a 'dad.' Now I'm a complete dad."

This change was the positive part of single fathering. What was the scary part? "For about a year," Jeff said, "I woke up every morning scared of being a dad. I didn't know if I'd get it right; I didn't know basic things; I didn't have any real support. Admitting I was scared helped me a lot. It made me reach out to friends and family."

Jeff and his sons are close. It is a closeness Jeff feels he wouldn't have had if he hadn't become a single parent. Jeff is friends with single mothers who also have assumed a new role and found in it parts of their own souls as parents.

Jeff asked his support group for their wisdom on what single dads need and can do. Many of the items on the list were similar to what the single mothers said. Being a single parent is in large part the same challenge whether you're a mom or a dad. Here are some issues Jeff's group added.

- Try very hard to give them rites of passage in adolescence. The boys really need it.
- Don't just parent your son, but mentor his best friend, too. Be a part of the boys' lives, have his friends over, take them to movies.
- Make sure to help your son find a male mentor other than you. When he starts competing with you and pulling away, he needs that other man.
- Don't teach him that his mother is a bad person or a failure.

There is an old Russian saying that parents are the sun and rain—take one away, and the child does not grow to full flower. Yet people like Jarelle and Jeff show us that with proper support, a single parent can help a child blossom.

### Increase Honor Activities in Schools

I am a believer in more rules rather than less for boys. For pre-pubescents, certain innovations like school uniforms ought to be considered, as is being done now in California in certain public schools. Uniforms reduce kids' tendency to spend too much time, money, and personal development in competing over who has what clothing. In whatever ways schools can reduce unhealthy peer pressure, it should. If uniforms are not going to be used, every school ought to have a reasonable and relatively uniform dress code.

Fifth, sixth, and seventh grades are good times for schools to provide written honor codes and principles to students. Adolescent boys like feeling heroic and important—they gain just as much of this feeling from following good rules as from trying to get around them. When a school provides an honor code for them to follow, it helps them navigate the difficulties of peer pressure. When a school does not, it relies unfairly on the boys' "inherent moral sense." Our pre-pubescent boys do have moral sense, but they need to know the rules and that they will be enforced.

### Media Use

After the family and school, the predominant moral and spiritual influence on our prepubescent boys today is, generally, the media. Our pre-pubescent boys are now seeking a great deal of what is sacred to them and their masculinity in action movies, video games, and television programs.

**Media Imagery and the Boy's Search for Honor.**   Our pre-pubescent boys continue to gravitate toward action movies not only for the spatial thrills and aggression activities but also because the action heroes often are models of honor, service, responsibility, and self-sacrifice. Whatever else we say about the "macho" films—despite the fact that the emotionality they model is sadly limited—they are, ironically, one of our culture's most popular tools of moral competency education for young males. Advertising pioneer David Ogilvy, in his *Ogilvy on Advertising*, reports a Gallup poll finding that males are actually *more drawn to* *male action stars than female sex symbols* because the male stars provide role models for which the males are starved.

In John Cameron's *T2: Judgment Day,* the second of the *Terminator* films, there is a scene in which the eleven-year-old boy's mother looks at the Terminator, played by Arnold Schwarzenegger, as the half-man, half-machine interacts with her son. She narrates in a voice-over that this Terminator is the perfect man—he will never let harm come to her son; he will help the boy in any way he can to meet his objectives, both in growing up and in getting away from the bad guys; he will help the boy fulfill his destiny; and he will sacrifice himself unto death to do it.

There truly is something very basic about stories of men acting honorably, something powerful for boys and girls, men and women. It goes down deep into the proving of a male's worth. If the boy sees only action films, he will not learn full moral life. He will not learn about empathy and compassion in the kind of depth he needs to learn them. He will not learn much about politeness. He will not learn much about compromise or about respect for the dignity of all things. Thus it is important that your son is exposed to different sorts of heroic tales. And it is it is important for you to *talk with your son about the moral competencies he is learning from Schwarzenegger and others.* A pre-pubescent boy is searching for the keys to the world of honor and needs adults to help him articulate what he is learning. It will be very difficult to stop an eleven-year-old boy from absorbing the world of action movies; it will be a shame to let him absorb that world without using it to teach him service, self-sacrifice, and the moral codes of compassion that do exist in those movies.

**Media Rules for Pre-Pubescents.** Having argued for our increased conversation with our sons about the media imagery they take in, I am not necessarily suggesting a significant increase in media use. The time and use ought to stay about the same as it was in the boy's pre-adolescence. We ought to factor into our "house rules" about media that, most probably, our son is already increasing his intake of media in ways we can't control, e.g., at friends' houses. In our house, however, if we don't want our son watching off-color shows, he is simply not allowed to watch them. He is, after all, only eleven or twelve years old, and still a boy.

Our restrictions continue to extend to video games, Game Boys, computer use, the Walkman, and the Internet. Unsupervised Internet access remains inappropriate. We might think to ourselves, *I've raised this boy well; I can trust him to be responsible about Internet use.* In fact, your son's primary imperative during pre-pubescence is to explore new worlds in relatively safe ways. Since his culture treats media as a safe environment, he himself will consider it so, and he will explore the Internet and other media stimulants for new ideas, new thinking, and, most of all, *new imagery.* We must treat unsupervised Internet activity as we would treat his trip, at eleven years old, into a big city. We would not allow him to go there alone, and we do not allow him to surf the Net alone.

Any video game use and exploration of the Net ought to occur *after* homework and chores. Most media experiences should be considered secondary to the core activities in a pre-pubescent's life. Family life is obviously one of those core activities. Hasbro, Inc., recently did a survey asking kids aged nine to twelve what they want more of in their lives. Ironically, 91 percent of the kids said they would like to set aside time to spend with their immediate family. Watching a favorite show together can satisfy the boy's desire for media entertainment and family time in tandem. Playing Monopoly or another game together can satisfy his enjoyment of games and competition in tandem with his need for core time with the family.

## JAMAL'S STORY

A father e-mailed me this success story with a note: "This made my eyes leak. I think it will touch your heart." It is a truly moving story.

Paul, in his late twenties, received an automobile from his brother for Christmas. On Christmas Eve, when Paul came out of his office, he saw a boy of about eleven walking around the shiny new car, admiring it.

"Is this your car?" Jamal asked.

Paul nodded. "My brother gave it to me for Christmas."

Jamal was astounded. "You mean your brother gave it to you and it didn't cost *you* nothing? Man, I wish . . ." He hesitated. Paul knew what he was going to wish for—that he had a rich brother like that. But what Jamal wished for jarred Paul.

"I wish," Jamal said, "that I could be a brother like that."

Astonished, Paul missed a beat, then he said impulsively, "Look, would you like to take a ride in the car?"

"Sure!" Jamal exclaimed.

They got in and took a ride. After a short time, Jamal asked, "Mister, would you drive in front of my house?" Paul again thought he knew what the boy was after—he wanted to show off to the neighbors. But again, Paul was wrong.

"Will you stop where those two steps are?" Jamal asked. Paul did, and Jamal got out and ran up the steps. In a little while, Paul heard him coming back, but he wasn't moving fast. He was carrying his handicapped little brother, whom he set down on the bottom step. Jamal sat down next to the five-year-old and pointed to the car.

"There she is, bro, just like I told you. His brother gave it to him for Christmas, and it didn't cost him a cent. Someday I'm gonna give you one just like it."

Paul bit his own lip to keep the tears back. He helped Jamal lift the little brother into the car and watched the shining-eyed older brother climb in beside him. The three of them took a holiday ride together. Paul later told his girlfriend that until that moment, he had never understood what Jesus meant when he said, "It is more blessed to give . . ."

# Part Four

## NURTURING THE TEENAGE YEARS OF A BOY'S DEVELOPMENT

The Age of Moral Intuition
(Thirteen to Eighteen Years Old,
and Beyond)

# NINE

# Puberty

NURTURING BOYS OF

THIRTEEN AND FOURTEEN

This story comes from the Jewish tradition. A rabbi and his wife were childless for a long time, but then finally had a child, a son, whom they raised lovingly. The boy was conscientious, well liked, and hardworking. Everything should have been safe and fine with him except that he felt a certain emptiness. He had a great yearning to know more, to understand more, to search beyond the village. One day he said, "I have heard of a great *tzaddik* [wise man] who lives far off in the mountains. I must journey there and talk to him about what I cannot find here in the village." His parents begged him not to go just yet, but the son was not to be dissuaded, so the rabbi and his wife determined that for his safety his father would travel with him. His mother packed food and suitcases for her son and husband, and hugged them good-bye.

Soon after father and son set off by coach, they came to a bridge, and one of the horses drawing their coach stumbled and the coach overturned. The rabbi and his son nearly drowned in the rushing river. They went back home, where they were reunited with the boy's mother. The young man told her about the short trip, and for a time was very happy to be back with her. But soon the emptiness returned, and he and his father set off once more. This time the trip was longer—they covered about half the distance to the *tzaddik* when Fate dealt them another blow. The axles on the carriage broke. Again they were forced to return home. Once more, the reunion was sweet, and the boy and his mother shared months together. But the boy awoke one day with his longing renewed. He and his father set out yet again, and nearly made it, when, at an inn, they met someone who had just left the *tzaddik*'s house.

"Don't go see him," the man advised. "I just saw him in a sin. He's not worth talking to." Disillusioned and depressed, the son agreed with his father that they should return home, where again they lived happily for a time.

One day, however, a new book was circulating in the hands of the young man's friends, a book about the *tzaddik*. This book by his former students praised him for his wisdom, dignity, nobility, and kindness. The young man went to his father and mother and said, "I am going to find the *tzaddik*, and this time I am going on my own." Indeed, the boy had become a young man and nearly an adult. His mother and father both gave their blessings, and he made the trip alone, encountering many adventures along the way.

When he arrived at the *tzaddik*'s Yeshiva (school), he discovered that the old man had died. He was sitting in mourning when one of the older students came up to him and said, "The *tzaddik* predicted you would come. He described you perfectly and said you would come after he died and we should give you this letter." The rabbi's son thanked the student and walked out into the courtyard, where he read the brief note.

*You will have yearned to find me when you were still a boy, as I have yearned to find you, for every yearning in the world is always returned by its companion. You will have thought me a great light, and you will have been attracted to that light, seeking it and meeting obstacles and yet never forsaking your search.*

*However, you will find me after I have died, and that is how you will know you are a man. You will stay in this Yeshiva and study until you have learned what you need to know, and then you will return to your people and become a light to others. God be with you.*

The rabbi's son stayed in the Yeshiva and studied, and later returned to his own village, where he became the rabbi. On his deathbed he had a vision of a young man seeking him, and he told his followers to watch out for this young man. His last words were, "I hope that he, as I have, will die thankful to have made the journey of love."

This tale captures much of the essence of a boy's journey toward manhood. Like the rabbi's son, your own boy enters his teen years with deep longings. He is changing rapidly, and he seeks direction and guidance. His parents still have much to teach him, but now he is looking elsewhere, too. He makes much of his journey in the company of his parents, but he must make some on his own. His closeness with both mother and father will be slightly different as he shares certain things with her but not with him, and vice versa. During his adolescence he will meet many obstacles, some of which will derail his journey, but he will feel the urge to move again, and finally he will set off completely on his own, and he will know himself to be a man because he will discover a clear sign of his own destiny. He will work toward that destiny all his life, gathering the energy, intelligence, and discipline to do so during the tumultuous years between boyhood and manhood.

The tale of the rabbi's son provides, I think, a spiritual model of the healthy male. Not only is it an allegory of every boy's life, but it directly inspires us to see our son's puberty, his times of manic search and times of laconic depression, and even his immoral acts during puberty and adolescence as a journey not just of and for himself but of and for larger mysteries. Your son is not just some boy in a mass of other young, gangly, confused teens. Your son is a sacred being on a sacred journey.

## YOUR SON'S THIRD DEVELOPMENTAL EPISODE: AN OVERVIEW

As boys begin their teen years, they enter the third developmental episode in their lives, the last we will cover in this book. After the three years that followed your son's birth (the infancy and toddler years), the three or so years that accompany and follow puberty can be, developmentally, his most challenging.

In the years around thirteen to eighteen, our boys are in the heart of adolescence. By the time they are about eighteen, they are thought to be "formed" individuals. Indeed, they themselves want to be formed: They want to have gained the sense of individual power and destiny they need to live fruitfully. Not all our sons will have gained it by eighteen, or even twenty-one, but the harder we work on parenting them, the more likely they will be successful.

"Adolescence" and "teenagers" are relatively new words in human development. The first time "teenager" was used was in an article in the *New York Times* in the 1940s. For most of human history, boys had to become men at around thirteen, as soon as puberty hit. They might have children already (which the extended family generally raised with them and their young mate), or be trained for war, or be initiated into the hunting party. Only recently have our children had the luxury of a nearly ten-year adolescence.

Teens are confusing partly because we've only recently been able to give boys and girls the six to ten years of adolescence we give them now. If all of us, when we first have our child, feel like we don't know enough about how to care for the little baby, we can be assured that we know even less about how to care for the teenage boy.

### His Biggest Task

During his teen years, your son will leave behind his boyhood. He will do so by becoming not only an adult but an *individual* adult. The first developmental episode dealt primarily with his personality, the second with his understanding of the rules and nuances of society. Now the primary task of the third is his own distinct individuality in the human community. The boy may come to buck authority; he may develop a great deal of idealism, and he will become quite creative. He is desperate to find opportunities to express himself. He still wants lots of protection and care from caregivers, even as he seeks opportunities. He also wants to test himself against his caregivers as he seeks his own emotional, physical, social, and moral center.

### His Thinking Is Not Always Consistent

Adolescent boys often seem to think so well—their abstract intellect now allows them to argue successfully against a parent's or teacher's logic—yet an hour later they'll seem to do a very dumb thing. The therapist Don Elium has a wonderful metaphor for this phenomenon: "The thinking life of boys this age is like a windshield wiper: thought, then pause; thought, then pause." Indeed, our adolescents can seem to pause right in the middle of making incredible sense. If we expect the adolescent to be absolutely consistent, we are missing the fact that his brain is still developing, and different parts of it develop in different sequences, especially now that it is accepting and learning to regulate the flow of adult hormones. Thus the brain gets thrown off very quickly.

One internally sanctioned way that adolescents self-navigate their up-down intellectual development is to become very task focused. By being intensely focused, they are forced to try to think consistently. While your son may sleep late and at times appear lazy, he will also probably become very stimulated by certain tasks for long periods of time—a sport, a debate team, chess, music, academics. As we encourage these tasks, we help him navigate his intellectual development.

### He Is in Some Real Emotional Turmoil

If they haven't already, many boys will now mask their feelings. A mom of three grown sons told me, "My sons used to cry, cuddle, climb all over me; then they became different. For a few years it was like I didn't know them as well anymore. They work masks over their feelings. I felt very sad sometimes, like I had been able to hold their hearts in my hands for so many years, then I couldn't anymore. Then suddenly something would happen and they couldn't get enough of my help and my love. I don't know why God makes it so hard for us to grow up. My sons have all turned out well, so I know it has all been worth it."

Many boys can become very volatile, darting around between feelings, going up and down in their emotions like a roller coaster.

As we will explore throughout the next three chapters, there are both cultural and biological reasons for the masking, the volatility, and even the withdrawal and "shutdown" that boys display for periods of time during the teen years.

## He Is Developing In the Age of Moral Intuition

For the most part, our adolescent boys *share* our moral values. Though they may rebel or "renegotiate" their relationships with us, they will generally not (again, unless there's been a trauma in their lives or they've been raised without much moral guidance) move too far from our moral system. Even as they experiment and explore, sometimes doing things we would consider immoral, usually they are not trying to subvert our moral system. Even as they may develop different political and economic views, they still will share our sense of service, of rightness, of justice. Our adolescents care a great deal about justice and personal dignity.

The third developmental episode is the age of moral intuition because it is the age during which our sons try to develop their *own* internal compass. The influence of peers will be severe for a time (especially between the ages of about thirteen and sixteen), but the boy will also be developing an "anti-peer" sense of morality. He will want to be *an individual of his own moral conscience who has the power to buck the peer group.* He will become very concerned with *individual* rights, especially his own.

During these teen years, your son will almost certainly do one or a number of things that twenty years later he will realize to have been immoral. Many of these you'll never know about. It's probably just as well. They are part of his journey toward individuality and moral intuition. Without making the mistakes and suffering—either publicly because he's caught, or privately if he's not—he can't *feel* what it means to hold himself to high moral standards.


## DEVELOPMENTAL MILESTONES

Having looked at the male's third developmental episode as a whole, let's now focus on developmental milestones in the years of thirteen and fourteen.

### His Encounter with Puberty

Not all boys begin puberty at this age, though it is the mean age. If your son has not reached puberty by age fifteen and a half, you should consult a doctor.

Because puberty dominates the lives of so many boys during the ages of thirteen and fourteen, we will deal with it in depth here. (If you would like a book to hand your pubescent son that is illustrated and that speaks directly to him about the material we will cover in this chapter, you might like *From Boys to Men: All About Adolescence and You,* which I wrote for boys aged ten and up.)

Because his hormonal changes have such a profound internal effect on him, let's begin there.

**Testosterone Pulls Some of the Strings.** Once puberty hits, testosterone levels peak—this is sometimes called "spiking" and "surging"—in the male body five to seven times a day. Testosterone is sometimes called the "risk" hormone because it pushes its host body to take physical and social risks. Males produce up to twenty times more testosterone than females by the time puberty is complete. There are gradations in testosterone amounts, of course. If you know a boy who is heavily muscled, likes lots of competition, and is taller than average, it's probable that he's at the higher end of the testosterone scale—perhaps he has around seventeen or eighteen times the amount of testosterone that his sister has. If you know a boy who tends to avoid heavy competition and physical aggression, feels uncomfortable in one-upmanship, and isn't heavily muscled, he probably has about ten or twelve times the amount of testosterone his sister has.

Testosterone in males affects physiology in ways scientists and doctors can track: For instance, it increases the ability of blood cells to utilize oxygen, giving teens long endurance for certain physical activities. It also affects male emotional, moral, and social development in ways we need to become very familiar with.

**A Male Way of Loving: Aggression-Nurturance.**   There are many ways to love. An easy way to express love is through kind comments, like "You're special, son; no matter what you do, you're great," or through empathic responses to a child's pain. These ways of loving are not aggressive—in fact, just the opposite, they are directly empathic.

There is also another way of expressing love that puberty reveals. See if you can detect it in these comments.

*When I was in junior high, I got trashed by the high school kids. A lot of us young guys did, and it was humiliating. But now that I'm one of the older guys, I can see it was good. If the young guys don't go through that stuff, get messed up and all, how are they supposed to belong in the big world? Now I have my friends because we went through a lot of shit together. We're loyal to each other.*

LEON, 17

*When I was in eighth grade, this guy Bruce and I just hated each other. We competed in everything. We hated to lose to each other. We got into fights. One day we got into a big fight in the park just down from the school. There were lots of people watching. We both got bloodied up, and we both got in a lot of trouble. I don't know why, but after that we got to be kind of friendly. We were friends in junior high. I still look Bruce up whenever I'm in Madison. We try to get a game of racquetball in—it's like we're kids again, beating up on each other—then we go get a beer and pizza and talk about the good life.*

FRANK, 46

One of the most interesting and, I believe, uncomprehended aspects of human life is the way males often nurture: not by avoiding aggression but by utilizing it as a tool for character development and bonding. Your sons will probably experience an increase in the drive to nurture and be nurtured through aggression, especially as they hit puberty.

Driven by hormonal and neurological components, as well as their male acculturation, young males bond to a great extent through aggression activities—like sports—and through countless subtle and overt forms of "initiation" activities—like the hazing of freshmen—by which males seek to help younger males find their place in social hierarchies. In a moment we will talk about how painful these initiations can be, and how vigilant we must be to guide them. But for now, let's explore how they work.

The writer Michael Novak puts it this way.

*Male bonding is one of the most paradoxical forms of human tenderness: harsh, hazing, sweet, gentle, abrupt, soft. Blows are exchanged. Pretenses are painfully lanced. The form of the compliment is, often as not, an insult. There is daily, hourly probing as to whether one can take it as well as dish it out. It is sweet preparation for a world less rational than childhood dreams imagine.*

A wonderful illustration of male aggression-nurturance was provided to me by a mother of a daughter and a son in their nurturing of their dog. The dog defecated on the floor of the family room. Dad and son wanted to keep the dog outside as a punishment (the dog was an inside dog and did not like being outside for prolonged periods). Mother and daughter couldn't stand his whining outside and brought him in. Jake, fourteen, put him back out.

Kristen, the daughter, fifteen, was overheard saying to Jake, "Can't you just be kind and let him in?"

Jake responded immediately, "I'm being kind. He needs to stay out so he learns."

"You're such a 'guy.'" Kristen sighed.

Kristen was intuitively right. Because of his hormones, his brain system, and his socialization, the male is often prone to nurture not by being "kind" first but by being "cruel" in order to be ultimately kind. Jake and his father wanted the dog to suffer so that he could learn how to behave. These males bypassed the dog's immediate need for closeness with the family in favor of developing his discipline. This discipline, in the males' minds, leads to better bonding over the long term.

Boys and men (and, of course, many women) come to rely on this kind of emotional bypass as one strategy of life. They try to return themselves and others to honor by putting themselves and others through paces and pain that, in the short term, impede closeness. These males are not unfeeling. Deep down, their very logic of feeling is different from the "verbal" logic of directly talking about emotion. The logic of empathy-nurturance is to protect self-esteem as immediately as possible by consoling the person in pain and by reflecting back, as soon as possible, that the person is worth affirmation and respect. The logic of aggression-nurturance is that self-esteem and self-confidence grow not only from consolation and praise but from disequilibrium—from "feeling bad until you have to decide how to make it right through honorable action."

Even adults engage in aggression-nurturing. Parents, teachers, and other caregivers almost universally report experiencing intuitive and subtle changes in themselves as they nurture pubescent and teen boys: an increase in their own sense, as adults, of "dishing it out" and "talking to guys the way they need to be talked to." As testosterone surges in the boy, we try to find ways to honor the young man he is becoming. Instinctively we know that while we may even become afraid of his new aggression, we must also respect that, well channeled, his aggression is a large part of what will make him a success and make the world go round.

Aggression-nurturance often happens best in organized group activities, like sports or debate team or in group family interactions. Again, Michael Novak writes,

*Sports (which are a modern equivalent of group hunting activity)*
*bring out in every ideal team a form of gentleness and tenderness so*
*intense that it is no misnomer to call it love; and coaches commonly*
*speak to their supposed macho males like golden-tongued preachers*
*of love, brotherhood, comradeship. Tears, burning throats, and raw*
*love of male for male are not unknown among athletes in the daily*
*heat of preparation, in the humiliation of doing plays over and*
*over . . .*

Lately, human culture, especially American culture, has gone through political and social rhetoric decrying aggression activities. Some pubescent and post-pubescent male aggression behavior is in fact dangerous and requires punishment. But if you are raising a son, you must come to terms with puberty not just as a physical change but as an emotional change as well. It is not a simplistic emotional life, and it will include some normal aggression in it. Be prepared for these possible and very natural changes in your son's aggressiveness.

- He may one-up a great deal.
- He and his friends may roughhouse dramatically.
- He may feel quite humiliated and may humiliate others.
- He may channel feelings that he once used words for into competitive activities he talks little about.

We will continue to explore these and other aggression-based male behavior throughout the next chapters, providing not only insight into them but good rules and strategies for handling them.

### His Emotional Development

The pubescent male is developing emotional language and perception at an amazing rate. Although they often conceal it, pubescent boys are very emotional creatures—whether in tears at a defeat or a hurt, or angry at an injustice. They also experience emotional contradictions. A pubescent male may perceive that his mother is feeling very sad, but his aggression pushes him toward verbally lashing out at her. Every child and adult is capable of contradictions, and pubescent males can be especially so. There is a wide spectrum of emotional life among pubescent boys, and personality types have much to do with it. Some boys wear their emotions on their sleeves and talk a great deal about them. Many other boys appear to be unfeeling.

One key to understanding the emotional life of pubescent boys is to avoid stereotyping or prejudging them. If we measure "feeling" only by talk about feelings, by shows of immediate empathy, and by networking of emotional relationships, we will certainly mislabel our adolescent males as unfeeling. But simultaneously, we must be very vigilant to make sure our son is not masking his feelings unnecessarily or to his personal detriment.

**The Dangers of Emotional Masking.**  Harvard researchers Deborah David and Robert Brannon have developed four "personas" to watch for in adolescent boys who are masking feelings.

- The "sturdy oak" persona. This is the male who tries never to show weakness.
- The "give 'em hell" persona. This is the male who goes for big risks no matter what.
- The "big wheel" persona. This is the male who is focused almost obsessively on being "cool."
- The "I'm not a sissy" persona. This is the male who fears talking about feelings that will brand him a "sissy" or a "girl."

Because it is natural for pubescent boys to mask emotions, I wouldn't worry about the show of one or even two masks. I would worry, however, if your son is showing all four, or if he's showing one or two so completely that he has shut off all other forms of emotional conversation.

Connected to this issue is the fact that our boys are emotionally neglected in the larger culture. We have broken down many of the family, church, and other systems by which we used to give boys greater opportunity for emotional conversation. Now we have to rely more heavily on one or two key adults to ensure that conversation. Should one of these key people be missing—like the mother or father—then the likelihood of dangerous emotional masking goes up. And even though it may appear that during puberty your son is pulling far away from his mother (something we'll discuss in more detail later), it is often the mother who is the most crucial emotional force in his life. Sons, especially sons of single moms, are very dependent on their moms to help them develop their ability to talk about feelings.

Every boy wants and needs to be proficient in both compassionate talk and action. For many boys, ultimately there will be greater emphasis on compassionate *action*. This focus is to be honored; yet we have done boys no good service as caregivers if we stop, in their adolescence, teaching them how to be compassionate in their words. In the end, *the mother and father, and others in the extended family and school, must model a life of feeling so that the pubescent boy can be comfortable in both aggression-nurturance and empathy-nurturance.*

### His Moral Development

Puberty is one of life's defining moral moments and a crucial time of moral development because the male is becoming

1. a greater product of aggression-nurturance and slightly less of empathy-nurturance, making his behavior potentially more high-risk and his responses to others' pain sometimes appear to lack compassion; and

2. more proficient at hiding his feelings to himself and thus cutting off previously available interactions by which he sorted out what was compassionate and moral behavior.

Professor Walter Williams of the University of Washington's Graduate School of Public Affairs, formerly a part of Lyndon Johnson's administration, has devoted much of his professional life to understanding perceptions of moral character. He recently pointed out what most of us intuit: that by the time males and females have gone through adolescence, "a woman is more likely to be seen as having a higher moral character than a man." We can go further and say that for males to be seen as comparable in moral character to females, they must do something heroic, like fight and survive a war.

Your son faces this fact, even though unconsciously, as he hits puberty. In his boyhood, he already may well have appeared less moral than girls. Then in adolescence his "high-risk" hormone can give him the appearance of moral laxness. Twenty years from adolescence, he will be a social success in large part because of his hormones and this socialization—he will invent something, create something, teach something, build something, nurture a family, and change the world in some way because of his intense male energy. He has to make it to that point, though, with his moral development in place.

As we discuss moral teaching and discipline techniques for boys of thirteen and fourteen, we will look at ways to channel his aggression and to keep him talking about his feelings. We will help him combat destructive socialization that tries to pigeonhole him into some sort of "machine male" who can't look within himself to find his own heart and soul. We will also combat destructive socialization that says because he is an adolescent male, he is inherently immature.

While we are trying to accomplish all this moral development with our pubescent male, we can expect him to be increasing his arguments with us about rules, and trying to compel us to alter rules. He will on the one hand develop an internalized sense of right and wrong—for instance, he won't steal because it feels intuitively wrong—but he'll also let his peers tell him what to do sometimes, even if it means doing bad things. His range of normal will be wide (see page 274).

### Risky Behavior During Puberty

A certain amount of risky behavior is normal for this age group, so it is important we try to develop a clear sense of what goes overboard into high moral risk and what is normal risk. I will present what we should consider to be normal risky behavior, signs of impending crisis, and crisis behavior itself. I hope my suggestions inspire your own intuitions. As always, although these actions fall within the range of normal, we still need to be vigilant caregivers and disciplinarians.

**Normal Risky Behaviors.**   These can include

- backtalk when he's angry at you; argumentation when he's not;
- choosing to do or say what peers want over what you and other adults may want;
- up to three or four "mistakes" or violations of school policies (but not involving violence);
- during the whole of adolescence, perhaps one or two run-ins with the police (nothing too serious—no felonies, no violence);
- cutting class, being tardy, even skipping school once in a while;
- experimentation with tobacco, drugs, and alcohol (nothing chronic);
- staying out later than he's supposed to a few times;
- worrying his parents once in a while;
- running away from home once in the whole ten years of adolescence; and
- sexual experimentation—in early adolescence, this may involve experimentation with other boys; in middle and late adolescence, experimentation with girls and ultimately intercourse (a discussion of gay boys follows later in this chapter).

**Signs of Impending Crisis.**   All of the aforementioned behaviors are within the range of normal risk for adolescents, and unless all or most happen together when the boy is in puberty, they need not be considered crises. What are warning signs that crises may soon occur or that your adolescent son is getting involved in dangerous, problematic moral behavior in some chronic way?

- He is being relentlessly humiliated by peers.
- He has bonded very intimately with a female and been rejected.
- He has no clique or group he feels he belongs in.

## The Range of Normal

It's normal for the boy to still wonder if you approve of him.

It's normal for the boy to worry a lot—about whether he's doing a sport or craft well, about whether he'll succeed in life, about whether he's liked by peers or girls.

It's normal for the boy to impose high expectations on himself; it's just as normal for him to avoid these and need you to impose them on him.

It's normal for the boy to be a little more like either Mom or Dad as puberty hits—if Dad isn't very showy about how he loves, the boy also may be a silent lover.

It's normal for the boy to want to argue a lot about anything that comes to mind.

It's normal for the boy to enjoy activities you find distressing—in 1998, 900,000 teen males watched the baseball playoff games, but 1.5 million watched professional wrestling!

It's normal for the boy to be judgmental of his peers' tastes.

It's normal for the boy to get involved in behavior that puts him physically, emotionally, and morally at risk—not to do these things every day, but to stumble into them now and then.

It's normal for the boy to crave material goods other kids have. As puberty ends, he'll become more individualistic in his taste.

It's normal for the boy to emotionally withdraw, to feel easily humiliated, to be unable to express his pain, and to need a lot of time alone to make himself feel better.

It's equally normal for the boy to come right to you for help.

- He is obsessively using media such as TV, computer games, or the Internet.

- He has mentioned suicide.

- He consistently reports feeling like a failure in life, or clearly feels it even if he never says so.

- He is a bully (and is unable to see what's wrong with his behavior).

- He is experiencing uncontrollable rages—three or more anger flashes a day, inappropriate physical pushing or hitting, and verbal threats.

- His grades are precipitously dropping.

- He is suddenly failing at an activity he has always loved.

- He is spending long periods of time alone in his room—withdrawing from you and all others.

These warning signs may indicate that your son is in trouble; they may also indicate that something very bad has already happened to him, which he is trying to manage through overt behaviors (perhaps he has suffered or is suffering sexual abuse, physical abuse, unceasing humiliation, depression).

**Signs of Crisis.** Your son may be undergoing an actual crisis. Here are some of the behaviors he may exhibit.

- Obsessive angry or enraged outbursts and confrontations with caregivers, or a complete cutoff of communicative relationship with caregivers

- Breaking house and home rules; not caring what parents or other adults think of his moral competency and discipline

- Absent from or tardy at school at least a third of the time

- Repeated violent behavior, violent acts, violent talk that frightens caregivers

- Getting caught by police for illegal action; being suspended or expelled from school for chronic behavioral problems; getting fired from a job, if he has one, for behavioral issues

- Living on the streets, homelessness, running away every few months
- Addiction to drugs or alcohol and/or chronic involvement with those who are
- Chronic sexual behavior inappropriate for an adolescent—promiscuity, unsafe sex
- Setting fires or vandalizing
- Involvement in a gang
- Mutilation of himself
- Breaking lots of your core rules for no apparent reason
- Development of an inappropriate fascination with weapons
- Involvement in repeated violations of school regulations, and violations of the law

If your son fits the category of a boy in crisis, you must get help immediately. Later in this chapter, and in the next, we'll deal more specifically with strategies for handling many of the specific behavioral problems.

### Separation from Parents

No matter the culture we study, males normally begin their journey of independence from the mother earlier than females do. Since females tend to mature earlier than males, we should expect females to begin the psychological separation earlier, but given what we know about how the male neurological and endocrine systems are formatted, the male's earlier drive to independence makes sense. He moves more quickly toward "standing on his own two feet" (1) because of his testosterone, (2) because separation is a psychological aggression response during the growing-up process, (3) because he is driven to prove his worth as a male as quickly and powerfully as possible, and (4) because this separation is modeled by other males (i.e., everywhere he looks, he notices that most males tend to be "more separate" than most females—doing less hugging, touching, and talking). And it is also often the case that while girls during separation can become immensely petulant, they are not generally as aggressive and do not generally engage in as many at-risk behaviors in order to show they are independent.

There are, of course, exceptions to what I have presented. Especially in the last decades, as we model more aggression responses for our young females, they too have become "harder to handle" during adolescence. Nonetheless, in most families, caregivers can think of one or more boys who became inscrutable, hard to talk to, and more difficult to discipline especially during the difficult and essential mother-son, then father-son separations. These boys truly want to exercise their freedom even as they are scared to death, in deep psychological ways, to do so. They become almost obsessed with "not being their parents." And they can often seem to spoil the very nest that has sustained them.

Our response to the separation is crucial, and throughout this chapter you will find assistance as you move through it with your son. During separation, the boy is at immense moral risk. He has relied on his parents and their traditions for his discipline and moral education. As he separates, he feels lost, often unconsciously and without the verbal skills to talk about it. Even if he won't admit it, he needs and wants honor codes, high expectations, curfews, routines, and rituals in place during this time. He needs reassurance that family and community attention and supervision are strong. He wants good discipline, for he is still very much on the journey of developing his own true self-discipline.

## DISCIPLINE TECHNIQUES

Most of the discipline techniques in the previous chapters will still apply. Here are important additions.

### Applying Curfews

Curfews are parent-imposed times at which the boy must be in the house. For all boys of this age, a curfew of around 8:00 P.M. on school nights is appropriate. A later one on weekends is appropriate. Curfews are not matters of trust or distrust. ("But, Mom, imposing a curfew means you don't trust me.") Curfews are part of a healthy discipline system.

While a curfew is necessary for all pubescent boys, an even more rigid curfew can be used as a discipline technique.

If the boy does something wrong, he may have to be home at 6:00 P.M. or 7:00 P.M. If it is a harsh offense, he loses his curfew entirely, as he is grounded. Curfews, grounding, strong reprimands, loss of allowance, loss of privileges, and extra chores all may need to be used in tandem, depending on the severity of the boy's offense.

### Holding to Core Rules

Disciplining pubescent boys (as with all children) requires us to adopt primary rules and secondary rules. We've discussed these before, but I raise this issue again here because during puberty, our boys need some rules to challenge and it is helpful to divert their challenges toward the secondary rules. The core rules, in large part, need to remain solid. Core rules may be: Don't disrespect your parents or God's name; do your jobs and chores; get your homework done; treat others— younger siblings, parents, and friends—with respect and kindness. Perhaps certain manners at the table are not as important to you, so here is where to give the boy some freedom, some joking belches, some potty jokes, as long as his pushing the limits is in good humor.

### Providing a Balance of Freedom and Responsibility

Throughout our boy's adolescence, it is essential we give him *a new responsibility for each new freedom*. If your son takes more freedom "to be himself" at the dinner table, he receives more responsibility to be himself in some other way that helps the family or community. Pubescent boys often want more freedom than responsibility—an impulse that can lead to a lack of discipline.

### Providing More Than One Disciplinarian

A good discipline system for a pubescent boy involves more than one trusted disciplinarian. While the sons of a single mother sometimes become her friends and allies as the family deals with the vicissitudes of single-parent life, just as often a single mother is at a disadvantage in providing needed discipline and structure to pubescent boys. To fully accomplish her goals as a disciplinarian, she may need to open her life to allies in her midst—the man she divorced, who may be a good parent—or perhaps another caregiver. A mother wrote me this letter.

> *My thirteen-year-old needed something I couldn't give, and I didn't know what to do. He was suspended from school for calling a girl a dyke. They got him on sexual harassment for that. He was caught shoplifting and got arrested. He only saw his father once or twice a month—there wasn't much there. My dad was single (my mom had died) so I asked him to move in with me. It took a while—my son knew exactly what I was doing and resented it at first—but then things started getting better—he bonded with his grandpa. Now my son doesn't get into that kind of trouble as much.*

If your son is showing the warning signs we reviewed of immoral and high-risk behavior, discipline techniques generally involve full community support—more personnel than just one parent—and a program of home, school, and social work to care for the boy.

If there is absolutely no one you can turn to, you may find you have to try to be two disciplinarians in one. Sometimes, a single mother has to become a harsher parent during her son's adolescence than she was earlier. She often has to change the way she speaks with him—become more paternal in her demands (i.e., more like a hard-edged dad). In a sense, she has to try to keep being the good listener and parent who draws him out emotionally, but also when concerned with his behavior and moral growth, she might become quite demanding and prescriptive. It's a hard job to be good at both all the time, but if the single parent has no allies, she or he will have to try.

## Rules to Live By

Rules and regulations are very important during puberty. I hope these inspire you to articulate and apply your own in your son's life.

1. A parent of a pubescent boy has the right to know who he's with and where they are.

2. A pubescent boy should understand that just because friends do it, say it, or believe it doesn't make something right.

3. A pubescent boy's cursing, cruel humiliation, and meanness are unacceptable.

4. It is appropriate for a parent of a pubescent boy to ask the boy why he has done something and to receive, within an appropriate time (this may mean waiting a few hours), an explanation.

5. Because a home is not just a place of conflict but also a place of joy, a pubescent boy should find ways to deal with his conflicts with parents that utilize good humor.

6. The home is still ruled by the parents, and children follow the rules; but since the rulers are starting to want more input now on what should be called "right" and "wrong," family councils and other family meetings should become a larger part of family life now, and all children must participate.

## MORAL TEACHING

As your son cries out for more freedom at thirteen and fourteen, you may be tempted to "let his own conscience be his guide." While this kind of letting go is important, and although the boy's basic character is generally set by the time puberty hits, he needs constant *moral confirmation* now, and *new moral challenges*.

- He needs continued moral debate (see the previous chapter, pages 233, 238 and 242).

- He needs his caregivers to point out wrongs and injustices in the world and help him shape his own opinions about what should be done.
- He needs to engage in moral discourse with challenging peers.
- He needs moral education and ethics curricula in his school.
- He needs parents *and mentors* to tell him they are available to him no matter what he has done or contemplated doing—they will always be there to listen and to help him find his way.
- He needs activities, sports, rites of passage, family events, and church groups that guide him toward teamwork, empathy, and service.
- He needs to be shown, by his parents and others, the grace of daily obligation—in other words, he has to fulfill his responsibilities to his family via chores, to his extended family via thank-you cards or other connecting points, and to friends and community via "doing the right thing."
- He needs to practice good manners, a minimum of cursing (especially around parents and other authorities), helpfulness beyond the call of duty. He practices good behavior now not because he's an obedient little boy or an approval-hungry kid but because he's becoming a man.

### Where to Draw the Moral Lines

One of the great challenges of raising adolescent boys is drawing moral lines with them. We don't want to overmoralize all risky behavior our boys get into, but we also don't want to let moral laxness develop. Here are some lines I recommend. Each parent must draw lines on some of these issues, and I hope these will help you decide on your own.

- While covering a teacher's car with toilet paper is an undisciplined and antisocial act, it is within the range of normal pubescent risk behavior. Throwing a rock through the car window should be considered immoral. Destruction of property is not pranksterism but violence.

- Taking a puff of a cigarette now and then is not immoral, but developing a smoking habit should be considered dangerous to the self and to others (secondhand smoke), thus a moral issue.

- While taking a puff of marijuana at an older friend's house is experimental, developing any consistent (once a month or more) use of any drug is immoral behavior.

- While sneaking a beer or other drink now and then is normal, any kind of consistent drinking habit should be considered immoral.

## The Temptations of Drugs and Alcohol

The temptation to use drugs and alcohol reaches a head when the boy is around thirteen years old, correlating with puberty. According to the National Center on Addiction and Substance Abuse, and the National Court Appointed Special Advocate studies in 1998, a thirteen-year-old is three times as likely as a twelve-year-old to know a teen who uses acid, cocaine, or heroin; three times likelier to be able to buy pot, acid, cocaine, or heroin; almost three times likelier to know a student drug seller; and more than three times likelier to be unwilling to report a student using drugs. In these studies, a majority of students polled said that the alcohol and drug problem in both middle and high school is getting worse, not better, and that alcohol and drugs are a primary risk area for them.

According to Joseph Califano, president of the National Center on Addiction and Substance Abuse, "Nearly half of middle and high school students say that their parents have never—*never*—discussed the dangers of drugs with them. Most parents don't even have drugs on the radar screen of concerns they think *their* children have."

Drug, alcohol, and tobacco use is high-risk and worth discussing with your sons. In our culture, it is a show of good parenting to be the first person your son comes to when he is afraid he might be stepping over the line from "normal risky" behavior to "highly at-risk" behavior and "immoral" behavior. The Century Council, a national anti-abuse organization, puts out a video, "Ready or Not: Talking to Kids About Alcohol," targeted to ten- to fourteen-year-olds. It is very good for private use, but also for use in schools and other institutions. Boys and Girls Clubs of America are Century Council partners and will know about how to get the video in your area.

While risk factors for drug and alcohol use rise in puberty, crises regarding their use don't generally show up until mid-teens, so we will deal in more depth with practical measures in the next chapter. If, however, you have a son in crisis regarding drugs or alcohol, jump ahead to page 321, and get help immediately.

### Handling One Common Problem: Cigarette Use

Recently, a mother wrote, "I opened my thirteen-year-old son's underwear drawer and found cigarettes hidden in the back. How mad should I be? What should I do?" Many parents have struggled with this question, as cigarette use is shoved on our young people through media and peers.

It is good for your son to see you righteously angry when he does something bad, something that scares you. Your son needs you to ask him what the cigarettes are doing there, how much he has smoked, how it felt to smoke, why he did it, who else he's doing it with, how he got the cigarettes, and so on. An interrogation—handled well—shows you care.

There is disagreement over whether to severely punish the first time you find evidence of cigarette use. Your intuition must guide you here. I am a believer in punishment the first time, because if there is obvious evidence of cigarette use now, it means he's been smoking a number of times before.

You and your son ought to decide together on the punishment, if you can. Grounding for a week, extra chores, and loss of television or phone privileges all are possibilities. Your son must also realize that being caught again will lead to more severe punishment.

It's important to handle the discovery of tobacco use—and drug and alcohol use (which we'll cover in the next chapter)—in a way that does not destroy your lines of communication with your son. You need to assure your son that it's always better to be honest than to lie, and always better to call you from a dangerous party or other situation if he needs you, *even if he will also get in trouble* for some of his activity there.

If your son's use of tobacco (or drugs or alcohol) goes beyond the experimental, then he needs help from your doctor, NA or AA groups, and perhaps even Social Services. Florida has begun a Teen Smoking Court for teen offenders. Police ticket kids younger than eighteen who smoke. These kids then go to court, pay court costs, and do community service. For chronic offenders, this system may be necessary for the country to use—it might help parents who obviously can't police their kids at school and on the street. It must definitely be augmented by a huge tobacco education campaign for youth.

If an adolescent is smoking (or drinking or drugging) at a time in life when you as his parent can't reach him—if he blows you off these days—it is important to look at confronting him with his other parent present, and with any other adults (or elder siblings) present whom he trusts and respects. Build a "confrontation team," then confront him. As with all problems, dilemmas, or tragedies in your son's life, cigarette use is a "family affair"—not necessarily something only one parent must solve, nor the boy himself, alone.

If your son is starting to smoke cigarettes as early as thirteen, or even earlier, he has a higher likelihood of using other addictive substances—i.e., drugs and alcohol—later, so watch for these as well.

### Handling Shoplifting and Stealing

It is not uncommon for boys to experiment with shoplifting either during puberty or even just before. Much of what we said before about handling cigarette use applies here: We handle shoplifting and stealing as serious issues, our punishments are severe and developed with the help of the boy, and we increase our attention to the boy's emotional and moral needs. The boy must return the stolen items, apologize, and make or do restitution as necessary to the victim of the theft. If shoplifting or stealing happens repeatedly, we will want to get professional help; once the police or courts get involved, the boy's life can be changed by the legal system in frightening ways. We must get professional help before that happens if at all possible.

## Building Spiritual Life

How wonderful it is for a pubescent boy to hear his parents challenging him to be increasingly spiritual. Now is the time to talk to the boy about what God is—not just to teach him doctrine, but to *engage his mind.* His ability to think abstractly is gradually outstepping simplistic dogma. For him, God is now becoming, in the words of Bishop Spong, "not a parent who will reward or punish for virtues and shortcomings. This God is rather a power, a presence that calls him into responsibility, into adulthood, into self-reliance, into living for others, and into contributing to the well-being of all humanity." This boy may for a while still hold to the edicts of a parent-God, but his mind is already shifting toward understanding a more complex deity, and if the shift is not nurtured, he and God may lose their bond.

Millions of boys are lost to spiritual and religious life during puberty because their caregivers either push a dogma too far and the boy rejects it, or they neglect open spiritual dialogue altogether. The boy wants to shape his own sense of the mysterious powers of life, and we must help him. The boy wants to develop his own moral intuition. He may end up believing exactly as we do, and he may become quite dogmatic, but at least he will experience his beliefs as his own if we help him challenge his own moral and spiritual intuition.

"Empedocles said, 'God is a circle whose center is everywhere and circumference is nowhere.' What do you think, son? What does that mean?"

"Have you read *Siddhartha* yet?"

"When you were little, we told you every word of the Bible was true. Now you should read the whole thing and see what you think."

"Have you read Chaim Potok's *The Chosen*? It's one of my favorite spiritual books."

What is God? What is nature? What is holiness? Why are we here? What are we meant to do? What am *I* meant to do? What is my destiny? What are the gifts I came into the world with?

All these are questions to engage boys in. They are growing, feeling, groping, experiencing themselves as beings of natural impulse. They want lots of outdoor activities, like Boy Scouts provides, lots of family camping or other travel or hiking, lots of time to contemplate themselves as creatures of divine nature.

### Sexual Morality

We will discuss sexual behavior in greatest detail in the next chapter. For now, normal sexual behavior generally runs in the range of self-stimulation (during puberty, it's not unusual for boys to masturbate many times a week), kissing a girl and perhaps giving or receiving a hickey, sexual stimulation through verbal teasing (some of which can hurt feelings), posturing about sexual conquests with other males, hurting girls' feelings, having his own feelings hurt, perhaps talking a girl into showing a breast or other private part, perhaps some touching of a girl's private parts, and perhaps some experimentation with other boys.

Sexual risk-taking becomes high-moral-risk behavior if the boy is already having intercourse at age thirteen or fourteen.

Because of the amount of actual sexual harassment going on among teens, and because of the amount of overreaction to normal adolescent gender struggle that exists in our culture today, it is essential you advise your sons on what sexual harassment means, and on what the risks are of sexual teasing, baiting, flirting, and force. Many pubescent boys are sexually harassing others without knowing the standards for appropriate sexual morality, particularly in a culture that flouts and flaunts sexual risk-taking in so many TV shows and movies.

*The best way to make sure your son knows what's wrong and what's right is to talk to him.*

- Repeatedly converse with him about your expectations for his sexual behavior.
- Teach him everything he needs to know to be safe even while showing him why abstinence is his best course at this point in his life.
- Encourage him to confide in you.
- Expose him at home and in school to lessons in respect, sexual morality, and sexual risks.

- Control as much as possible his stimulation by "adult" sexual programming. A *Playboy* magazine now and then is normal for boys this age. Watching adult videos on the sly is within the range of normal. He might "sneak" these—but they are not things to buy for him or encourage him, at age thirteen, to model.

- Teach him about sex, love, and commitment. He is old enough to see that sexual intercourse is a sacred act, different in quality from sexual petting or masturbation. Talk to him about these distinctions. Men must especially tell their stories to sons—these discussions are intimate for him (even if at times uncomfortable), and they help build the father-son bond.

In all areas of high-risk behavior—drug, alcohol, and cigarette use, and sexuality—studies consistently show boys lowering their at-risk limits if they are involved in spiritual development. This behavior is to be expected—each of these high-risk acts is a way the boy is trying to belong. To the degree he feels he belongs in the universe through spiritual life, he will be less inclined to force his belonging through other acts.

**Develop Age-Appropriate Dating Practices.** Pubescent boys should not date. By "dating," I mean one-on-one solitary time spent with a peer female. It is not appropriate for a thirteen- or fourteen-year-old. Time with females can be spent in groups or in supervised activities. A boy who is just starting puberty is not mature enough to regulate his own hormonal and emotional life to the extent that dating, which is a mating activity, requires. Sixteen is generally an appropriate age to formally begin dating.

A boy who is coupling, dating, or mating at the age of thirteen should be considered an at-risk youth. He may not be getting the love he needs from people he is mature enough to appropriately bond with. He may be compensating for that lack by bonding with someone in a manner that his maturity will not be able to handle.

### Helping Guide His Emotional Impulses

Puberty for any child is very much about learning to control emotional impulses. The moral community to which parents, educators, mentors, and peers belong is one that tries to help the pubescent male to *experience, express,* and, when necessary, *expel* his own feelings in personally and socially appropriate ways. In the midst of all the hormonal, brain, and social changes, our sons are nearly desperate to learn how to guide emotional impulses to successful and well-disciplined conclusions. "I feel hurt," the boy is crying, even if silently. "What do I do?" "I feel a crazy anger. What do I do?" "I'm afraid. Should I stop doing the thing that's scaring me, or do I just have to stuff it and do the brave thing right now?"

**Help Him Feel His Feelings.**   It is essential that not only Mom but Dad and other men as well model healthy emotional expression for and with the boy. The boy needs hugs, pats on the back, handshakes. He needs people he trusts to teach him that it takes as much courage to express his emotions in healthy ways as it takes to hit someone.

It may be quite normal for your son not to talk to you a lot about his feelings these days. His behavior should become worrisome only if he is not talking to anyone else about them either. If he is isolated and is not relying on you or peers to share feelings with, then professional intervention may be needed. *He needs one or more individuals or groups in his environment with whom he shares his innermost feelings.*

Boys in adolescence are very capable of "naming" their feelings, and we need to encourage them.

"Are you feeling afraid, son?"

"Nah."

"Are you sure?"

"Well, maybe a little."

"Of what?"

In our emotional conversations, the sentences may start out small, but at some point, if we keep helping the boy name the feeling—"I'm afraid"; "I'm sad"—he will probably open up.

Parents of adolescent boys are often unclear about whether repression of feelings should ever be encouraged. We are in an interesting dilemma in our present culture about this issue. We have almost a phobia about boys or men repressing any feelings except their anger. Yet I encourage you not to see your parenting as unsuccessful or your son as emotionally stunted if he represses many feelings. *All human children, male or female, must learn to repress feelings in order to mature.* Whining, complaining, outbursts—a great deal of this behavior has to be weeded out of our emotional system during adolescence so that we can grow up. To rampantly "express" feelings whenever one has them is just as often a sign of immaturity as it is a sign of emotional success. Maturity is as much a matter of our equanimity and our ability to transcend emotional impulses as it is a matter of emotional expression. It is just as useful to be proud of a quiet, nonexpressive boy as a loud, expressive one, as long as both are showing their feelings in ways that are appropriate to a given situation at a given time.

Pubescent boys need the safety to cry, yet it is useful to realize that by nature they probably will not cry as much as girls. Pubescent girls have increased levels of prolactin—the hormone that controls breast milk production, mammary glands and tear glands. Girls' tear glands are, on average, 60 percent larger than boys' by the time they reach age fifteen. Boys more naturally and by socialization tend to process more of their feelings through physical anger, and it is this tendency we must monitor.

**Help Him Make Appropriate Choices Regarding His Anger.**   Some boys get angry a great deal during puberty. It's their body's and brain's way of expressing their hormonal surges and disequilibrium. Boys also can become very angry because they model constant anger from a caregiver. Other boys become angry excessively as an expression of trauma they've experienced—humiliation or abuse. If a boy is getting angry but handling it—going to his room, or going for a run, or hitting a punching bag—and not hurting others with his anger, then he is to be congratulated for his self-control as well as nurtured in calming himself down.

But when does his anger have moral implications? We must allow his anger to be expressed, and we must honor legitimate anger. But we must not allow him to rely on anger and rage too often, nor to humiliate or hurt others with it in bullying ways.

Here are questions you can ask yourself regarding your son's anger. I adapted them after reading a quiz developed by Dr. Ichiro Kawachi and others at Harvard who study anger. I have added answers that you will have to measure as accurate or inaccurate according to your own intuitions.

1. How many times a day (or week or month) does your son swear out loud?
   If it is every day, there is cause to worry.

2. How many times a week (or month or year) does he break something in anger?
   If it is once a week, there is cause to worry.

3. How many times a year does he physically fight in anger with another?
   If it is six times a year, there is cause to worry.

4. Would you consider him "hotheaded" or "bad-tempered"?
   If so, is he showing it physically and verbally in inappropriate ways?

5. Have other people you trust called him hotheaded or bad-tempered or implied that he fits these descriptions?
   If so, it's probable that you and your son should take steps.

6. Does he get angry, then often feel ashamed afterward?
   If so, he himself knows he needs help controlling his anger.

7. Does he seem unable to stop himself from lashing out?
   If so, get help immediately.

8. Has he gotten angry enough to hurt another physically?
   Again, if so, he needs help.

9. How often is he disrespectful to you in anger episodes?
   If it is often enough to make you even the least frightened, it is definitely too much.

If your son is swearing, hitting, disrespecting parents and authorities to an extent that you and at least one other caregiver believe is inappropriate, his pubescent years are the right time for you to address this behavior—through anger-management programs, reconnection of the boy with a tough father or other caregiver, martial arts, church youth activities, counseling, and school alternatives. *No boy wants to be excessively angry.* As much as we can help the boy develop self-regulation of anger, he will be thankful, even if he resists us.

**Creating Standards for Fighting.** There is a great deal of debate about when a boy should hit back. I teach the "three strikes" rule. If a boy has been taunted once, he turns the other cheek; if he's taunted a second time, he gives a warning and he gets help as needed from friendly peers or other adults; if he is taunted or attacked a third time, he strikes back. *In nearly every case, if the first two strikes are handled with dignity and by engaging his community to help him, the third strike will not occur.* There are bullies, however, who won't quit, and there are boys who refuse to reach out. They want to deal with problems on their own. Puberty is a time of relatively undisciplined behavior in many males, thus a time in your son's life when you and other trusted adults need to be very active in the home, school, church, and neighborhood in teaching both honorable fighting *and* nonviolent methods for dealing with conflict. If your son gets in one fight a year during junior high, he is probably within the range of normal.

## A HEALTHY MORAL AND EMOTIONAL ENVIRONMENT

Your pubescent son will want to determine more and more of his own environment. He'll want to make his own room into a private haven. He'll seek peer environments more than before. You will be losing control over certain aspects of his environment, even over some of his friendships. And yet your son, even if he says the opposite, will not want you to give up too much control over his life. Your son wants to explore new relationships and environments, but he still wants and needs the safety of what is tried and true. The art of parenting a pubescent boy lies in being *simultaneously authoritative and adaptable*—no small feat.

### Family and Community Life

It's essential that parents and teachers are part of the same community spirit, for in a sense, parents and schools are coraising the pubescent boy. If parents' emotional and moral standards are significantly different from the school's (and vice versa), the boy experiences the kind of developmentally confusing inconsistency that, earlier in life, he experienced if Mom and Dad were divided as disciplinarians.

And although your son is gradually becoming more independent from you as parents, he still needs you to be *deeply* involved in his life. He needs at least one parent to be around (or another trusted caregiver) when he comes home from school. He needs you to go to his recitals, sports events, and plays. He needs you to go work out with him at the gym or take him to the movies. He needs you to drive him to activities—not just rely on an older sibling. Your pubescent son wants the alone time with you as you drive him—and might like even more alone time with you as you stop for a bite to eat together en route from somewhere to somewhere. This kind of time can be nonthreatening to the young teen, and good conversation can ensue.

The boy needs you to take an interest in his schooling and school environment. Many parents give up going to parent-teacher conferences when their children get to junior high, which is a mistake. The child needs to see how much we care about his school life. He needs to hear our opinions about his school, and talk to us about his own. He may need us to intervene once in a while on his behalf (and he may fear we'll intervene too much).

He may still need us to help motivate his study habits. It is still appropriate to help him schedule homework, music practice, and exercise time. Simultaneously, it is good to wait a little before reminding him of an obligation—if he runs his life well without you, praise is a good thing to give; if he needs the reminding, we remind.

A grandmother shared with me this story. At dinner one evening, her grandson said, "You remember I told you about that girl, Hailey? Well, she wrote me a letter. She asked me why I was so smart. I told her because I read a lot and my mom and my grandma don't let me watch too much TV. She watches too much TV. I'm glad I don't." At thirteen, this boy wants these rules and regulations. He likes the fact that his family and community care enough to help him run his life.

### A Best Friend

If your son is one of those boys who curtails his conversation with you a great deal, you might wonder if he's doing okay. One of the best ways to know is by asking yourself, "Does he have a best friend?" And: "Is this person of high quality?" We find that most "best friends" for our thirteen- and fourteen-year-old boys are other boys—at this age they are too young to mate with girls. However, every once in a while, a boy of this age will have a "best friend" who is a platonic female. If your son has no best male friend, it is worth wondering why. Or if that best friend is a "druggie" or otherwise morally at risk, it is worth intervening—talking to your son about the trust he is putting in this person, and trying to find out why he is placing his trust in someone like this rather than in parents, other peers, or other mentors. He will most likely need professional help if he is distrustful of you and trustful only of a dangerous best friend.

### Mentors and Role Models

Another sign of your son's health over these two years and into the next four or five is his discovery of mentors and role models. A good environment for your pubescent son is one with positive role models from the larger culture—like Michael Jordan, or an honorable government figure, or even characters he feels close to from books and other media—and one or two adults other than Mom and Dad who are positive, active mentors. If he has none of these, now it is essential for you to try to find them for him before it's too late. If the boy has a favorite teacher or coach but is shy about approaching him as a mentor, you as a parent can help bridge the gap. Now is also the time for grandparents and other extended family members to become more active. Older siblings also can become mentors, and agencies like Big Brothers and Big Sisters and Boy Scouts can provide mentors and role models.

### The Need for Respect

Pubescent boys are almost desperate for respect and will seek environments in which to gain it. They will very quickly "turn off" a teacher or other adult (including a parent) who doesn't provide it.

While we as parents cannot control how boys gain this respect in many environments, we can control how we give respect in our homes. Now we must respect our son in new ways. If we used to be "talkers" rather than "listeners," now we become listeners, asking our son what he thinks of things rather than forcing our own opinions on him. By doing so, we help build his sense of self-respect. If our son is a belligerent or morally at-risk boy, now is the time to increase our authoritative presence—make sure he sticks to rules. At this time we also expect adultlike behavior to a much greater extent than before: Most boys want and need to be brought to and shown higher standards and earn respect by meeting them.

Now is the time also to really try to bring out our son's natural chivalry. One mom told me that while she had always trained her sons to be helpful, she started thinking of helpfulness in terms of "chivalry" when they started getting taller and stronger. "It was like a lightbulb went off in my head," she said, "when Paul got to be as tall as me. He wasn't just being helpful—he was learning chivalry." Saying to him, "I'm tired; the groceries are heavy; I need you to lift that—thanks, son, you're a great help," helps him develop the kind of manners that chivalry entails.

*Now is the time when Dad and/or other trusted males must show their respect for their sons and help their sons show respect to others.* During puberty, some boys will experiment with "dissing" their mothers. Mothers and fathers should monitor this behavior closely, and fiercely discourage it.

*Pubescent boys are becoming men, and they yearn for men to respect them.* Much of a pubescent boy's acting out behavior will be unnecessary if he feels respected by his father and elder men. It will be unnecessary because he will realize, however unconsciously, that he does not have to constantly prove himself—his father and other trusted men already see how manly he is.

Boys gain a great deal of self-respect through *action, through doing things.* It is a cardinal rule of male adolescence that *every boy needs a craft.* Perhaps his craft is his sport, or carpentery, or even ballet. He will probably have more than one. If he has no craft, we need to make sure to help him find one. Playing video games, or that kind of passive activity, should not be considered a craft.

### Homosexuality

Somewhere between 5 and 10 percent of our pubescent males will know that they are "different." They will not be sexually attracted to girls. The environment we raise our children in today is not generally one that understands or supports males who are homosexual. They face a society that continues to think of them as perverts. They face parents who may be afraid of them and even reject them. They face peers who humiliate them.

We now understand that to a great extent, homosexuality is biological. Studies over the last decade have found that there is a structural difference in the hypothalamus of the brain that controls sexual orientation. Studies also have confirmed that homosexuality runs in family lines, giving it an additional genetic component.

Understanding homosexuality as biological is difficult for some people because it seems counterintuitive to simple notions about the human reproductive process. Those people who condemn homosexuality as "unnatural" are participating in a condemnation based on the idea that a nonreproducing human is to be suspected.

Thousands of years ago, following an edict like "Go forth and multiply" was more necessary because we needed to build up human population in order for humanity to flourish. Now, just the opposite is true. There is no specific biological reason to compel all humans to have children; in fact, it would be better if fewer of us did, given the environmental and social problems overpopulation produces.

Biologically speaking, this new circumstance will gradually work its way through human thinking and we will gradually become more accepting of homosexuals. Our adolescents who know themselves to be homosexual desperately need us to step forward into this new thinking, especially if we are their parents or mentors.

If you have a homosexual son, know that *in nearly every case* your parenting did not "make" him homosexual. In most cases, he was not sexually abused; nor will he turn out to be a sexual abuser—the vast majority of men who commit sex crimes are heterosexual men. Know also that the difficulties he will face in his society are enormous. He may never quite feel he fits in. He may suffer from depression, addiction, and other psychological problems because of the social stress he is under. Get help for him immediately for these emotional stresses from professionals who understand him. Never withhold love, attention, or caring. If he needs a little extra help or protection during adolescence—which is a time of great humiliation for gay males—give him that help, even if that means transferring him to a school where people are more open-minded than at the huge, relatively unsupervised local school. As quickly and diligently as you can, help him find two or three activities he excels in, and support him in enjoying these—perhaps drama, or debate, or a sport—so that he can steadily develop self-esteem. These all are things you would probably do with any child, yet with a gay son there is often a need for you to be even more vigilant. The gay boy in our culture, especially in adolescent culture, is like a pariah, and you may be challenged to do even more to help him find a sense of belonging. Certain churches, like the Unitarian-Universalist denomination, have Welcoming Congregations that specifically welcome gay individuals and offer them community. Finding this kind of community with your son is invaluable.

I recommend also that parents and caregivers of gay children be open to the wonderful gifts these children bring us—especially the gift of courage. Gay boys, facing all that humiliation and hate, nonetheless get through adolescence and flourish. They are very courageous young people and can inspire us all.

Some young men will go through a phase of thinking they are homosexual when they are not. Some adults worry that male-on-male sexual experimentation will lead to a son's becoming homosexual. This is doubtful. Males experiment sexually with other males during adolescence, but if the male is not already biologically a homosexual, he will most probably not become one.

Some groups are arguing great success in "converting" homosexuals to heterosexuality. It's important to note that most of the "converts" were not biologically homosexual in the first place, and many who are "converted" today will, after a few years, probably discover that they cannot go against their own biology.

Should you belong to a church or other group that condemns homosexuality as immoral, I hope you will never condemn the boy in your life or community. If you feel you must criticize, please criticize the *action,* but not the individual's whole being. We should hold *all* teens to sexual standards of temperance, abstinence from intercourse, and responsibility. Apply these standards equally among homosexual and heterosexual teens, and you will very likely be upholding ethics that match your religious values and that will help your son.

### Media Use

Television, movies, magazines, video games, CDs, CD-ROMs, the Internet—all the media for pubescent boys are both potential moral pitfalls and learning opportunities. Going to movies with your son, talking to him about the television he watches, watching with him—being involved in his media life—is essential as the pubescent boy's mind and hormones grow at exponential rates and need help in interpreting and managing all the stimulations he receives.

A father told me about taking his fourteen-year-old son and the son's friend to see the movie *Good Will Hunting,* a film about tough young men who grow up with the help of one another. The father and boys went out for coffee after the movie and talked a long time. One of the boys admitted (it had been hard to cover up) that he had cried in one particular scene, and talked about why. The father and the young men were finding in the story their own moral and spiritual moorings. This use of the media is a positive one during a boy's puberty years.

A single mother told me about how scared she was becoming of her son's growing need to objectify women and girls. She overheard her thirteen-year-old call girls bitches, and say to a friend on the phone he couldn't wait "to bone one." She had known for a few months that he had some hidden *Playboy* magazines. She asked him to get one and didn't leave him alone until he did. After telling him how she felt about his words, she opened the magazine to the centerfold and talked to him, unabashedly, about what he saw there. She confronted him with the humanity of the woman in the photo, and told him, in tears, how it made her feel, as a woman, to hear her son talk about girls and women in dehumanizing ways. She neither shamed nor condemned him for wanting the magazine, and she did not take it away from him. What she did was make him feel guilty for his own *words*. It also was a positive way to use the media during the boy's puberty years.

It is still appropriate to allow a pubescent boy only supervised Internet access. It is also still appropriate to make sure the boy finishes his homework and chores before he watches TV. Limited video game use is appropriate, as well as limited TV viewing. Decision-making and choice-making skills are important to build in pubescent boys, and requiring them to select an hour to two hours of TV/video stimulation per day not only protects them from overuse but encourages them to take control over what they view.

### The Rituals of Life: The Second Rite of Passage

Rites of passage are a lost art, yet our pubescent boys hunger for them. For more than two decades, anthropological studies have confirmed that, biologically, males need rites in order to mark their passage into manhood. Males have needed these rites since hunter-gatherer times. If I ever had any doubt that males are "hard-wired" in certain ways based on the past tradition of hunting, it was allayed by Richard Krause, an educator in Montgomery County, Maryland, who told me about a jury selection process he participated in. There were twenty-five people sitting around, nineteen women and six men. To alleviate the boredom, the bailiff decided to start a crossword puzzle. At one point he said, "Okay, folks, what's a four-letter word that starts with 'h' and ends with 't'?" All six men, in unison, called out, "Hunt!" What Richard found so interesting was that none of the men was a hunter by trade or recreation, and also, only the men called the word out.

The majority of today's boys and men do not hunt prey with weapons, but they seek the challenge that the hunt implies. When we give our sons a rite of passage, we give them a chance to hunt, through the ritualized heroic quest, for who they are. The rite can last five days or one week or two or three weeks. When boys aren't given these rites by their families, they nonetheless go out and try to prove their manhood through high-risk, self-created rites of passage. They may form gangs to hunt with and often damage their communities in hopes of proving they are becoming men and ought to have the respect of men.

A rite of passage during a boy's puberty can happen spontaneously. A mother in Seattle told me about how her fourteen-year-old son had been acting out severely for about a year: He was tardy, truant, had been backtalking, was disrespecting his mother, and was experimenting with drugs. This mom sent her son for two weeks that summer to stay with his father in Baltimore (the divorce had occurred when the son was ten). The boy came back a changed person. He told his mother he felt bad about how he had treated her, became "a hugger again," and started the fall semester as a young man who cared about his schooling and his own success. He had taken a spontaneous rite of passage that did not involve wilderness experience or too much ritualization. For this boy, getting away and bonding with his absent father was an immense life change.

One day I received a heartfelt call from a mother whose son, Owen, fourteen, had just gone with his best friend, John, also fourteen, to South Africa. The story was almost breathtaking for its rite of passage. John's mother had read a statement in *The Wonder of Boys* that in both a literal and a symbolic sense, once your son becomes taller than you, it's time to find him a rite of passage into manhood. Since both Owen and John were playing adolescent games with their parents—backtalking, dissing, disobeying—and since John's mother was originally from South Africa, she called Owen's parents and made an offer. "Let's send both of them this summer to visit my uncle Joss for three weeks." The trip required a considerable expense and a great deal of courage on the parts of both the parents and the sons.

While in South Africa, the boys hunted with Uncle Joss, worked the ranch, and fulfilled certain ritual traditions. One ritual that moved the boys was hunting a boar and, after killing it, cutting the liver out and wiping the blood of the liver on their faces. This whole trip was such a "different" and "cool" experience for these previously sheltered American boys that it had a profound impact on them. Because Joss was a good mentor and teacher, the boys developed a deep sense of the sacred natural world, and of themselves as important parts of the natural life cycle.

Owen came home a more loving boy and a more respectful and trustworthy young man. John told his mother, "I can do anything now. I'm a man now." It was, in fact, easier now for the parents to see them as young men, and to respect them in the way they craved.

**Facilitating a Pubescent Rite of Passage.** When your son was ten or so, he should have gone through his first rite of passage (see chapter 7). Generally, the following rite is appropriate for a thirteen- or fourteen-year-old, but you can modify the timing to fit your own intuitions. It is very effective to do this rite at a time when you believe your son is at least halfway finished with the fundamentals of puberty—the two-year growth spurt, especially, and the development of early teen muscle mass.

In creating a rite of passage of your own, you might want to focus on these specific things.

- The rite is an adventure experience that takes place away from home, often in a wilderness area.
- The boy is led through it carefully by elders, parents (particularly fathers), teachers.
- The boy can do it alone or with other peers (generally other boys).
- Everyone is involved in aspects of it—the mom and other women are important as well as the men.
- Rituals are important. One mom told me about her fourteen-year-old's rite of passage experience in the Cascade Mountains in Wash-

ington State. At the end of it, the leader had all the boys wash the feet of their parents. The son, mother, and father all were in tears as the boy performed this ritual of respect, love, and humility.

- Childhood must be symbolically left behind. Often burning rituals are used—the boy burns a childhood toy or other accoutrement.

- The boy should hear men talk about what it means to be a man, in detail and variety—no stereotypes, no gross chauvinisms, but real talk about the character of manhood.

- The boy should make one or more statements to his community about his worth as a man, his plans, his dreams.

- The boy should perform in some way in front of the whole community. In a bar mitzvah, for instance, a boy publicly reads from the Torah.

ICA Journeys, on the World Wide Web, is a very good resource for learning more about rites of passage for both boys and girls.

## A DOCTOR'S STORY

Recently a grown man, a physician, recalled being fourteen years old. He remembered that his father had made him dig fence posts all that summer. It was backbreaking, painstaking work. There were no power tools then, just the manual posthole digger and many football-field lengths of fence to put in. He resented having to dig the fence posts. He resented his father; he resented his life. Even when he would feel the daily exhilaration of hard work and accomplishment, he would downplay those in his mind in favor of absolute resentment.

But then, looking back on it as a man and as a father himself, he realized what his father had been doing, and he realized the immense wisdom of it. His father was giving him a mission. His father was directing his pubescent energies of aggression toward service, compelling him to contribute to his family and his land. His father was giving him a job, an activity through which he could learn, himself, in his own body, what it feels like to contain human energy, to direct it, to endure, to persevere. And his father was giving him a way to be of value as a man.

Though puberty is a very challenging time, it is in many ways a very simple time. Our boys aren't as complicated as we think. If we've raised them well, they'll follow us anywhere, including into a task that nearly breaks their backs. This physician had a wise parent who had the guts and follow-through to build his son's character during puberty.

Our sons during puberty are like this doctor who went on from digging postholes to being a healer. By moving through his pubescent years in a constant embrace of mission, direction, healthy action, and service, he became a man who served the world.

# TEN

# The Middle Teens

## NURTURING BOYS OF

## FIFTEEN AND SIXTEEN

Karen Wong, forty-two, told me about her fifteen-and-a-half-year-old son, David. Her story mirrors the lives of so many families.

David was the kind of kid who, when you asked "How was your day?" would respond, "Okay, I guess." When you wanted information, he was a vault.

But then when he was staying at Dad's house—Karen and her husband had split up ten years before—he would call his mom and talk to her for an hour. Karen recalled a Saturday night after he'd come back from a party, at about 11:30 P.M. He had felt spurned by a girl there. He called his mother and talked, while she listened, half asleep.

"More freedom! More freedom!" Karen laughed as she told her story. "This was always his cry to us. 'Give me more freedom! Just let me be myself!' His father and I get along well, so we kept talking, kept adapting, made sure we were pretty consistent in both houses with the rules.

"Then one day we discovered a new twist to things. David came to me and said, 'Mom, I'm really mad at you.' For days he had been in a weird mood and I didn't know why. We sat down at the table, and he said, 'How come you don't make me do my homework? Terry's mom and Lurent's mom say, "Do it, or no party Friday night." "Do it, or no camping over the weekend." But you don't.'"

Karen told me that she was a little shocked. She said to her son, "David, we were trying to follow your lead. You are getting old enough to see that when you don't do something you should, there are choices and consequences."

"I guess," he replied, his eyes down for most of this conversation. "But it seems like you have other things to do, or you don't care about me."

Karen, wisely, did not take this bait. She did understand, however, that her son was not as mature as she and her ex-husband had thought. "How far are your grades falling?" she asked.

"I'm getting two Cs." This was another shock. David had always been a good student who wanted to go on to a good college.

Karen told David how much she respected him for talking to her about this and he hugged her, something he hadn't done in a while. Then they got on the speakerphone with David's dad and worked out a new plan for keeping David motivated and helping him find limits to his extracurricular activities.

About a year later, when he was nearly seventeen, David did mature enough to handle his academic work with complete independence. Karen heard him crying, again, "Just let me be myself!" and *this time* he saw that he was better able to follow his own internal impulse to be free.

## DEVELOPMENTAL MILESTONES

The middle teen wants to be *himself,* an individual who is *different* from parents and the past. At some point, he will want to be an individual, different from even his own peers. His great task is to become a separate human entity who gains respect for what *he does and he is.* While he may decide to take on the respectable mask of his family, church, neighborhood, or clique, *he* will decide. *He* will try to select fragments of each social group and mandate and bring them together into a whole which *he* is.

### His Individuation

To fully individuate, your son needs to have the *freedom, responsibility, and opportunity* to construct his own identity, within the set limits and discipline systems he's used to. If he has not had consistent discipline before puberty, it's hard for a parent to impose it in his middle teens. If he has suffered significant abuse or other trauma before puberty, he may very well manifest the trauma stress now, wrapping his search for individuality in destructiveness toward the world that has hurt him. If he lacks appropriate social opportunity—food, shelter, clothing, racial equality—he is also more likely to act out his needs with destructiveness.

There is a vast range of individualization behavior among middle teens. Some "rebel"; some do not. Some have a girlfriend; some simply have many friends who are girls. Some wear the clothes others do; some wear costumes that seem strange to adults. Some stick close to their family religion; others emphasize the breaking down of the regimen, religious principles, and previously held rules.

Over the last few decades, inspired by the adolescent rebellions of the sixties, we've held the myth that for a boy to fully individuate, he has to be a rebel. Yet for the majority of our sons, rebellions are small rather than huge. The sixties were a fertile anomaly, not a model for the wider expanse of human history.

Recently I read a "Parent's Coalition" brochure put out by law-enforcement officials that said, "It's natural for children at a certain point in their development to rebel against parental authority." The use of the word "rebel" shows how we have, over a few decades, come to assume that rebellion is normal. I would argue that the word "renegotiate" is more developmentally accurate. *Rebellion* implies a destruction of authority, while *renegotiation* is what all but the most lost youth want. Most male teens want parents and other authorities to remain as stable resources in their lives. Only if a teen is being brutalized or neglected by the authority system will he want to destroy it. If your son is respected, listened to, consoled, challenged, and directed toward higher principles, he will navigate the middle teens with vigor, dignity, and good character.

Saying this is not to imply that rebellious and dangerous behavior will not occur. We will cover many of these dangerous behaviors later in this chapter.

### His Intellectual Development

You may very well find your middle-teen son almost obsessive about his homework, his debate team, his research, or other academic pursuits. If your boy is a learning-disabled or "special-needs" teen, this time may be quite difficult for him. It's hard for the special-needs boy to feel less than intense shame, and he will need extra care from his parents and teachers.

The middle teens are also a time when many boys begin to fall behind girls academically. The issues in the school system we discussed earlier hit a peak in adolescence. In our high schools, just less than 70 percent of the D's and F's are received by boys, and the majority of the A's by girls. Being vigilant about helping your son stay motivated for academic and intellectual work is a must, and later in this chapter we'll explore this idea further.

### His Emotional Development

By ages fifteen and sixteen, middle-teen boys are fairly well formed in their emotional responses. While they can always learn better emotional skills, we should not expect them to be very different at age twenty-five than they are now. If they talk a lot about their feelings, they probably will as adults. If they don't talk much, they probably won't as adults.

Middle-teen boys are deceptive in their need for love. Often they will not show how much they need you to let them know that they are worthy and special.

A mother wrote me about saying, "I'm glad you're my son," to her sixteen-year-old at dinner. The six-foot-two young man looked a little shocked. "Really?" he said. "Of course," she said. The young man reached over and gave her a big bear hug. He needed her approval, but she rarely saw this need because he seemed to like building the tough shell around himself that so many of our young men do.

Acculturation among peers continues to be a strong factor. While some peers help young males to express their feelings, many accuse expressive males of being "fags" and "sissies." As always, we do what we can to guide our son away from this kind of stereotyping.

**Biological Differences Between the Ways Adolescent Boys and Girls Process Emotions.**  Brain scans of adolescent males and females show that when under stress, a male's brain is more active in the region linked to quick tension release and physical responses. A female's brain, on the other hand, is more active in regions of the limbic system linked to quick verbal responses. The initial neural activity—the "source" of the response—happens in males in the reptilian brain (which controls quick aggression responses), while in females it happens in the cingulate gyrus, the part of the brain linked to emotional processing. This evidence correlates with male-female differences, especially in handling *stress and sadness.*

When middle-adolescent girls and boys experience rejection, sadness, pain, and stress, boys are much more likely (some studies estimate them to be about ten times more likely) to act out that stress with some kind of socially destructive or isolating act. Thus while part of the male-female difference in emotional responses lies in the fact that boys are socialized to be more physically active in dealing with stress and girls are socialized to "talk about it," the differences are biological.

As we've noted earlier, progesterone, the "bonding hormone," exists in large part to bond the female to her offspring, though it has myriad other applications. When under stress, a female, driven by this hormone, is more likely to seek out an immediate bond for assistance. The girl is more likely to have a conversation with a parent, peer, or friend. The male, driven by testosterone, is more likely to become aggressive—which can include being violent to himself or others.

He is socialized also to be more independent, so in the end he spends more time emotionally isolated, navigating internal impulses with less help. We must come to terms with this fact as we parent and mentor our middle-teen boys. *They risk emotional isolation, and we must make sure they don't fall into it.*

**Painful Separations.**   Emotional isolation can become worse as the middle-teen male navigates his normal adolescent separation from his mother (and then father). In order to individuate and become an independent adult, the boy must pull away from his mother. But the pull away is painful, especially if he is bonded with a single mother and has had, for years, no other similarly trustworthy bond. Sometimes these boys involve themselves in aggressive, even violent, behavior, and we punish them for it without realizing that a great deal of their aggression stems from their feelings of despair at having to pull away from the single trustworthy influence in their lives.

We can look at other primates for a stark illustration of this process. Many people will remember growing up during the sixties and seventies with the *National Geographic* television specials about Jane Goodall and the chimpanzees. Her work with primates provides a parallel to the human adolescent male during his times of separation anxiety. In her book *Through a Window,* Goodall writes about Prof, one of a mother chimpanzee's many sons, who was going through adolescence.

"For Prof, weaning [among chimps this is the physical act of separation that takes place during adolescence] was a time of despair, but because he was a male, he was far more aggressive in his misery than Pom [his sister] had been. Once he actually tumbled backwards right into a stream—and young chimpanzees are frightened of fast-moving water."

When a young male feels despair, he is more likely to make a risky response. Because this reaction is harbored deep within human and primate adolescent biology, we must treat it with real care and give it great concern. I believe that one of the main causes of violent and at-risk behavior among sons of single mothers is this biological/emotional response to mother-son separation. Our teen boys are struggling with their emotional impulses nearly alone.

### His Moral Development

Your middle-teen son often will be immensely compassionate. A teacher told me about a freshman boy who wasn't coming to first period—he was home, sleeping. The teacher organized a meeting between herself, the boy, and the principal, in which she explained to the student how much extra work he was causing her, and how much it disturbed the order of the class. The boy looked her in the eye and said, with real regret, "Mrs. Daley, I'm sorry. I just didn't see it your way. I didn't see how one guy could cause that kind of trouble, but you're right, and I'll do better." He acted more responsibly after that. His tiny rebellion and selfishness gave way to more powerful feelings of compassion.

Middle-teen boys can seem very tough and gruff, and often are, but just as often they are walking on the edge of great compassion.

## DISCIPLINE TECHNIQUES

Despite all their rhetoric to the contrary, middle-adolescent males want to be self-disciplined. Let's look at some crucial strategies by which we adults can help them. Some of these have appeared in previous chapters, but I'm revisiting them here because this is the very time when many parents relinquish such methods.

### Providing Rules and Consequences

Your family will benefit from a list of rules (even if oral) and clear prescriptions for which consequences will follow if they are broken.

Middle-teen males need help with deterrence. Knowing the rule and the consequence helps them deter themselves from a dangerous, bad action.

**It's Okay for Him to Suffer a Little.**   Natural consequences need to be felt and suffered by the young man. If he humiliates a younger sibling in an inappropriate way, he is acting immaturely and loses a privilege—perhaps use of the car. He has not earned the right to have an adult privilege. Your respect for him can be shown as he handles the difficulty of losing the car and then you admire him.

**He Needs to Make Mistakes.**   By age sixteen, some of our sons can become perfectionists. They can seem to think that if they make a mistake, they are shameful, terrible people. It's important to encourage your

## The Range of Normal

It's normal for the boy to be very judgmental of others, parents, and at times himself.

It's normal for the boy to appear selfish and unable to admit his own flaws.

It's normal for the boy to go through various phases of liking one parent more than the other.

It's normal for the boy to become competitive with his father and buck his authority.

It is normal for the boy to want to avoid prolonged explanations of feelings or actions, either on his own part or on his parents'. The boy often prefers concrete, quick conversations.

It's normal for the boy to be very concise—and expect it from you—until he finds something he really needs or wants to talk about. In that case, he can be almost selfishly invasive of your time, and can go on for hours.

It's normal for the boy to get into a phase of arguing *everything*.

It's normal for the boy to feel unchallenged intellectually, and to complain of boredom.

It's normal for the boy to want to take on more authority at school—start a club, a school newspaper, a new sport, a new book a week.

It's normal for the boy, if he is not academically inclined, to feel this fact harshly and to compare himself unfavorably to others. The middle-teen years are a time when a young man comes to know his own flaws—even if he won't admit them aloud—and he can feel easily hurt by them.

It's normal for the boy to be afraid of failure. Recently, I asked a group of middle teens what they most feared. Every one of them replied: "Failure." These boys are scared of not making it in life. This fear is normal but can get easily masked in males who practice bravado, posturing, or stoicism, or who use some other armor that covers deep insecurity.

It's normal for the boy to use words when he needs help, but it's also normal for him to use quick physical responses, too.

son to make mistakes and to grow from them. Doing something wrong and getting caught is useful. No one is ever too old for this truism.

### Creating Discipline in Your Verbal Interactions

We often benefit in conversations with middle teens by using very concrete words. While allowing the young man to argue on and on about a rule or consequence can be entertaining and lead to some good moral debates, we should end the discussion when it needs to end. "Son, that's interesting, but you knew the rule and you broke it. Now it's time to accept your responsibility."

**Show More Than Tell.**   A middle teen will often resist being *told* what to do, but he might accept being *shown*. Show him what to do by being a good role model and by doing things with him. *He is not too old for you to do activities and work with him.* He still wants the bonding time. Furthermore, if you can engage in moral service activities to-gether—through church or social-justice committees—he will be seeing your sense of justice in action, which is better than always hearing your "opinions" about things.

**Praise and Criticism.**   Your son still needs a higher ratio of positive reinforcement to negative. Think about praising your son at least twice as much as you criticize him. I don't mean to say you should critique his behavior less, but if you're going to critique it a lot, make sure to admire and respect him even more.

**Disagreement.**   Discipline and decorum are to be followed even when parent and middle teen disagree vehemently—about politics, reli-gion, a set of friends, a family procedure, a rule. At a minimum, during a disagreement, neither child nor parent ought to name-call or inter-rupt. These things may indeed happen, and decorum may fall apart—but the chaos need not be sanctioned in the family. The family always needs to be a safe place.

### Practicing Creative Discipline

Teen males are certainly creative about the trouble they can get into. We need to be equally creative about how we discipline. With a chuckle I recently read about a father in Alabaster, Alabama, whose sixteen-year-old son got his third speeding ticket and stayed out past curfew one too many times. The father chained his son's pickup to a tree and put a sign in the window: "This is what happens when a teenager does not mind." The truck remained chained there for six weeks. "I hate being that rough on my boy," the dad said, "but if he ain't going to listen to me, I have no choice."

A wonderful resource for tips on how to provide discipline for teens is *Teen Tips,* by Tom McMahon. It has inspired me for years.

### Practicing Immediate Accountability

Regarding teen discipline, Missouri Attorney General Jay Nixon recently said something very wise: "When we study juvenile delinquency we find that the severity of the punishment for a first offense is less important than the fact that the parents or someone else *gives* a punishment." He related a story from when he was a teenager. His mother told him to be home by 9:00 P.M., but he came home at 9:30. This was typical middle-teen behavior—forgetfulness, testing authorities, independence seeking. In his words, "I didn't get the death penalty, but I got punished—I didn't get to use the car for a week." We need to make our teen boys immediately accountable when they mess up.

### Holding Appropriate Expectations of Young Men

We live in an interesting time regarding middle teens. We've just ended about two decades of thinking that being a good parent means letting them do much of what they please. It was a noble experiment, one that grew partially out of our confusion about what "adolescence" and "teenager" mean. Earlier in the century we thought of these terms as meaning "big child," and so made our sons' lives rigid. Later, we thought of them as meaning "young adult," so we tried to treat our teens like adults by giving them freedom.

Now we have come to find the middle ground. Our teens are both children and adults. While we can give them some latitude, we also must hold them to high expectations.

Even if you have a boy at high moral risk, your expectations for him can fit the ones below. Discipline techniques and discipline systems for middle teens go much better if the boy knows our expectations.

- It is appropriate to expect your son to communicate with you— even if for a time he communicates only by creating conflict. At least he's communicating.

- It is appropriate to expect him to respect the core rules of your house. If he wants one of these changed, he needs to call a family conference (see chapter 6). Secondary rules might change on their own, just by attrition.

- It is appropriate to expect him to fulfill his responsibilities for chores and other work around the house.

- It is appropriate to expect him to put work, homework, and other responsibilities above entertainment.

- It is appropriate to expect, if the family is in financial need, that he contribute to the family from his work paycheck, if he works.

- It is appropriate to expect him to save money toward college and the future.

- It is appropriate to expect him to be courteous toward elders and authorities.

## MORAL TEACHING

There is an old story from the Muslim Sufi tradition. A young man met God one day. God said to him, "I like the way you live your life. I am going to grant you one wish. What is your wish?"

The young man replied, "I would like to go about the world doing good without even knowing I'm doing good."

"Why do you want to be ignorant of your own good deeds?" God asked.

The young man replied, "I have had to think every act out to try to see if it is right or wrong. I do not mind this, for every moral thought is an act of humility in your creation. But if I could have one wish, I would wish also to just do good as a part of my being."

God was very impressed with this young man. God thought this such a unique and wonderful wish, He granted it not only to the young man but to all human beings. Now all humans have the capacity to know what is right and to do what is right as an inherent part of their being.

This story is about the essence of middle adolescence, in which the teen is becoming capable of true moral intuition—of knowing what is right and acting on it as a part of his very being. He does the right thing not only because he is obedient and because it brings him social approval but because he has the ability to choose, by moral intuition, the right act.

Moral teaching during these years is very compelling when we add this notion of intuition to all the earlier teaching. These boys still need help dealing with temptations; they still need help being obedient; they need people to verbally and intellectually spar with—in other words, they need pieces of everything we've already given them, as much as they need us to let go of boyhood simplifications. They need us to help them develop *their* intuition so that, at a party, at a business meeting, in a future crisis, at a community gathering, these young men do the right thing because it is their nature.

### Holding High Moral Expectations

He needs you to teach him the most moral thing to do in a situation. His peers will easily take on the job of teaching him the least moral thing. He'll disagree with you and even argue, but he'll be in the middle of a bad situation one night and will intuitively remember the high standards you've taught.

Practically speaking, this kind of moral training often means that we appeal to the higher moral principles he is developing. Laurence Steinberg and Ann Levine call this "appealing to the adolescent's better self" in their wonderful book *You and Your Adolescent.* They suggest you say these sorts of things to your teen.

## Rules to Live By

Providing middle teens with reasonable rules does not show we distrust them or "still treat them as children." It shows we care about them and want them to act like adults. Adults live by strict rules. Because we are coming to see our middle teens as adults, we can engage them in helping us set the rules.

Here are some rules that build trust and introduce some flexibility.

1. A middle teen will call his parents and tell them where he is and/or where he is going. This rule is followed not because a son is mistrusted but because it's considerate to tell people you love where they can reach you if there is an emergency or if you are needed. Worrying one's parents is a "rite" of middle adolescence, but it is not something to encourage.

2. Some appropriate silence will be respected: If a middle teen doesn't want to talk, he won't be forced to. But parents will ask him what he did, how he spent his time, and how he is doing—because they care about him. And if the parents think something is wrong or he is hurting in some way, they will consider it appropriate to break down the silence.

3. A middle teen will help his parents create the reasonable rules of the house.

4. A middle teen may not call his parents names, curse at them, diss them in public, or in other ways humiliate them. Parents have the right to ask a son not to use certain kinds of language—as a son has the right to ask his parents to desist from language offensive to him.

5. A middle teen's privacy will be respected, but not to the extent that he is allowed to put a lock on his door. The parents' privacy will be respected by the son as well.

6. A middle teen is required to share certain meals with the family, and certain outings with the extended family.

7.  A middle teen still needs to come home at a set time every night, perhaps somewhere between 9:00 P.M. and 10:00 P.M. on week-nights, and later on weekends.

8.  A middle teen needs to support the family as much as he can, and his parents will support his endeavors as much as they can, with words, finances, motivational help, and encouragement.

9.  A middle teen may not use the car or any other family item to en-gage in an activity that is morally offensive to the parents.

10. A middle teen will get his work done before leisure or entertain-ment, or negotiate a way to accomplish both in time.

These rules imply a certain kind of son—a son who will obey and who will accept consequences when he doesn't; a son who will take part in his family's happiness; a son who will be a little patient in his develop-ment of his independence. If parents and other caregivers have done their job up to now, the son will be this kind of Good Son. He will be de-railed by now if he is experiencing severe trauma—residual effects of a parental divorce or other destabilizing set of events—or was raised with-out his needs for moral and discipline development met in earlier years.

As this chapter continues, we will continue to look at how to help ado-lescent boys who are in a state of emergency or otherwise destabilized. Other fine resources are *A Parent's Guide for Suicidal and Depressed Teens*, by Kate Williams, *You and Your Adolescent*, by Laurence Stein-berg and Ann Levine, and *Toughlove*, by Phyllis and David York and Ted Wachtel.

"Wouldn't you like to be known as a responsible (or caring, sincere, honest) person?"

"This is a favor we are asking of you. Think about it as a good deed."

"Try to look at this from my point of view. What would you do if you were the parent?"

"I'm tired and grouchy right now, and I really need your full cooperation. Thank you."

"How do you think it sounds when you talk to your brother like that?"

"We're trusting you to do what we've asked while we're gone. Can we depend on you to do that?"

"We expect you to be a responsible person, even when those around you aren't. We probably do expect more of you than some other parents expect of their kids. But we expect a lot of you because we think a lot of you."

This last one is so important, and so often missed by parents. Often parents of middle-teen boys think that because the child sometimes resists our expectations, we should back off. Just the opposite is true: We need to have very consistent expectations for *the highest good.*

### Using Stories, Moral Puzzles, and Moral Debates

When I travel to high schools to speak, I give students a moral story and invite debate. "Three boys did such and such to another boy. Was it moral, or immoral?"

Moral stories and parables—for instance, from the Bible or folk tales—used to be a central part of our ancestors' lives. Sacred texts from all over the world contain heavy doses of parable and fable, which provide young people with entertaining moral puzzles to stimulate their development. In rites of passage throughout human history, adolescent males have been told stories and been required to construct their own of who they are and how they fit in the moral and spiritual paradigms of their culture.

While most of the moral teaching that parents can give a young man has already occurred by the time he becomes fifteen, he nonetheless remains open to moral and spiritual tales and is striving to figure out how he fits in his culture's mythic story. For the most part, young men today do this activity *without the presence of elders, and through imagery disseminated through media.* To some extent, we each need to take back the role of storyteller and story listener in our sons' lives—asking them what they're reading and why; directing them toward books and movies that build moral intuition. Listed in the Appendix at the back of this book are suggested books and movies to inspire moral discussion with boys.

### Sexual Morality and Romance

While many middle teens will neither have intercourse nor find true love, fully half *do* have intercourse by the time they are sixteen, and many *do* feel they are finding true love. How shall we help them navigate these waters?

Sexually speaking, middle-teen males are hormonally driven toward frequent ejaculation. They'll accomplish much of this act through masturbation, wet dreams, and sexual fantasy. Sometimes they'll pursue it in the company of females. Because testosterone provides heightened sex drive, middle teens need to learn a great deal of self-discipline and self-regulation in regard to sexual functioning.

As a culture, we provide the *highest amount of sexual stimulation to our youth and the least sexual teaching.* I have never lived in or studied another culture that provides its youth with thousands of sexually stimulating images and yet gives them almost no concomitant sexual education. At sixteen, your son probably absorbs twenty to forty sexual images a day and generates at least that many images in sexual fantasy, but perhaps gets a lesson in sexual morality and maturity once a month, if that.

The biological components that build sexual fascination in the male are often not shared by the female. Her hormones and brain system direct her somewhat more toward "romantic fantasy" than toward overt sexual fantasy. Because middle-teen boys and girls often are poorly trained in their own internal imperatives, nor know each other very well yet, they don't know how to care for each other well. It is our job to teach them; it is their job to experiment *based* on what we've taught. The key mistake modern culture makes in matters of sex and teens is that it *believes youth should learn most of their skills by experimentation rather than by previous teaching.* In fact, in order to do right by our sons, we must *teach* them a great deal about sexuality—*constantly* discuss sexuality and true love with them; answer questions as they ask and even when they don't ask; provide them with our own life stories, our own pitfalls and learning experiences; and direct them to other people and literature on the subject.

In addition to discussion, of course, we must help our sons develop along a healthy sexual and romantic path by providing useful parameters. Here are some parameters I hope you'll find useful in your care of your middle-teen son.

1. Dating is allowed to begin at sixteen—this is "alone dating": no group, no supervision. Girls are getting more aggressive about wanting to date guys, so part of getting our son to wait involves teaching him ways to bond with girls without dating.

2. Our son's room is never locked when there's a girl in it unless we have made a special arrangement condoning his sexual activity.

3. We instruct our son to meet a girl's family before he takes her on a date. We also require him to bring the girl home to meet us.

4. Even if he is with a girl, he is required to tell us where he'll be. Just because he's dating doesn't mean family courtesy goes away.

5. We teach him that sexual intercourse is a sacred act. We talk to him about all the other ways to discover sexual gratification with a female that do not involve the act of penetration.

6. If he is not going to abstain from sexual activity, we teach him to wait between six months and a year to get to know a girl before having intercourse; we encourage other forms of gratification during this time. We tell our own stories of growing up if these will help inspire him to see that he can be patient.

7. We teach him to accept "No!" from a girl. We teach him to talk about sex with a potential partner before pursuing it.

8. We teach him that he can resist emotional manipulation by girls. He need not attach his whole developing self to one girl's love for him.

9. We show him that no matter the question he has, he can come to us and we will help him find an answer.

10. Publicly—e.g., in school—caregivers should teach middle teens *both* abstinence and contraception. While abstinence training alone is appropriate for early teens, it is not realistic for many middle teens. These middle teens must learn to use condoms to protect against disease and pregnancy.

11. We make sure our sons understand that sex and love are moral issues. If the young man gets a girl pregnant, he's just as responsible as the girl.

12. Grown men must make sure to volunteer to go into schools and talk to young males about these issues, augmenting what we do at home, and fulfilling the duty men have to raise the next generation of males in their community.

It is generally good to remember that no matter how you've raised your son, he lives in a highly sexualized culture, so he may not be as resistant to "temptation" as you think. Fadi Auro, a middle teen in El Cajon, California, recently made this analogy: When a group of people get into a swimming pool and keep walking around in a circle in the water, there comes a point at which they no longer need to walk— the whirlpool-like momentum of the water carries them. This, he said, is what it's like to live in our sexualized culture. It is immensely difficult, especially for testosterone-driven boys, to resist the internal and external pulls toward teen intercourse. They need all the help they can get in order to be sexually responsible.

### Handling a Son Who Has a Drinking Problem

A dad recently wrote me about his sons, ages fifteen and sixteen: "I know they drink at parties. I've restricted my fifteen-year-old pretty well. But my sixteen-year-old has started drinking more than just on Saturday night. I think it's starting to affect his schoolwork. What should I do? Is he becoming a chronic drinker?"

He may well be. The parents of this boy, and others like him, should definitely worry.

Alcohol education needs to begin in early adolescence as a concerted effort by family, school, and media. Nearly all boys will experiment with alcohol at some time during adolescence. As with cigarette experimentation (a puff now and then, or a drink now and then), we don't need to overreact. It's all part of the risk-taking behavior normal to adolescent boys and adolescents in general. We need to provide education about what's right, provide discipline as needed, and move on.

*But if we have any questions at all about whether our son's drinking is going beyond normal experimentation, we must get second and third opinions.* School counselors, the other parent, extended family members, friends who have already raised teens, and professionals are our allies. Once we determine our son is drinking inappropriately (more than once in a while on a weekend night if he's pubescent or older), we need to confront him (with other allies beside us, if needed) and provide the discipline needed.

When confronting your son and his peer community, try to fully understand what the youth are doing and whether you yourself hold some myths about their behavior. The most predominant myth is: *Oh, he's just taking a sip at the party.* In all likelihood, he's getting drunk, not just sipping, especially if he's fifteen or older. *Studies consistently show that teens generally drink to get drunk.*

Recent studies, like a sweeping one conducted by the National Institute of Alcohol Abuse and Alcoholism, have provided us with valuable information on teen drinking. Every parent needs to know the following.

1. Adolescents who begin drinking before age fifteen are two times more likely to abuse alcohol later in life than those who

begin drinking after age fifteen. *A thirteen-year-old who has begun drinking is 44 percent more likely to become an alcoholic even if his family has no genetic history of alcoholism.*

2. Binge drinking and frequent drinking is increasing *not only among high school students but among middle school students as well.* Twenty-five percent of tenth-graders reported binge drinking (more than five drinks at a party) within two weeks of the survey; so did 15 percent of eighth-graders.

3. While both male and female teens drink, boys are more likely to drink more at a given time, to binge drink more, and to become violent more while drinking. Alcohol affects male and female hormonal systems somewhat differently. *Among teen males, alcohol use correlates with rape, violent behavior, and other crimes.*

4. Our kids don't know as much as we may think. A recent survey of teens conducted by the American Academy of Pediatrics found that almost a third of them didn't realize that a can of beer is as intoxicating as a shot of vodka. The survey also found that about half considered a "designated driver" a person who "drinks less than I do."

5. *Sixty-four percent of teens ages sixteen to nineteen responded to a survey about alcohol use by admitting that they had consumed alcohol in the previous month.*

6. The average age when our teens begin drinking is fourteen, even if heavy drinking may not show up till a year or two later.

7. Media use affects alcohol use. A Stanford University study found that teens who watch a lot of television and music videos are more likely than other young people to start drinking. *Alcohol is the most common beverage shown on television commercials and in TV shows.*

What is the most profound influence on whether your son will drink? Studies show it is *you*, the parents. If you don't drink much, your son most probably won't either. A responsible model creates a responsible son. If you insist on responsible behavior regarding alcohol (as with tobacco and drugs), your son is likely to be responsible. Debate the issue with him; talk about it; show him the research; insist on alcohol (and tobacco and drug) education programs in schools; help him navigate peer pressure.

Studies show that peers are the second most profound influence on whether your son will drink (media is the third). If all your son is doing is hanging out with inappropriate drinkers, he will probably drink. If he's going to parties where there is booze, he'll drink. We never need to allow our son to consistently go into a situation where there will be substances dangerous to him (and illegal for his age). It is better to stop whatever we're doing and give him a fun substitute for that party—take him to do something he's always wanted to on that night instead of letting him go to the party.

If you have lost control of your son in regards to drinking, then teen AA programs become important. *If your son is drinking inappropriately, he is at high risk for criminal behavior and legal trouble.* This situation should be considered an emergency. If a family "intervention" is needed, it must happen immediately. Programs like Toughlove also are very useful. For more information on this issue, the American Counseling Association (800-347-6647, ext. 222) provides resources through the Century Council. One good resource for schools is the thirty-minute video and student activity guide on teen drinking called "Brandon Tells His Story." This powerful program, oriented to helping educate teens (and even scare them in a healthy way), won the Freddie Award from the American Medical Association.

### Challenging Teen Drug Use

A mother recently wrote that her son, age fifteen, "had very red eyes the other day when he came home from school. I smoked marijuana when I was younger. I knew the signs. I confronted him, and he promised never to smoke again, but he wouldn't tell me who gave him the marijuana. He insisted he's never done any other drugs. I was very upset, but tried to stay calm. I got his dad on the phone, his grandpa, who he really trusts. Even though Ricky got embarrassed and ashamed, I think all the family attention did him good. I think it might have brought us all closer, too. But here's my question: Should I have grilled him about who he did it with, and then called the other kids' parents? Should I have called the school? I'm never sure where the line is—I don't want to kill his independence or embarrass him among his friends."

As we have said before,

- *If you have followed a good discipline system throughout the boy's life, and if there is no genetic tendency for the boy to abuse substances, most probably he will not do much more during his teen years than explore substances.*
- It is in general a good idea to stay calm when confronting him.
- The boy nevertheless needs to experience some severe punishment, which he himself may help devise—a significant loss of privileges, a new curfew for after-school life, being grounded for an extended period.
- *We don't show we care for him by letting him get away with an illegal behavior—we show we care by extending consequences to his actions.*

Should we interrogate our child until he tells us who else was involved with him in the dangerous and high-risk behavior? Depending on his age, we should. If our son is a middle or late teen, we should ask and insist. It is our duty, and the young man must understand it that way. Generally, if we are at all close to our son, we will probably know who his friends are, anyway, and we will not have to interrogate. If the young man absolutely won't "tell on his friends," we have to treat him like a young adult and try to get him to tell his friends that they are at high risk. If we are in any kind of mentorial relationship with the friends, we can talk to them ourselves. But we must keep trying to *find out who the friends are, and to involve their family systems.*

Your own intuition will have to tell you if this involvement will do more harm than good in your relationship with your son and community. Except in the most tenuous and fragile parent-adolescent relationships, I find that the adolescent community *needs the adults to ferret out who is troubled and come together to help them.* If one of the other kids is definitely involved in dangerous behavior, especially in a consistent way, your son needs to "be a man," step up to the adult's table, and get adult help.

On issues where there is a possibility of larger crisis later—addiction, car accidents, falling grade performance, and criminal activity, all of which are possible once drug involvement begins—it is important to put *community safety ahead of our son's "need for independence."* Our sons have, throughout adolescence, ample opportunity to "become independent" and "remain loyal to their peer group." Drug activity is not one of the opportunities we must protect. Among my relatives and yours just a few generations ago, it would have been anathema to allow growing children to get involved in dangerous activity without some kind of intervention or supervision.

There is no reason for us to be different now.

## A HEALTHY MORAL AND EMOTIONAL ENVIRONMENT

"Programs that succeed with young men understand the tremendous need that boys have for information and guidance," write Carol Beemer and Joy Fallek, social workers who work every day with middle teens. This is the kind of environment we must furnish our young men.

### Trustable, Adaptable Parenting

Studies continually show that the single most important moral and emotional influence on the lives of middle teens are their parents. Parents still are the people the middle teen wants to trust. He trusts them when parents keep their promises. He trusts them when parents apologize for saying or doing hurtful things, and fess up when they've made a mistake. He trusts them when parents display clear authority *and* adaptability.

**Allow Him to Experiment with Trust.**   Lucia Herndon, a reporter for the Philadelphia *Inquirer,* told me about her sixteen-year-old son. "He comes to his father and me for money and permissions," she said, "but when he comes to me, it's like he always feels invaded by me. But he'll get the same exact response from Dad that I gave, and he's all right with it." She gave a wonderful example.

Son: "I need twenty dollars."

Dad: "What for?"

Son: "The movies."

Dad: "Okay. Here. Be home by ten, right?"

Son: "Okay."

Lucia noted with a smile, "If I'd said the same thing to him, he'd scowl at me."

This month he might like Dad, next month Mom. This fickleness is very normal. If the parent who is "on the outs" for a period takes it personally, the son's trust is traumatized. He needs to be able to pull away and come back through these testings and experiments. His home environment ought not be severely disrupted by a parent's outrage at the testing and pulling away. Lucia handled her son's pulling away with serenity, and it paid off.

**Maintain Consistent Rules in Both Houses.**   If there has been a divorce and your son lives in two houses, discipline and moral intuition are more easily built in a middle teen when there is consistency—*especially on core rules*—in both houses. If in Dad's house he can stay out till any hour, but in Mom's he has to be home by 10:00 on weekdays, he is at a moral disadvantage. The longer the list of conflicting rules, the more time he spends trying to decide *which* core rules are right.

If divorced parents cannot agree on core rules, talk to your son about why you hold *your* rules. You need not shame the other parent, but you can try to help the boy develop his own intuition.

**Let Him Always Know You Are There for Him.**   The middle teen needs to know you are there for him. He needs to know he can call you at any time for help. He needs you to let him know that even if he's drunk or done something wrong, you will help him. He still wants you to go to some of his games and recitals, and he especially wants the parent there who has not been there much before.

## Work and the Workplace

Should my middle teen get a job? This is a question many parents ask.

Some parents say, "I don't want him working, I want him concentrating on school."

Others say, "I want and need him to work—it's good for his personal development and it helps the family."

Geoffrey Canada, author of *Reaching Up for Manhood* and president of the New York–based Rheedlen Centers for Children and Families, says this about his experience with youth and work: "Many of the young people at Rheedlen graduate from high school and go on to college because of one thing—work. We have found work to be a very effective tool in keeping boys involved in school. For millions of teenagers growing up in America, school is something that they feel only marginally connected to." Rheedlen Centers specifically connect a boy's schoolwork with job work.

Experts like Canada agree that work in the middle-teen years is good for lower-income boys, but what about middle-class or high-income boys? The National Research Council and Institute of Medicine recently released a study that tracked teens and the workplace. They found that *eight out of every ten American teenagers hold down a job sometime during their school years.*

They also found that young people who work more than twenty hours a week, no matter their economic background, are *less* likely to finish high school and more likely to use drugs and enter the criminal-justice system. The strain of home, friendships, romance, school, and more than twenty hours of work is often too much.

Work for teens is an important way for them to learn punctuality, money management, responsibility, loyalty, fairness, empathy for working parents, and self-sacrifice. I started working in restaurants just before I turned fifteen. It was an essential part of my passage into manhood. I highly recommend it for teen males fifteen or older. As with everything, though, it needs to be tempered by your intuition and by the principle of moderation.

Here are some keys for making "work" work for you.

- Make sure your son is contributing to the family budget, not just spending his money on new shoes, candy, movies, entertainment.
- Make sure he's working a reasonable amount of time for his physical, emotional, social, and moral maturity—generally less than twenty hours per week.
- Make sure you get to know his workplace situation, even if it means dropping in just to meet the manager.
- Help your son prioritize—if he gives up athletics for work, is this the right priority? At ages fifteen and sixteen, a boy ought to try to participate in one sport, enjoy healthy academic success, work, and, if possible, do another extracurricular activity—like music, drama, or art. This scheduling will require good time management not only on your son's part but also on the family's.

In the first developmental episode of a boy's life, we tried hard to teach him obedience and cooperation; in the second, social rules and manners; now, in the third, teaching him responsibility is absolutely crucial. Helping him work effectively is one of the best ways to do so.

### The School

Though we have covered this topic elsewhere, it is essential we not forget that after parents, teachers are often the most profound elder influence on the middle teen. From sex education to ethics curricula, the schools are moral educators of our children. Honor codes and rules must be posted and enforced. And parents and schools must develop deep bonds—parent-teacher and administrator-parent—so the school is not just a warehouse of bodies but an environment of the soul.

A mother wrote me about her fifteen-year-old son: "He has been a good student but now is getting bad grades. He and I are kind of estranged, so I can't really find out what's going on.

Our adolescent boys drop out of school four times more than our adolescent girls. As we've noted throughout this parenting plan, we must constantly be vigilant about our sons' school life and performance because there are many ways in which our schools let our boys down.

While many adolescents in academic trouble have shown signs earlier, many do not until now. Many boys do fine in earlier grades as they get a lot of attention and stability in life; then that stability disappears—perhaps because of a divorce or other trauma—causing male fragility to manifest in an attention or impulse problem in adolescence. In this case, school performance hinges on divorcing parents returning as quickly as possible to healthy caregiving roles and, if needed, getting the boy counseling and getting the new extended family involved. *It is not unlikely that a young man will have a delayed reaction to the divorce trauma, manifesting it in diminished school performance a few years after the actual traumatic event.*

Many adolescent boys also lose focus on schoolwork because of excessive TV, video game, or Internet use.

Other issues we've been able to identify are

- learning disabilities or other neurological problems, especially reading problems;
- lack of male role models in classrooms;
- when adults don't stress homework over parties, the adolescent boys stray;
- overemphasis on one activity—perhaps one single sport;
- obsession with a girl or intense relationship with a girl he's too immature to handle;

- bad teachers, boring classes;
- the young man feels disrespected by teachers and/or humiliated by other students; and
- rebellion against parents with too-high expectations or parents who have hurt the son in some way.

It is also important to note that a boy may just be a C student, and that's that—at least for a time. For a year or more he may hinge his identity and sense of peer belonging on the desire to be "normal" or "average."

### Media Use

To a great extent, we can no longer control our fifteen- or sixteen-year-old's media use. Still we should not avoid issuing rules or opinions. To shuck this responsibility would show we don't care about his development. Part of the parent's and teacher's job during a teen's middle adolescence is to deepen the conversation with him about the growing power of media in his life. Parents still need to go to movies with him and talk afterward, and watch shows that he likes (which we may not like) and debate their moral content.

Now is a good time to think about allowing private, unsupervised Internet access. Like driving a car and dating, having this privilege is an appropriate rite of passage for a sixteen-year-old. If your son is mature enough to know how to handle the Net, you might hold a celebration as you give him the reins. At some point your son will probably start exploring the painful and desperately sad pornography on the Net, and you will want to decide if he's mature enough to handle the chaotic and absolute freedom the Net represents. I hope you'll still talk to him about what he sees on it.

Your son will probably go to movies and listen to music he chooses, but he needs an elder who tries to help him find the hidden parables in what he's seeing and hearing. I recall playing my own father an album by Rush—a 1970s heavy-metal band. He read the lyrics and realized which Ayn Rand books they were based on, got me those books, and started me on a very challenging search through the moral system Rand represented. This action led to many conversations between my father and myself. Like most teens, I gained from having a "third person" in the moral dialogue. It wasn't just my dad and I, but Ayn Rand was in it, too, a buffer between us.

Time in front of the screen still should be monitored. If your son is coming home from school and watching many hours of television, he's living an unhealthy life. A few hours of TV, video, and movies combined—two to three hours a day—ought to be the maximum. Some days he'll just want to "zone out" for more than that, so, again, sports events and weekends can be exceptions.

### The Rituals of Life: The Third Rite of Passage

In their freshman or sophomore year of high school, our boys benefit from a third rite of passage. Getting a driver's license is a built-in rite, as is the move from junior high to high school itself. Yet each young man needs more.

Each young man needs a rite in which being a man is celebrated. Each boy needs to spend time, during this rite, with people who know how to celebrate the great adventure that maleness is. This third rite can be like the second, which we detailed in the previous chapter.

Outdoor adventures are good venues for rites at this time, since the boys have so much physical energy. Boy Scouts also encourages this kind of outdoor adventure. My own *A Fine Young Man* is a resource for developing this rite, as is the book *Boy into Man,* by Bernard Weiner.

### CAMERON'S STORY

Cameron was one of the middle teens in Don Meyerhoff's seven-week Alternative Program for high-risk boys. Don is a volunteer in this program, a paramedic by training who had been a high-risk boy himself. As an adult, he became a Big Brother for many years. Now he volunteered

in this Pennsylvania program to help drug-addicted, alcoholic, even violent boys. Like many alternative-education programs around the country, this one relied on adult volunteers who could really talk to the kids,
handle their dissing, and gradually build trust. Building trust isn't easy,
as Don can attest.

In week two of the program, Don talked about high-risk behavior
with the boys—they booed him and talked to one another, withholding
their respect and common decency.

Don came back and kept trying. In week three he showed a video,
and a tall, angry Cameron, sixteen, threw an acorn at him. With
Cameron in the lead, so did most of the other boys. Don received a bar-
rage of acorns. He showed his anger verbally and left the room.
Cameron and the rest of the boys assumed he'd never be back.

Week four came, and Don was back. He knew how to talk to these
guys. He told them they were assholes but that he had been one, too.
He told them they were testing him and pushing him and trying to
get him to hate them the way they felt other adults hated them. He told
them he wouldn't hate them. He told them he'd keep coming back, and
he did.

In week five, Cameron came up to him to talk. He told him he and
the other boys were surprised he would put up with them. "You put up
with more than my dad ever did," Cameron said, "and you don't even
know us." Over the next two weeks, Cameron, as the ringleader, led the
others in giving Don a modicum of respect. By the end of the seven
weeks, Don had become trustworthy to the boys; he had become, in his
words, "a constant. These kids had so few constants in their lives, they
were ready to find one. They just needed to try to break me down. Once
I couldn't be broken down, they trusted me. They were hungry to trust
me, actually. That day after the acorns was a breakthrough for Cameron,
at least, and I think for some of the other boys."

Unfortunately, like so many programs, this alternative program was
barely funded—it couldn't extend beyond the seven weeks. In a sense,
it created a "constant" in Cameron's life, then pulled that constant away.
Yet Cameron did form a small bond with a man of character, and took
on just a little more character himself.

Don kept one of the acorns thrown at him. It hangs from a chain on the rearview mirror of his car. Don told me that when he glances at it in his car he thinks of the tall, rude, but morally and emotionally hungry sixteen-year-old, and hopes the boy will remember what it means to be a man.

# ELEVEN

# Pre-Adulthood

NURTURING YOUNG MEN OF

SEVENTEEN, EIGHTEEN, AND BEYOND

I was researching and teaching at Ankara University in the mid-1980s when I met Mehmet, an eighteen-year-old who constantly got in trouble at school and on the street. He got in fights, and had already had one run-in with the police. I wanted to reach out to Mehmet and some of his troubled friends. Somewhere along the line, I don't remember exactly when, I decided to try to become friends with them as a way of helping. I was only ten years older than they were, anyway.

Even though my Turkish colleagues warned me against it, I invited my students to call me by my first name, and I went out with Mehmet and his friends to the backgammon cafés. I told my wife, "I'll be able to create trust with these guys. Maybe I can really help them." My plan was heartfelt, but it didn't quite work. Mehmet and his friends kept getting into trouble. And now they got into the additional trouble of cheating on my tests and generally rebelling against me. Mehmet's attitude not only went opposite of my hopes but affected the whole classroom. He felt free to treat me like a buddy in class, damaging the kind of authority any teacher needs to control a large classroom (I had sixty students in one class, almost three hundred students total in my five classes).

For weeks, as my Turkish colleagues helped me sort through the mess I'd made, I felt very humbled and did a lot of thinking and growing. I remembered that back in graduate school in the U.S., when I was a teaching assistant at Eastern Washington University, I had tried similar moves with certain male students—especially ones like a red-haired freshman named Eddie and a bored sophomore named Josh—who were hard to discipline. In nearly every case, when I tried to be "one of the guys," I reached negative results. These young guys liked me for a while, but then ended up disrespecting me. They needed elders who were friendly authorities, but not "friends." They needed to be able to trust me, not because I dissolved my authority as an elder but because I held my authority in a balanced and dignified way.

Mehmet, Eddie, and Josh were searchers after themselves—every pre-adult male knows he's in the midst of an intense identity search. I had to make mistakes to discover how best to help pre-adult males find themselves. No doubt you have made or will make your own mistakes. A boy's pre-adult years are sweet, rich, but confusing for those of us committed to shepherding the male in his late teens and early twenties into adult life.

## DEVELOPMENTAL MILESTONES

Throughout the years of his pre-adulthood, your son will probably become focused on a set of activities and visions—getting to college, work, sports scholarships, academics, music, or even, like Mehmet, making trouble. What is going on inside these young men? They'll tell you some of what they are experiencing, especially if they trust your authority and your friendship. They may have renegotiated their relationship with you in their middle teens, and now may start growing closer to you again. Or they still may be pulling away. As you watch their signals, you will notice many ways in which they are adults, yet many ways in which they remain kids. They can vote at eighteen; they sign up for the draft; they may have had sex for the first time. They may act like young men on their own, but then an emotional setback can make them wish they were boys again, innocent and sweetly beloved in their parents' arms. While they generally behave with moral competency, they can suddenly fall into a series of absolutely stupid acts, making you think you've failed as a moral custodian.

### His Intellectual Development

By now you'll have a clear sense of who your son is intellectually. For many pre-adult males, academic interests will clarify themselves. Even though these may change in college or once he enters the workplace, he will still probably have some clear direction. For others, the junior and senior years of high school are intellectually unclear—the young man feels adrift. During the pre-adult years, some parents can let go of having to motivate their sons to do homework, and others have to push the boy to fulfill academic obligations nearly every day.

Cognitive development in the brain is pretty much complete by now, although the young man will keep learning things all his life. Your son has, in cognitive terms, nearly an adult's brain.

### His Emotional Development

Even if he doesn't express it, your pre-adolescent son will fear failure and at times become depressed when he fails. Stakes are now getting higher for him, and he will have to experience some real pain of failure—not getting into the college he wanted, or breaking up with a beloved girlfriend. He will need to talk about his feelings, but he also may find other ways of handling his emotions—including holding long silences.

He may very well find himself less emotionally developed than the girls he's trying to learn about and love. In the pre-adult years, males intensively try to develop emotional maturity commensurate with that of females. These young men realize, even if unconsciously, that if they are going to be emotional equals, especially in verbal skills, to females, they may have some real catching up to do.

Adults often try to measure a young man's emotional maturity by the quantity or quality of his romantic friendships. This is not a bad measure, but it is certainly incomplete.

Your son may be very focused on seeking a mate. Simultaneously, your son may lack any real interest in young women. Both extremes are normal for this age. A young man's interest in a mate depends a great deal on how shy he is, how much he's enjoying other activities, how he feels about his worth, and how much opportunity he has to meet young women. Your son may feel completely committed to one mate, then become very attracted to another. This behavior is not necessarily "immaturity." In our culture, mating maturity is not defined by staying with one mate during the teens and early twenties (unless of course the young people have become pregnant). In fact, it is easy to argue that the norm for mating maturity in the pre-adult years is and should be safe experimental behavior that can last well into the twenties.

## His Moral Development

In the movie *Con Air,* a thriller about a man who has to rescue airplane passengers from a band of escaped criminals, Nicolas Cage's character kills another man in a barroom brawl and ends up in prison. Just before he kills, his wife sees his anger rise up and nearly take him over. She says, "I just saw that guy again. I was hoping the Army would make that guy grow up." He had been immature years before when she first knew him. Then he entered the Army Rangers and "grew up." But then outside a bar he and his wife are accosted by some drunks, and in his rage, Cage's character loses control, kills, and is imprisoned.

I've brought up this incident in workshops and asked participants whether Cage's character's action was right or wrong. Some have answered that he was defending himself. Others have answered that he should have shown more restraint, should have walked away from the three men who were goading him rather than use his physical skills to fight them.

From one point of view, he is immature and uncontrolled; from the other, he's mature and protective.

Your son is living in *both* realms now. Part of him agrees that turning the other cheek is right. Another part looks with pride upon protecting and defending himself and others. Much of your son's internal thinking and self-assessment now will be about the *grayness of moral-*

*ity.* Your son may not talk to you about it a lot, but he needs you to provide a sympathetic ear when he does want to talk about the moral, emotional, and intellectual grayness of life. If you hold very rigid views and make him uncomfortable with his search for his own moral center, you may alienate your son in his normal development. In school, church, and among peers, your pre-adult son is taking moral measurements constantly, deciding where he fits in the spectrum of rights and wrongs, and committing more and more to adult codes of moral conduct, especially when those codes are presented by schools, universities, the military, churches, and other institutions.

## DISCIPLINE TECHNIQUES

There is little to add to the discipline techniques already established. Curfews, grounding, high expectations for behavior, clear rules for behavior, and how to handle disagreements all remain useful.

It is important that a pre-adult understands that there are consequences, rewards, and punishments. Conversing about these with a pre-adult is often easier than conversing with a middle teen. A lot of the "rebellion" of the middle teens mellows by pre-adulthood.

### Providing Discipline for the "One Bad Act"

I have dealt with so many young clients who committed the "one bad act." This is the bad act that nearly derails their young lives. It may happen during puberty, or middle adolescence, or pre-adulthood. It is the act of getting drunk, then smashing car windows or even trying to force himself sexually on a date. It is the adrenaline rush of racing another car that leads to an accident in which a friend is hurt or killed. It is the act of punching a coach or breaking Mom's most precious heirloom out of anger. This "one bad act" actually may happen two or three times but is usually not a chronic condition. Chronic bad action during pre-adulthood is an indication of a true "high-risk" youth, whom we'll discuss in a moment.

## The Range of Normal

It's normal for the boy to isolate himself for certain periods of time. This isolation may not be unhealthy because it is during isolation when a lot of one's own character and identity emerge. If it goes on more than a few days, then he's probably depressed and needs you to help him through some form of family or professional intervention.

It's normal for the pre-adult to have had sexual intercourse by age eighteen. However, if your son has not, he's in no way abnormal.

It's normal for the pre-adult to do fairly well at following core rules but to have targeted in his mind some that he wants to break.

It's normal for the pre-adult to take on more responsibilities than he can handle; it's also normal for him to go through a "lazy" period. Should he go to an extreme in either way for prolonged periods—hyperresponsibility to the point of panic attacks, or laziness to the point of drops in personal progress (schoolwork, athletics, social interactions)—it is important to get family and professional help.

It's normal for the pre-adult to feel clearer now about what his strengths and weaknesses are. Your son might say, "Dad, I'm a 'B' student—just get used to it." This is his way of drawing clear lines around his identity.

It's normal for the pre-adult who once was very cliquish now to want to belong to a broader group of friends. There is a drive in the middle teens and pre-adulthood to create an identity that is separate even from peer cliques.

It's normal for the pre-adult to enjoy opportunities to nurture younger kids. Some of this nurturing will involve direct empathy—"Here, I'll help you with your homework." Some of it will be aggressive—"You dork, you don't know what you're talking about."

It's normal for the pre-adult to face (if he hasn't already) the dilemma of competing loyalties. He may pick his girlfriend's point of view over his mom's or dad's. This choosing can be uncomfortable, but it is very normal and can show healthy developmental progress.

It's normal for the pre-adult to be noticeably like you in ways you've modeled, even if inadvertently—if you've cursed a lot, he may enjoy cursing. Simultaneously, he is internally feeling the urge to *not* be like you in a number of ways he has both unconsciously and consciously selected.

It's normal for the pre-adult to become very idealistic, and argumentative when his ideals are attacked.

It's normal for the pre-adult to seek his destiny and want to know his own fate. He hasn't learned yet that he can't completely plan his destiny and that his fate is always going to be something of a mystery.

It's normal for the pre-adult to seek safe places (especially home, friends' houses, "hangouts") in which to talk about, think about, and wrestle with the angel that is his own budding identity.

It's normal for the pre-adult to want respect and admiration from family, mentors, peers, and the larger culture. He will go to far lengths to get it—whether it means working extra hard at school or athletics, or becoming angry at you until you treat him with respect, or solidifying himself in an antisocial activity, like a gang.

Connor was seventeen when he committed his one bad act. He and friends got drunk and took baseball bats to car windows. "It was a thrill," he admitted, "an adrenaline rush." They had been cruising around, got bored, saw a man close his car door as he went into his house, and one of the pre-adult males in the car said, "I've got a bat in the trunk. Let's go out past Sullivan to that new subdevelopment and do the windows." The most sober of the group, Connor, argued against it, but even he gave in to the peer pressure. He and his friends smashed the car windows then fled, but someone peeking out a window got their license-plate number. Connor and his friends sobered up and got scared. They talked about what they would do if they got caught, and if they'd pay anonymous restitution if they didn't. None of them told his parents. Forty-eight hours later, the police came to the driver's house, and gradually all four youths were brought in. Since Connor and another youth were seventeen, they had to wait for their parents. The other two youths, both eighteen, were questioned, booked, then released. All the youths were handcuffed and spent time in jail cells. One of the youths, the one who was usually the instigator of trouble, postured his lack of fear, but the other three were obviously scared. In the end, the case came to court and the youths had to pay damages, receive counseling, and do community service for six months.

Connor said, "Even my friends at school thought we were a bunch of stupid freaks for doing what we did. I'm just lucky I was under eighteen—my record's okay. My friends who were eighteen have a record for life. I was ashamed of what I did and learned a lesson. When I saw my parents' faces that night at the police station, that was the worst. They had raised me right and treated me well and trusted me and I had let them down. It took a long time for them to trust me again."

I think the majority of middle-teen or pre-adult males commit at least one bad act like Connor's. They may not get caught—most do not—but they never forget what they've done, and they wrestle with their own feelings and grow morally from the action.

Some youths, of course, do get caught, and your son may be one of those. A great deal about your son's character, your own, and others' gets measured in the process of disciplining this act. You learn the quality of your son's peers—often finding that his own peer group looks down on him for what he's done. This humiliation is part of his punishment. You also learn about your own son's conscience by how he feels when he's caught. And you learn that no matter how well things are planned out, and no matter how much you believe in your son, he, like you, is a flawed person. He is learning all of this, too.

Punishment must include not only restitution but counseling if needed—from family members or professionals—and service work.

The restitution is the natural consequence of the bad act; the counseling is the community's (including your own) partial ownership of the youth's act; the prolonged service activity is the society's statement to the youth that from the negative will come a positive, from the bad act will come a commitment to help others.

Sometimes parents will feel so let-down by a son who has committed a heinous act that they will withhold trust for longer than necessary, or punish more than necessary. Yet if your son is a "good kid" before the act, he's a good kid after the act. His character has a flaw, but his whole being is not flawed. He must receive discipline so that he can build self-discipline, but if he is condemned, he may never regain his self-trust.

**The High-Risk Youth.**   If you are a single mother or other caregiver with a son who frightens you, you have a high-risk male in your home (see chapter 9 for specific warning signs). He may be to some extent antisocial and even dangerous. Your son will almost surely need the intervention of another kind of social system—alternative programs, the military, youth corps, the criminal justice system, an Alcoholics Anonymous or Narcotics Anonymous group, inner-city social programs, church interventions, or Toughlove-type programs.

It is essential that you not face alone the changes you will be required to facilitate in this young man's life. Two books deal specifically with issues faced by these young men: James Garbarino's *Lost Boys,* and Aaron Kipnis's *Bad Boys.* If you have any question at all about whether your son is a high-risk male, or how to handle him, contact school counselors, appropriate state agencies, and, if need be, neighborhood action committees your local law-enforcement officials have set up. One clear way to know if you need help is if you are afraid of your son. Another is if you are constantly afraid *for* him. If you fit either of these categories, be prepared to have to institute radical measures—even if at least a complete change in the way you provide discipline and structure in your family and home.

## Rules to Live By

The list of Rules to Live By in the previous chapter still apply in this chapter, for the most part. You can definitely expect more maturity from pre-adult sons, and give them some more latitude in following certain rules: Every month or so, you might want to hold a family council with your son to regularly negotiate rules. "Son, do you think any rules or expectations should change now?" Often your son will be satisfied and ask for no changes. Just as often, he may make concrete suggestions. Negotiation is a crucial skill in the middle-teen and pre-adult years—it teaches him compromise and helps you and him stay bonded.

## MORAL TEACHING

Again, much of what applied in the middle teens continues to apply in the pre-adult years. Our own moral debates with these young men must continue. Ethics curricula in the school should continue. A young man's moral intuition becomes largely united with *action*, and so he may become quite engaged in a "cause" during these years—a fight at school over whether his student newspaper can print something, or working for a political candidate. One of the reasons why different religions and cultures send pre-adults on "missions" (such as in the Mormon culture) or "trips back to the old country" (such as Israelis do in sending pre-adults to Europe for two to three months) is that the young person is at an age when the home's or community's moral teaching is augmented by moral travels away from home.

By age eighteen, some boys already will have had experiences, quite comprehensive ones, outside their own town, city, or country. They already will have bridged different cultures. Many others will not yet have done so. Either way, the pre-adult has reached a stage of brain, biological, and cultural development when it is useful to pursue moral education through a journey.

### Encouraging Moral and Spiritual Education Through Travel

When a pre-adult goes off to college, he is fulfilling many functions—getting away from home, getting an academic and/or athletic education, experiencing more of the world—and he is also adventuring into new moral landscapes. This last function we have not noticed as well as I think we should. College environments generally allow the young man to "live the questions," as the German poet and thinker Rainer Maria Rilke talked about in his *Letters to a Young Poet.* Here he writes to a college-age young man:

> *I would like to beg you to have patience with everything unresolved in your heart and to try to love the questions themselves as if they were locked rooms or books written in a very foreign language. Don't search for the answers, which could not be given to you now, because you would not be able to live them. Live the questions now. Perhaps someday, far in the future, you will gradually, without noticing it, live your way to the answers.*

Rilke calls on the young man to realize that he is not yet fully able to handle the answers—he is at the age when he must question, and find joy in questioning.

You can help your son "live the questions" by exposing him to new ideas, new people, new elders, new mentors—something college does. If possible in your lifestyle, you might also encourage him to take on the mission of quest and travel for at least a summer, if not more. Perhaps he can take his old car (when I was a pre-adult I drove my 1962 Rambler American around the western United States) and make some trips around the state. Or perhaps you can help him fund a trip to Europe, Africa, or Asia, or wherever his family lineage can be found. If you and he belong to a religious group that sponsors work around the world, perhaps he can spend time pursuing one of these.

There is nothing like travel for opening the soul. I am convinced that one of the reasons our young men read so much science fiction is because they hunt and adventure through the pages into the world of ultimate travel, ultimate quest.

### Encouraging Service Activities

General Colin Powell, the leader of the Alliance for Youth, recently told a crowd of high school students: "While we're giving resources to you, in turn we want you to find a way to serve in your community, because we honestly believe that service is a virtue that you should take into your life. Make sure you save some of yourself to give back to your community."

Every pre-adult is looking for his path to service and for service activities. When a young man contemplates what job he'll have after college, the instinct of service is there: He's not focused just on making money but, if we've raised him toward moral competency, also on what job will help him serve his family, his culture, his people. He hopes to have a good job so that he can raise children. He wonders, throughout his being, how to find work that also serves his own soul and, through that union, that helps him bring success not only to his wallet but to all those whom he touches. He wants to see how his work is a service activity itself.

Young men are idealists—they want to be happy in their work, and they know, even if unconsciously, that the highest measure of their work is how it serves. We see this desire illustrated when we hear of a basketball star who gets a huge contract and immediately buys his mother a new house and sets up a foundation for a charity. Most of our boys know they will ultimately measure their manhood to some great extent by the mark of service they leave on the world. Though many of our young men appear selfish and money hungry today, I find that far fewer fit this bill than fit the bill of the Good Son. While we can help them bring their sense of service to the forefront by helping them find education and work that satisfies them, we can also directly point out available service activities to them.

Throughout a boy's high school years, it is important that you engage, as a family, in the kinds of service activities mentioned in earlier chapters—nursing homes, homeless shelters, Meals-on-Wheels. This activity ought not end for your family just because the boy can drive the car by himself or is otherwise entering adulthood. *Schools also must en-*

*courage and sustain service activities for young people.* In the same way that each high school should have an ethics curriculum, it should involve youth in service work.

### Teaching the Art of Relationship

By ages seventeen and eighteen, most young men have attempted at least one serious love relationship. Even if they have not, they still need to learn the rules of relationship, the dynamics, the potential crisis points. While they will make all their own mistakes, those mistakes will come at a worse cost if parents and mentors have not, during the boys' pre-adulthood, talked to them about the realities of relationships.

Husband and wife Steve McCormack and Kelly Morrison are professors at Michigan State University, where they teach pre-adults the rules of relationship. They take the best research and shape it to show young people that relationships are journeys in which everything from eye contact to posture to conversation to sexuality to childrearing are steps along the way, and each needs to be understood.

Here are Professors McCormack and Morrison's "rules of love," which I've adapted. I hope you will talk to your sons about these very directly.

1. *Abandon the passion delusion.* It is natural for passion to dissipate within weeks or months of entering a relationship. Expect this and get ready for it.

2. *Romantic feelings can't be forced.* You can't talk yourself or anyone else into falling in love. Why we fall in love and with whom is, in large part, a God-given mystery. Forcing love or sex on someone is one of life's most immoral acts.

3. *Relationships are hard work.* For love to last, both parties must work hard, just as they would to raise a family, build a career, or even spend six months rebuilding a car.

4. *Honorable commitment to a mate is an ongoing process, not a final product.* The honorable commitment we have made to our mate is something we reinvest in every day and constantly learn new things about. It is not a product of the wedding itself, or of the first sex act, or even the first child. It is ever new.

5. *Maintain independence, other friends, and solitary activities.* Couples that last are couples that spend a good amount of time apart, each pursuing his or her own activities and friendships.

6. *Cultivate mutual interests, activities, and values.* Couples that last share basic life values and enjoy many of the same activities. Even at age fifty, they still go on dates together.

7. *Develop between yourselves your own "rules of the relationship."* Communicate about these as frequently as needed. Develop rituals for communication, like the classic "What did you do today?"

8. *Decide how you two will communicate and practice your honesty.* Not everything about one's past or present ought to be shared with a mate.

9. *Conflict and confrontation are good.* Healthy conflict and confrontation are part of making relationships work. If the couple is having trouble with these, they need to get help from elders they trust who are good at working through problems. Dudley Weeks's *The Eight Essential Steps to Conflict Resolution* is a good resource for troubled individuals and couples.

10. *Be friends with each other, and be kind to each other.* We need attention and respect from each other. We will continue to love each other if we're kind.

There are probably many other things you want to teach your son about relationships. He needs you to teach them to him. My own book called *Love's Journey* is about the twelve stages of relationship we all go through during our lives. You might find it helpful in teaching your son.

### Handling Money and Work

It is good to think of money and work as moral issues in your pre-adult son's life, especially since he is becoming an adult for whom so much of his life will be spent at work and in pursuit of money. As much as possible, it is important not to push a pre-adult too hard toward earning money at all costs. He needs to be realistic about what kind of work will help him make a living, but he doesn't need to obsess. By the same token, laziness is never to be encouraged.

Credit-card companies inundate families with mailings. Given the dangerous levels of debt that have been built up in this country—at least partly due to credit-card companies targeting youth who are not yet even gainfully employed—it is inadvisable to allow your son to have his own credit card until he has more than a part-time job. (He may sometimes use your card with your direction and consent.) Perhaps he will not get his own until he's out of college and working full-time. But since at age eighteen your son can get a card without your knowing or giving consent, this goal may not always be realistic. In the end, it is generally best to at least hold off on letting the son have his own unsupervised card till his eighteenth birthday. Also, during this time, you may not want to cosign a card for him because you'll be legally responsible for bills. A better option is to be the primary borrower on a card and let him cosign. He can build credit, but the credit-card bills and statements get sent to you for oversight. Should he spend more than you and he agreed, you close the account.

Overall, our sons need financial education. It is essential at this time to give your son a crash course on how your own checking account works, what grace periods are, what minimum payments are, and other aspects of financial life, including national and statewide financial markets. John Rosemond's *Teen-Proofing* is a good resource for educating your son on these and other teen issues.

### Having Faith in Our Sons

One of the great moral difficulties we have in raising these young men is knowing whether we can fully trust them. We want to, but we are often unsure of what they're doing and whether they realize all the consequences of their actions. Often our pre-adult sons drift somewhat far away from us, and we worry. I received a letter recently that moved me deeply. I hope it provides you with not only some answers but also inspiration to "live in the question."

*My son, Jerry, was seventeen when this happened. You need to know that he and I had been pretty close until he was about fifteen. He went through a time of not really being very close to either his dad or me. He was close to his grandfather, but his grandfather died when he was sixteen. This brought us all closer, but then Jerry pulled away again by getting into a relationship with a girl who was two years younger (just fifteen when he turned seventeen). We didn't approve of the relationship and I even called her parents and talked to them. This created a lot of problems again in our relationship with Jerry. The weird thing was, Jerry was brought up in a more moral and disciplined way than this younger girl. She was allowed to have unsupervised parties. Jerry had come home drunk from some of them, and I know he became sexually active with her. She was very mature. She had friends who had drugs, something Jerry had never wanted to be involved in before. Anyway, enough preamble—here's what happened.*

*One Saturday night he was due to go to a party at her house. I was feeling very sad about what had been happening between him and us. I had been making a list of my mistakes in handling it. I'd left the list on my desk upstairs. Jerry was up in his room getting ready. I was downstairs in the family room looking at his baby albums and crying. Everything seemed to be falling apart, I couldn't reach Jerry, his father was being stoic. ("It's going to work out," my husband would say, "it's a phase. He'll be okay.") I felt I had nowhere to turn and I was depressed and sentimental.*

*Without my realizing it, Jerry had gone into my study and seen the list. He'd gone in looking for tape, he said. He came downstairs with my list and saw the baby albums and the state I was in. He set the list down on the table and looked at one of the photos. "Did I really look like that?" he asked, turning the pages. It was slow at first, but somehow we got to talking, and I had a lot of memories and so did he. Then he picked up the list and said, "I don't know what you want from me, Mom. I just want you to let me be myself but you won't do that."*

*I said, "What I want is for you to be a good man. I don't care anymore if you're having sex with her, or if you're doing drugs. You won't let me in to care about that. But I still care about you, about your heart and your soul. I raised you to be a good man and to have the strength to know the difference between doing right and doing wrong. That's the person I care about. I don't want you to lose your character. I don't want you to wake up one day and realize you've become someone you yourself don't respect."*

*He got mad. "You just feel like you failed as a parent and now you want to keep me from happiness by pulling all that morality crap." He picked up my list and crumpled it up. "I'm leaving. You can find this in the trash." He went out the back door and got in his car and gunned it and left.*

*You may think this story has an unhappy ending, but it doesn't. That night around midnight I heard his car. He had a midnight curfew and he did abide by it almost all the time.*

*He walked in the house and saw me and said, "Mom, I just want you to know, I broke up with Heather. I don't want to talk about it." He went up to his room and went to bed. I finally fell asleep around 2:00 A.M. after waking up my husband and telling him.*

*The next morning, Jerry came down to breakfast and started talking. He talked about how lost he had been feeling the last few months, how he hadn't been proud of himself, how he had had fun but he had felt weird too. We talked for about an hour, and he said at the end, "You know, Mom, if you hadn't kept trying to talk and fighting with me, I think I might have really gone off the deep end. You never gave up on me."*

*I cried and gave him a big hug, and he cried too.*

*After that day, we became friends again, or maybe in a new way. He trusted me again, and I realized that deep down I had always somehow trusted that he would do the right things in life. It was sure a rocky time, but I wouldn't have traded it for anything in the world, now that Jerry is grown up and doing great.*

I believe, as this mother does, that if we have raised our boys well, there is no reason to think they are not basically trustworthy. My experience tells me that they are deeply moral, loving human beings who will do the right thing. In the end, they will not let us down. They will do things their own way by late adolescence, but it will not look too different from how we did things when we were their age. I am one who has no right to carry any illusions about adolescent boys being perfect, or being complete already, or being men yet. I was none of these at seventeen. I was still searching, still trying to find the limits of my youth, still trying to become a free human being, and unsure how to resolve the contradictions of limitations and freedom that are inherent in the human condition. I needed and received what Jerry received—parents who never gave up.

## A HEALTHY MORAL AND EMOTIONAL ENVIRONMENT

When it comes to dealing with seventeen-, eighteen-, and nineteen-year-olds, intuition is worth 99 percent, and expert advice about 1 percent. The sheer amount of variety in maturation at these ages makes it nearly impossible to generalize about these young men.

However, here some things to aim for in the environment you share with your son.

### Supervision

We must ask, "Is my son ready to enter an unsupervised environment, or is he the kind of young man who needs continued supervision?"

Pre-adult males need clear supervision, perhaps less in the form of "parenting" and more in the form of "mentoring." An eighteen-year-old who goes to a college and lives in a dorm or fraternity house known mainly for partying is probably entering an environment that is too loose for him. He is being encouraged to break the law by drinking underage. And he is being told by his peers that he now needs neither parents nor mentors.

This situation does not fit the developmental needs of pre-adults. Pre-adults still need their parents to help them find motivation, a safe place for self-exploration, and financial and other support; they need mentors to take a specific interest in their emotional, moral, and spiritual lives; and they need their school, craft, or trade environment to provide them with clear guidelines.

As you explore which high school and college, vocational school or workplace your son will spend his pre-adult years in, you may want to look closely at him and speak frankly about what kind of supervision and mentoring he needs, and where he can get it. His intuitions may match your own.

### Responsibilities

It is useful to ask, "Am I giving my son enough responsibility to balance the freedom he's gaining?" In our son's junior and senior years of high school, we must help him find a new responsibility for every new freedom he gains. If he is allowed to stay out late at night on weekends, he might find some commensurate way of being responsible around the house during the day. If he is allowed to have a party at home, he must supervise cleanup. If he gets the family car for entertainment, he must also use it to ferry younger siblings to activities. If he is enjoying unsupervised Internet access, he must also spend some of his Internet time searching for things important to the whole family, such as helping to plan a vacation. Many parents think they must let their pre-adult sons breathe for a while and not be too burdened. In fact, our pre-adult boys may complain that certain responsibilities are burdens, but those very responsibilities also make them feel a continued bond with the family.

### The Mentor

Somewhere in his environment, he wants the presence of a mentor. This person may be someone in our extended family or a coach or teacher or professor who takes a special interest in our son. This mentor may come from our son's workplace, or spontaneously from some other environment he never spent much time in but in which he is nurtured and which he comes to care a great deal about.

There is an old Chinese saying: "When the pupil is ready, the master will appear." When our son is ready, the mentors will appear, as they have, we hope, throughout his boyhood. There is something of an urgency on our part to help them appear to our son, because he is moving away from us and now needs a "transitional parent." We cannot force a mentor on our son, but we can provide our pre-adult son with environments—like a trade or college, like sports or clubs—in which he can find one.

### Adult-Adult Conversation

Your intuition tells you how best to converse with your son. It tells you when he's ready for real adult-adult conversation. As you observe and modify your conversations with your son, heed this tip: When talking to him, focus as much as possible on what you have in common—personality and character traits, moral and spiritual beliefs, observations of reality, hobbies and interests. Don't get bogged down in how you differ *unless there is a substantial and direct moral or other gain to be made for your son.*

### Media Use

It is still useful to ask yourself, "Is my son using the media responsibly?" By age seventeen, your son will probably be using media as he wishes. Yet I hope you will continue to be actively involved in his life of story and imagination. I hope you will help guide him away from many hours of television and video games per day. I hope you will go to films with him now and then and discuss them. I hope you will ask him to educate you on the media he is viewing and the songs he listens to, so that you will not lose your bond with him in this area of life.

While your son may no longer want to have TV family nights, he may well surprise you by dropping back into one suddenly. This is to be encouraged.

And certainly, if he is involved in anything dangerous regarding media—heavily pornographic Internet use, obsession with slasher films, or just too much quantity—you are the authority he needs (and unconsciously wants) to help him stop.

In the end, I still think you should discourage your son from having a television in his room. It is good for your son to use a family area to entertain himself, and it keeps the family just a little closer. Especially if you are noticing any kind of unhealthy isolation in your son, requiring him to use family space for some of his TV viewing reduces the chance of isolation becoming unhealthy.

Because young people are story hungry—they look for myths and stories that give shape to their lives—they need more than one mode of gaining access to those important stories. You have cause to worry if your son's only major way of gaining stories is through visual media. If he has no spiritual or other institution through which to hear about life issues, if he has little access to stories through school, if you and your extended family spend little time with him telling the stories of your lives, he may rely totally on media stories—and these are not enough.

### The Rituals of Life: The Fourth Rite of Passage

When a young man graduates from high school, he experiences a rite of passage that goes something like: "Yeah, school is over! Now life can begin!" When he turns eighteen, he can vote or join the military— another rite of passage. When he leaves home for college, he experiences yet another rite of passage. Together, all these might constitute his fourth rite of passage.

Yet I suggest augmenting these with a special rite created by the young man and his family. The quest and travel we spoke of can be this rite, in which the family is involved in sending the young man off, perhaps with a celebratory party.

This fourth rite could include a significant "letter of passage" written to your son by you (and hopefully all parents and extended family will write their own to him), in which you tell him the story of his life as you've known it, and give him your blessing. Probably parents, but perhaps someone else in the extended family, ought to create a scrapbook of the son's growth and achievements. Letters and this scrapbook can be given to the son in a ceremonial way, perhaps at a graduation party.

## MARCEL'S STORY

Marcel's mother, Judy, spoke with me about her eighteen-year-old son. She was very proud of him and of how she and her ex-husband (they divorced when Marcel was nine and his brother seven) raised their two boys. Both Judy and her ex were the kind of parents the boys always knew they could count on. Judy had a strong bond with Marcel, strong enough that he called her one day to confide in her about some disturbing things.

After a couple of months at college, Marcel went to a party, where over a period of hours he used cocaine, some mushrooms, pot, and booze. In the past, he'd experimented with drugs and had drunk his share of high school beer, but never anything like this. He was calling Mom the next day to say he felt very sick and wasn't sure what to do. Though he never quite said it, he was scared.

Judy panicked in a way any mother might, but also because she was a drug and alcohol counselor and had seen what binges do to people. She got enraged; she made threats; she told Marcel he should come home for a while, or that she or his father should go to Marcel.

Then she calmed down and asked him what he needed right now, whether he needed medical help.

Marcel said he would wait a day and see how he felt. He thought he was just badly hungover, not terribly ill. Because Marcel's father was paying for his college, Marcel asked Judy not to tell him. Marcel was afraid his dad would pull the funds. If Marcel would go to rehab classes of some kind, which she could find and arrange for him, Judy agreed not to tell Dad.

At first, Marcel agreed to go, but as the next month progressed, he wavered. He registered, but then didn't show up. A week later, he went once—but he never returned. His mother confronted him again on the phone, and he said, "Mom, I saw that morning how much it upset you. I haven't done anything since that night and don't plan on doing that again. It wasn't right for me to do it to my body, and it wasn't right to scare you like that." In telling me the story, Judy laughed, and said, "At that moment I should have realized what a great son I'd raised, what a wonderful man he was becoming—but I was still scared, upset, and wanted him in rehab." She insisted he go, and threatened to tell his dad. He begged her to trust him.

"Mom," he said, "I'm a grown man now; you have to trust me, just like I trusted you by telling you what I'd done." This gave her pause, and she said she'd put off telling his dad.

In the next month, Marcel got a part-time job, and his grades were good. When Marcel came home for Christmas break, Judy asked him if he'd done anything regarding his "problem." Marcel said, "Mom, I've handled that already. I'm doing fine; I learned my lesson; it's my life now, let it go."

As Judy recalled this conversation, she remembered with tears in her eyes the beauty and the pain of being a mother of a young adult—how wonderful it was to see that he was a man who had "separated" from her, a man who had handled his own moral dilemma with his own intuition and honor (though still with a little help from Mom). When Judy told me the story, Marcel was twenty-three, in law school, and married. Drugs and alcohol were not a problem for him.

"I'm not done being a mother," Judy told me. "I never will be. But now"—she smiled—"I'm the mother of a man."

As you finish your hands-on parenting of your son, as your son leaves pre-adulthood for young adulthood, you, like Judy, will probably still feel the terror of his crises just as much as the triumph of his successes. I hope you will be able to look back at how you parented him—at how you fulfilled your own parenting plan and also adapted to the spontaneous explosions of human life. You can never be replaced in this young man's life. You are the earth from which he grew.

# Epilogue

Mark Twain, when asked how he succeeded in capturing so well the human adventure on paper, responded, "I keep it simple." He did not mean simplistic. He meant that deep down, the human journey is one of simple pains and simple pleasures, and the truly wise author of the human plot needs to remain focused on the daily hurts and triumphs. As a parent, as an educator, as a therapist, I try to share Twain's vision. I have experienced strict moral authority and intense religious tradition in my own boyhood; and I did things in adolescence that were highly experimental, as befitted the experimental years of any young man. Like many of you, I have lived in the worlds of both "conformity" and "creative chaos." I think there are important lessons in each world.

In *The Good Son*, I have presented a guide for how to raise your boys that I hope builds a bridge between the two worlds. I hope you have found that *The Good Son* envisions a world for children that is ripe for exploration and new developments, but also one that begins from the foundation of an ordered, authoritative, intimate family.

Let me leave you with this thought: In our times, one of

the most important questions humanity faces regards the purpose of males and masculinity. Who are our males? Why are they here? What do they need? How are they essential to human life? As you raise boys, you not only are a hands-on caregiver but also are providing the answers to our civilization's questions. You are not just a parent—you are a visionary. Even while giving the boy in your care a life purpose, you are also shaping humanity's perception of boys and men.

In *The Good Son* we have come together to develop a plan for accomplishing one of the single most important tasks of any caregiver in a human society: to build a loving, wise, and ethical man. My thoughts are with you as you continue your journey toward this goal. You are needed, and your hard work will be rewarded.

# Fifty Books and Movies That Stimulate Moral Growth in Boys

Books and films can be seen as gifts of a culture that is in search of a moral center. They can help build compassion and discipline in males, and raise moral questions for boys to contemplate.

In order to assist you and the boys you know in male moral development, I have included below twenty-five books and twenty-five films, each of which has an important moral lesson for boys. I hope you'll use them to stimulate dialogue with the boys in your life.

In making this brief list I have not included sacred texts, like the Bible, though I hope you will generously visit sacred texts with your sons.

## BOOKS THAT STIMULATE MORAL GROWTH

The earlier we start reading to our boys, the better. Especially when boys become toddlers, and then as boys learn to read, books and stories with overt moral lessons ought to comprise at least half of their reading time. As boys become older and don't want us to read with them, we often think we must rely on schools to provide books and discussion. But reading the same book as our middle school or high school boy, and talking to him about it—even presenting him with books we read in our childhood—is a wonderful and essential part of family life.

### For Early Reading Experiences

*My Little Golden Book About God,* by Jane Werner Watson. This collection of stories gives children a sense of spiritual security. It is best read aloud to your son; as he gets older he may enjoy reading it aloud to you. In this storybook, God gives each of us an inner voice that teaches right from wrong. As you read this book with your little boy, he'll benefit from questions you pose about the voice of God that is inside him.

*Aesop's Fables.* This ancient collection of little stories with big morals might be read aloud to any growing boy, even before he can have a dialogue about the fables. Aesop wrote mainly about human character but used animal figures, making the tales perfect for the toddler or early school-age child. To be sure the messages of these fables get through, especially to the younger boy, it's good to do a fun question-and-answer period after each story.

*The Giving Tree,* by Shel Silverstein. This book tells the heart-wrenching story of a tree that sacrifices everything for a little boy. Even upon becoming an adult, the boy does not seem to fully appreciate the tree's self-sacrifice. But readers understand and are inspired toward compassion by the story. The reading of this story to a boy should be accompanied by good conversation about selfishness.

*What Is God?,* by Etan Boritzer, illustrated by Robbie Marantz. For people who have left traditional religion but still seek a universal spiritual life, this is a classic. In rhyming prose it pays homage to all the world's religions, and to the sense in each of them that there is a greater force caring for us all.

*Stevie,* by John Steptoe. This is a touching story of early friendship and loss between two African-American boys, and shows how boys can hide their affection for each other—even from themselves. It is just right to be read aloud to children up to school age or given to a boy who is beginning his first reading experience.

## For Elementary School Boys

*The Little Prince,* by Antoine de Saint Exupéry. This intergalactic fable takes the little prince to earth, where a fox teaches him the secret of life. If reading it aloud to children, you should go slowly and let the child (and you) savor it. It electrifies the imagination, and the lessons can become the heart of family discussions over a period of weeks.

*When Dinosaurs Die,* by Laurene Krasny Brown and Marc Brown. Through the lives of a modern dinosaur family—they look almost human and could live next door to you—readers learn about what death is and how to handle it compassionately. Deep feelings are explored as Harriet the hamster dies and is given a memorial service. This book opens feelings in a school-age boy who may not have been able to explore issues of death and loss directly before.

*The Children's Book of Virtues,* edited by William J. Bennett. Prompted by the popularity of his collection *The Book of Virtues,* William J. Bennett gives us this smaller, illustrated children's book. It is a gold mine of stories about morality. Sunday schools can pick out a story; parents can pick out a story; teachers can pick out a story. This collection can be mined for months, even years, on end.

*The Chronicles of Narnia,* by C. S. Lewis. Heroes, heroines, giants, magic, God, wizards, witches, swords, battles, banquets, love, loss—all these themes and more are covered in these seven volumes by one of this century's foremost authorities on Christianity. The Chronicles are fantastical, filled with spiritual and moral allegory. In reading or talking about these with your son, you might call special attention to the moral decision making each of the children goes through, and the way these decisions are often inspired by the divine figure, the lion Aslan.

*Grimm's Fairy Tales.* These stories are a treasure of moral allegory, as are different fairy tale collections from all over the world. Throughout human history, fairy tales have been used by teachers and parents to describe symbolic and allegorical journeys to moral life. All classrooms will benefit from bringing fairy tales out of the nursery school and returning them to the forefront of moral teaching. Once I even used a Grimm's fairy tale to facilitate a discussion among 500 middle and high school students on teen pregnancy issues. All of us were mesmerized by how powerfully a tale many thousands of years old mirrored the issues faced by today's young people.

### For Middle School Males

*Harry Potter and the Sorcerer's Stone,* by J. K. Rowling. In this magical tale, a boy becomes a wizard at twelve years old, an event that complicates his life but also gives it meaning. Most appropriate for middle school boys, *Harry Potter* provides a role model of a boy who must grow into a life of purpose and courage.

*The Education of Little Tree,* by Forrest Carter. An Indian boy learns what is required of a young man of integrity after suffering a family tragedy. This book shouldn't get overlooked by middle school curricula. It is a valuable, inspiring story about how a boy grows up in the face of adversity. Boys who are going through divorce, deaths in the family, or other painful times in their development will feel befriended by the book, and also morally awakened.

*Bless the Beasts and Children,* by Glendon Swarthout. Perfect for middle school readers as well as adults, this short novel tells the vivid story of a band of adolescent outcasts at a summer camp for boys. Although ultimately tragic, the book can generate a powerful discussion about the anger that exists between kids and parents, and the ways in which kids sometimes torment one another.

*The Shiloh Trilogy,* by Phyllis Reynolds Naylor. *Shiloh, Saving Shiloh,* and *Shiloh Season* make up a trilogy of books that are very appropriate for middle school boys. They involve early adolescent boys in relationship to a beagle named Shiloh, whom one boy rescues from an abusive owner. Their adventures teach boys a great deal about honor, integrity, and compassion.

*The Book of Virtues for Young People,* edited by William J. Bennett. In this collection of stories about ethics, morality, and integrity, William J. Bennett chose themes more appropriate to late-elementary and middle school boys. Like his *Children's Book of Virtues* and his original *Book of Virtues,* this one is filled with inspiration and moral stimulation.

*Lord of the Flies,* by William Golding. Still a staple of many middle and high school reading lists, Golding's chilling classic depicts what happens when adult authority disappears in the world of boys. Discussions about this book will lead classrooms and families into the darker questions of human nature. This is a realm our boys benefit from searching through, especially with trusted adults to help them understand the moral consequences of our darker selves.

### For High School Males

*To Kill a Mockingbird,* by Harper Lee. In one of the most important novels of the twentieth century, a father is at the center of racial strife in a southern town.

His children, too, wrestle with some of the most important themes of growing up. Courage, conviction, moral duty, compassion—all are tested. Racism itself becomes a worthy topic in discussions about this book, and in a way that guides young readers deep into their own prejudices and intrinsic desires to do what's right.

*Sophie's World,* by Jostein Gaarder. Sophie's life is changed one day when she receives two questions in the mail: *Who are you?* and *Where does the world come from?* Her suspenseful search for the answers to these questions inspires young adults (and adults) to ask the questions for themselves and make their own search. This book is just right for high-school-age boys who lean a little toward the philosophical.

*Ender's Game* and *Seventh Son,* by Orson Scott Card. These books begin a science fiction and a fantasy series, respectively. In Card's series, boys grow to manhood by discovering and accepting their moral and spiritual destinies. Every moral competency is covered in these books, in the same way C. S. Lewis was able to create a drama that seemed to absorb every key theme of human development. A Mormon, Card imbues his vision with virtue and values, yet, like Lewis, never becomes overwhelmed by doctrine or proselytizing. While each book in Card's series is a good template for moral discussion, classrooms will probably benefit most from the first in each. Some students will get "hooked" and pursue the others themselves.

*Siddhartha,* by Hermann Hesse. This story of a young man's spiritual and moral development is loosely based on the Buddha's life. Few novels match it for moral and spiritual content. If a young man is clearly touched by this book, he also ought to be provided with Hesse's *Narcissus and Goldmund.* Because of the sophistication of language, Hesse's books are best read by very mature high school readers.

*The Last Temptation of Christ,* by Nikos Kazantzakis. This is a fictional story about Christ's moral and spiritual struggles. Though some educators might worry that it is controversial, I hope they will at least suggest the book to young males who are spiritual searchers. Jesus Christ is an immeasurably powerful moral role model for young men, and becomes even more powerful as he becomes real to them.

*The Adventures of Huckleberry Finn,* by Mark Twain. Like nearly all of Mark Twain's books, this one is about people (most often boys and young men) trying to develop character in both ordinary and extraordinary circumstances. Huck Finn's story is worth mining not only for its humor but for its finely interwoven moral dialogue about human character and ethics.

*Sheehan,* by Terry Trueman. This short young adult novel is told from the point of view of an almost completely disabled high-school-age boy named Sheehan. He cannot talk, cannot even respond to most cues from his caregivers. But he has a spiritual and moral point of view that is startlingly powerful. The novel raises questions not only about what might be going on inside the minds of those we consider retarded (in the way *Flowers for Algernon* did a generation ago) but also about a family's and culture's duty to the severely disabled.

*The Lost Boy,* by David J. Pelzer. This true account of a boy's journey through foster home life is immensely powerful. It builds compassion in anyone who reads it and leads to very important discussions about what constitutes a family, the resilience of the human spirit, and the development of character despite attempts by an outside world to crush the spirit.

*The Chosen,* by Chaim Potok. Once a high-school-age boy (and some mature middle school readers) discovers Potok's books, he may not rest until he reads them all. *The Chosen* is still considered Potok's classic, and for good reason—it is the story of Jewish boys growing up in New York and has become a universal tale of all boys who seek their own individuality within and without the blessings of their families and religious traditions. Friends Reuven and Danny struggle together to discover a spiritual and moral center.

## MOVIES THAT STIMULATE MORAL GROWTH

When we think of movies that offer moral gifts to our children, we must also think of ourselves as the moral teachers. For parents, mentors, and educators of boys, movies shouldn't be considered mere entertainment but also teaching tools and the means to the end of raising an ethical man. All twenty-five movies suggested here are useful moral parables. They best serve the moral needs of our boys and young men if each of us remains involved in encouraging discussions about them.

I am listing each film in the youngest age group for which I feel it appropriate. I hope you won't limit the application of the movie to the listed age group if you feel it appropriate for another. *The Lion King,* for instance, can be seen by anyone—I enjoy it as an adult. On the other hand, I hope you'll think carefully about a younger boy seeing a film listed for an older age group. For instance, the war films listed could harm the growing minds of little boys.

### For Pre-School and Early Elementary School Boys

*The Lion King.* This animated Disney movie tells the story of a lion "prince" who loses his father and flees, feeling that his father's death was his own fault. Befriended, and inspired to become a moral and compassionate man, the prince becomes the king and returns his beleaguered kingdom to prosperity. This movie is good for late toddlers and school-age children, and it is useful in class discussions in high school ethics curricula.

*Mulan.* This animated film tells the story of a girl who must dress up as a young man in order to save her family's honor and prove herself. It is funny, filled with adventure, and exciting for both girls and boys. Young boys take to it as much as girls, and learn about duty, hard work, telling the truth, doing your best, loving your family, and growing up.

### For Later Elementary School Boys

*It's a Wonderful Life.* This movie is about a man who doesn't realize his own worth until it's almost too late. I've watched the film with young men, only to find all of our eyes brimming with tears. It is an important film about family, courage, and character. While appropriate for little boys, it is useful also with young adults.

*Titanic.* In all the hoopla surrounding this blockbuster film, its moral content did not receive enough discussion. In large part, this is a film about the strength of character a young man of twenty-two possesses. Good for boys of around ten and older, this film provides a role model of self-sacrifice, courage, and integrity.

*Simon Birch.* This film tells the story of a disabled boy who seems to know intrinsically the real meaning of self-sacrifice. He is humiliated by society but has a inborn sense of character that inspires. Good for boys of around eight and older.

*Three Wishes.* Two boys and a single mom are struggling when a mysterious man enters their lives. He teaches the boys what it means to endure and to discover personal self-confidence. This film is appropriate for boys around ten and older. Boys who are facing the death of their father or a divorce may find it especially inspiring.

*Beethoven Lives Upstairs.* This film is a made-for-TV movie about Beethoven as a mentorial boarder in a ten-year-old boy's house. Music and the arts constantly provide backdrop for a boy's development of self-discipline and self-worth. This film, suitable for ages ten and up, captures a boy's relationship with music, with a mentor, and with life's lessons.

*Stand by Me.* This film is a classic about how boys nurture one another and yearn to be morally and emotionally cared for. Four boys are challenged to understand what is right, and try to do it together. This film is suitable for boys ten and older. It inspires parents, mentors, teachers, and students to explore such themes as right and wrong, loyalty to friends, parent-son relationships, and peer pressure.

*High Noon.* In this Western classic, a lone sheriff must display matchless courage. For boys who have no choice but to face down a bully, this movie may be of special inspiration. It is appropriate for boys eleven and older.

## For Middle School Boys

*Scrooged.* This humorous Christmas morality play tells the story of a warped TV executive who learns the meaning of compassion. Especially at the Christmas season, this film is good for both home and school.

*Dead Poets Society.* A teacher mentors boys growing up at a boarding school. The film captures the beauty and the grief that male friendship can carry. As the boys find the opportunity to be good young men, they also discover the freedom to make critical mistakes, and experience the consequences. This film is suitable for some middle school and most high school audiences.

*Men Don't Leave.* A very moving depiction of the relationship between a single mother and her sons, this film challenges middle school and older boys to understand loyalty, family love, and how hard they have to work to be responsible men.

*Paths of Glory.* For any boy who thinks war is "cool," this classic depicts the brutal realities and moral agonies of World War I. A harsh film that should be seen only by boys thirteen or older, *Paths of Glory* can stimulate powerful moral dialogue about just and unjust forms of authority.

*White Squall.* Troubled young men, mentored by a husband and wife, face adversity within themselves, in nature, and in society when their ship is destroyed. Each young man must face his own moral confusion. This sea drama is suitable for some middle school boys and boys in high school.

*The Karate Kid.* Despite having a Cinderella-like theme, this family classic provides a model of how a boy can transform his life through hard work, dedication, and perseverance—particularly with the crucial guiding hand of a beloved mentor.

Martial arts and mentorship are beneficial to any boy either being bullied or unable to control his own aggressive urges.

*Hoosiers,* like many other sports-oriented films (e.g., *Breaking Away, Rudy*), depicts young men struggling to develop character, discipline, and courage against the backdrop of athletics. It is suitable for most middle and high school boys, and some late-elementary-age boys.

*He Got Game.* This film is about a father who has abandoned his son and must reconnect with him in order to facilitate the son's development in basketball. The movie powerfully inspires young males to come to grips with their fathers' impact on their own development of heart and soul. It is appropriate for boys of twelve and older, and should be accompanied specifically with discussion of how fathers and sons teach each other forgiveness for human failings.

### For High School Boys

*Saving Private Ryan.* This World War II film is very much about the male search for self-worth. Captain Miller and a few men strike out across France to try to find Private Ryan, whose three brothers have been killed. They and he learn about duty and the terrible toll of war. As Ryan remembers the incident from his own old age, he still wonders if he has earned the right to have remained alive. The violence in this film makes it unsuitable for boys younger than middle adolescence.

*Gallipoli.* This film painstakingly depicts the blossoming friendship between two young men, and then shows how one of the most ill-fated military campaigns of the twentieth century destroys them. *Gallipoli* provides an excellent opportunity to discuss the ambiguity of war and the sometime failure of command. Because of the film's violence and subject matter, only mature young men should see *Gallipoli.*

*Schindler's List.* This classic of the Holocaust provides a forum for discussing the character both of nations and of individuals. Schindler starts out exploiting a group of Jews for profit against the backdrop of the Holocaust, but ends up saving as many as he can. This movie is brutally honest about human violence and should be seen only by mature young men.

*Boyz N the Hood.* This film about gangs and growing up black and male in the inner city is useful in the homes and classrooms of high school boys. It depicts how an environment can strip males of one kind of honor and entice them with another. It does not take moral shortcuts, and inspires in-depth dialogue about what young men need in order to feel whole.

*A Simple Plan.* This movie presents a moral allegory about men who begin their own demise with one simple immoral act. It is a superb starting point for discussions about what morality is, how we become tempted away from moral competency, how one bad act can snowball into tragedy, and how muddy our personal ethics can become once we start trying to rationalize obviously bad behavior.

*Blood In, Blood Out* is a long but intense film about young Latino inner-city males who struggle to find a moral center. It is a morality play that follows the lives of three young men as they make different but intertwined moral choices. Because of its violence and language, it is not suitable for middle school or younger audiences.

*Unforgiven.* This film by Clint Eastwood was said to have changed the Western genre forever. While this statement might be an exaggeration, the claim makes sense when the film is viewed from a moral standpoint. William Munny, a former thief and killer, is transformed by a wife whom he nearly worships for her moral strength. She dies, and three years later he is involved again on a trek through his old behaviors. Suitable for high-school-age boys, this film challenges boys to decide what part inborn character, alcohol addiction, environment, friendships, and love all play in the development of ethics and morality.

*On the Beach.* This is a chilling film from the Cold-War era about human technology outpacing human ethics. Although the message is about the devastation of nuclear war, the movie holds a perennial warning about our delicate hold on life in an era in which environmental devastation threatens. Humanity's journey of dominance over the natural environment is an ethical theme every high school male benefits from grappling with.

*October Sky.* This is a moving, true story about a boy who has to juggle his own desire to be a rocket scientist with his moral duty to his family and town. The question asked by the film is this: How can a young man be free to find himself while still doing what's right by those he loves? Every high-school-age male must face this question in his own way if he is to fully become a man.

# Additional Resources

In this bibliographical list are books that have been useful to me over the years, as well as new discoveries. This list is only a beginning.

## THE EARLY YEARS

The American Academy of Pediatrics. *Caring for Your Baby and Young Child: Birth to Age 5*. New York: Bantam, 1993. The Academy also puts out a volume for children ages five to twelve and ages twelve to twenty-one.

Ames, Louise Bates, Frances L. Ilg, et al. *Your One-Year-Old*. New York: Dell, 1976. Ames and Ilg have written one volume for each year of a child's life up to age ten, then an additional volume for ten- to fourteen-year-olds.

Brazelton, T. Berry, and Bertrand G. Cramer. *The Earliest Relationship*. Reading, MA: Addison-Wesley, 1990.

Eisenberg, Arlene, et al. *What to Expect in the First Year*. New York: Workman, 1990.

———. *What to Expect When You're Expecting*. New York: Workman, 1988.

Greenspan, Stanley and Nancy Thorndike. *The Essential Partnership*. New York: Viking, 1989.

The Philadelphia Child Guidance Center. *Your Child's Emotional Health*. New York: Macmillan, 1993.

Hirsch, E. D., Jr., and John Holdren, eds. *What Your Kindergartner Needs to Know.* New York: Doubleday, 1996.

Kaplan, Louise J. *Oneness and Separateness: From Infant to Individual*. New York: Simon & Schuster, 1978.

Karen, Robert. *Becoming Attached*. New York: Warner, 1994.

Leach, Penelope. *Babyhood*. New York: Knopf, 1990.

Lieberman, Alicia F. *The Emotional Life of the Toddler*. New York: Free Press, 1993.

Spock, Benjamin, and Michael B. Rothenberg. *Baby and Child Care*. New York: Dutton, 1985.

White, Burton L. *The First Three Years of Life*. New York: Avon, 1975.

"The Growing Child Library" is a wonderful series of newsletters and publications packed with developmental information and support for the growing child and his growing parents, divided by age groups: birth to twelve months, thirteen to twenty-four months, twenty-five to thirty-six months, thirty-seven to forty-eight months, forty-nine to sixty months, and sixty-one to seventy-two months. Contact: Dunn and Hargitt, Inc., 22 N. Second Street, P.O. Box 620, Lafayette, Indiana 47902.

A video-based parenting guide that is very helpful is the "Active Parenting Library," provided by Active Parenting Publishers (800-825-0060).

## ADOLESCENTS AND TEENS

Cline, Foster, M.D., and Jim Fay. *Parenting Teens with Love and Logic.* Colorado Springs: Pinon Press, 1992.

Giannetti, Charlene C., and Margaret Sagarese. *Parenting 911.* New York: Broadway Books, 1999.

Lerner, Richard M. and Graham B. Spanier. *Adolescent Development.* New York: McGraw-Hill, 1980.

Steinberg, Laurence, Ph.D., and Ann Levine. *You and Your Adolescent.* New York: Harper, 1997.

Rosemond, John. *Teen-Proofing.* Kansas City, MO: Andrews McMeel, 1997.

Stone, Douglas, et al. *Difficult Conversations.* New York: Viking, 1999.

## REGARDING BOYS

Bassoff, Evelyn S. *Between Mothers and Sons.* New York: Dutton, 1994.

Beausay, Bill. *Teenage Boys!* New York: Waterbrook, 1998.

Brown, Keith Michael. *Sacred Bond: Black Men and Their Mothers.* Boston: Little Brown, 1998.

Elium, Don and Jeanne. *Raising a Son.* Hillsboro, OR: Beyond Words, 1992.

Garbarino, James. *Lost Boys.* New York: Free Press, 1999.

Garcia-Prats, Catherine and Joseph. *Good Families Don't Just Happen.* Holbrook: MA: Adams Media, 1997. The authors are raising *ten* boys.

Gurian, Michael. *Mothers, Sons and Lovers.* Boston: Shambhala, 1993.

Hunter, Mic. *Abused Boys.* New York: Fawcett, 1990.

Kindlon, Dan, Ph.D., and Michael Thompson, Ph.D. *Raising Cain.* New York: Ballantine, 1999.

Moore, Sheila, and Roon Frost. *The Little Boy Book.* New York: Ballantine, 1986.

Sommers, Christina Hoff. *The War Against Boys.* New York: Simon and Schuster, 2000.

## GENERAL PARENTING HELP

Medved, Michael and Diane. *Saving Childhood.* New York: HarperCollins, 1998.

Mountrose, Phillip. *Getting Thru to Kids: Problem Solving with Children Ages 6 to 18.* Sacramento: Holistic Communications, 1998.

———. *Tips and Tools for Getting Thru to Kids: Innovative Approaches for Pre-Schoolers to Teens.* Sacramento: Holistic Communications, 1999.
Pipher, Mary. *The Shelter of Each Other.* New York: Putnam, 1996.
Reder, Alan, et al. *The Whole Parenting Guide.* New York: Broadway Books, 1999.

"Turn Off the TV" is a family games and activities catalog useful to any parents looking for alternatives to TV use (800-949-8688).

For those parents looking for a more religious- or fundamentalist-based parenting approach, the works of James Dobson and John Rosemond are very valuable.

## DISCIPLINE ISSUES

Crary, Elizabeth. *Without Spanking or Spoiling.* Seattle: Parenting Press, 1979.
Dobson, James C. *The Strong-Willed Child.* Wheaton, IL: Tyndale House, 1985.
Giannetti, Charlene C., and Margaret Sagarese. *Parenting 911.* New York: Penguin, 1999.
Kurcinka, Mary Sheedy. *Raising Your Spirited Child.* New York: Harper, 1991.
Nelsen, Jane. *Positive Discipline.* New York: Ballantine, 1987.
Whitham, Cynthia. *Winning the Whining War and Other Skirmishes.* Los Angeles: Perspective Publishing, 1991.
Wyckoff, Jerry, Ph.D., and Barbara C. Unell. *Discipline Without Shouting or Spanking.* Deephaven, MN: Meadowbrook, 1984.

## TEACHING MORAL AND SPIRITUAL ISSUES DIRECTLY

Damon, William. *Greater Expectations.* New York: Free Press, 1995.
———. *The Moral Child.* New York: Free Press, 1988.
Dosick, Wayne. *Golden Rules.* New York: Harper, 1995.
Eyre, Linda and Richard. *Teaching Your Children Responsibility.* New York: Fireside, 1984.
———. *Teaching Your Children Values.* New York: Fireside, 1993.
Kushner, Rabbi Harold. *When Children Ask About God.* New York: Schocken, 1989.
Nolte, Dorothy Law. *Children Learn What They Live.* New York: Workman, 1998.
Schulman, Michael, Ph.D., and Eva Mekler. *Bringing Up a Moral Child.* New York: Doubleday, 1994.

The Reverend Bruce Barth of the Bethany Lutheran Church in Baltimore, Maryland, is involved in creating some very interesting and state-of-the-art moral development programs for young people that involve direct mentoring from church members.

Another powerful grassroots program is led by Charles Davis in Seattle, of Counseling Associates in Lynnwood, Washington. Called the Integrity Umbrella, it provides guidance for moral development in families and communities.

## AFRICAN-AMERICAN FAMILIES

Comer, James P., M.D., and Alvin F. Poussaint, M.D. *Raising Black Children.* New York: Penguin, 1992.

Hopson, Dr. Darlene Powell and Dr. Derek S. *Different and Wonderful.* New York: Fireside, 1992.

Staples, Robert. *Black Families at the Crossroads.* San Francisco: Jossey-Bass, 1993.

Williams, Gregalan. *Boys to Men: Maps for the Journey.* New York: Doubleday, 1996.

A very powerful community program in Houston focuses especially on African-American boys. It is the Fifth Ward Enrichment Program, headed by Ernest McMillan.

## ADD AND ADHD

Hallowell, Edward M., and John J. Ratey. *Driven to Distraction.* New York: Touchstone, 1994.

Stein, David. *Ritalin Is Not the Answer.* San Francisco: Jossey-Bass, 1999.

## FATHERING

Braver, Sanford L., and Diane O'Connell. *Divorced Dads.* New York: Tarcher, 1998.

Brott, Armin. *The New Father: A Dad's Guide to the First Year.* New York: Abbeville Press, 1997.

Bryan, Mark. *The Prodigal Father.* New York: Three Rivers Press, 1997.

Davis, Reginald F., and Nick Borns. *Solo Dad Survival Guide.* Chicago: Contemporary Books, 1999.

Klatte, William C. *Live-Away Dads.* New York: Penguin, 1999.

Parker, Ross D., and Armin A. Brott. *Throwaway Dads.* New York: Houghton Mifflin, 1999.

Pitts, Leonard. *Becoming Dad: Black Men and the Journey to Fatherhood.* Atlanta: Longstreet, 1999.

Sullivan, S. Adams. *The Father's Almanac.* New York: Doubleday, 1992.

Gurian, Michael. *The Prince and the King.* New York: Tarcher/Putnam, 1992.

I have not included a section here on mothering because nearly all books about parenting are targeted to mothers. If you are a new mom who has left a profession to care for a child, the transition can be difficult, and two books may help: *The Stay at Home Mom,* by Donna Otto (Eugene, OR: Harvest House, 1997), and *At-Home Motherhood,* by Cindy Tolliver (San Jose: Resource Publications, 1994). A wonderful online resource for moms can be found at www.momsonline.com.

# Notes

## INTRODUCTION

### The Declining Moral Health of Our Sons

For violence and crime statistics, see *Violence: Reflections on a National Epidemic,* by James Gilligan (New York: Vintage, 1996), and *Body Count,* by William J. Bennett, John J. DiIulio, and John P. Walters (New York: Simon & Schuster, 1996).

For mental health information, consult the American Academy of Child and Adolescent Psychiatry.

For teen pregnancy statistics, consult the National Campaign to Prevent Teen Pregnancy.

Reporter Ann O'Hanlon, in *The Washington Post Magazine,* recently wrote about moral issues in school.

> *Educators speculate about what's causing the increase in disciplinary problems. Dual-career families. More violence and trouble in society, which rubs off on children. The influence of television, with its emphasis on instant gratification and glorification of violence. The notion that selfishness is more acceptable than it used to be, for parents and kids alike . . . But no one is happy with their explanations. In the end, educators like Prince William School Superintendent Edward Kelly acknowledge that they don't fully understand the changes they're seeing in the classroom. "I'm just not sure why it's happening," he said.*

*Bad Boys,* by Aaron Kipnis (San Francisco: Jossey-Bass, 1999), is a valuable statistical resource.

Statistics can be checked in *A Fine Young Man* and the sources and government

Web sites referenced in chapter 1. Most statistics are available from the U.S. Department of Justice, as well as from the Bureau of Justice Statistics.

### The Good Son Parenting Plan

*The Good Son* is the third volume in my series of books on the needs of boys in contemporary life. *The Wonder Of Boys: What Parents, Mentors, and Educators Can Do to Shape Boys into Exceptional Men* focused on the emotional and social development of boys in general, especially boys from birth to adolescence; *A Fine Young Man: What Parents, Mentors, and Educators Can Do to Shape Adolescent Boys into Exceptional Men* focused on the emotional and social development of adolescent boys (between ages nine and twenty-one). Neither focused primarily on moral development and discipline, and neither presented a step-by-step parenting plan you could reference at whatever age you find your boy. *The Good Son* has taken fifteen years to complete, and provides that plan.

*The Wonder Of Boys*, by Michael Gurian (New York: Tarcher/Putnam, 1996).

*A Fine Young Man*, by Michael Gurian (New York: Tarcher/Putnam, 1998).

## PART ONE: THE CHALLENGE OF PROVIDING DISCIPLINE AND MORAL DEVELOPMENT TO BOYS

### One:  What Does It Mean to Have a Son?

MORALITY IS SOMEWHAT DIFFERENT FOR BOYS

Good sources for understanding biology and gender include:

*Brain Sex,* by Anne Moir, Ph.D., and David Jessel (New York: Laurel, 1987).

*A Celebration of Neurons,* by Robert Sylwester (Alexandria, VA: Association for Supervision and Curriculum Development, 1995).

*The Developing Mind: Toward a Neurobiology of Interpersonal Experience,* by Daniel J. Siegel (New York: Guilford Press, 1999).

*Essentials of Neural Science and Behavior,* by Eric R. Kandel et al. (Norwalk, CT: Appleton & Lange, 1995).

*Firestorms in the Brain,* by Daniel G. Amen (Fairfield, CA: MindWorks Press, 1998).

*Human Sperm Competition,* by R. Robin Baker and Mark A. Bellis (London: Chapman & Hall, 1995).

*In the Shadow of Man,* by Jane Goodall (Boston: Houghton Mifflin, 1988).

*Neuroscience: Exploring the Brain,* by Mark F. Bear et al. (Baltimore: Williams and Wilkins, 1996).

*On Killing,* by Lt. Col. David Grossman (New York: Little, Brown, 1996).

*The Runaway Brain,* by Christopher Wills (N.Y.: Basic Books, 1993)

*Sex on the Brain,* by Deborah Blum (New York: Viking, 1997).

Phon Hudkins, director of the Human Ethology Research Interchange, is an invaluable resource for biocultural material (Suite 927, 2401 Calvert St. N.W., Washington, DC 20008).

. . .

In exploring biocultural factors, it is useful to remember that many of the inherent qualities our boys and girls (and men and women) exhibit exist because, for 99 percent of our human development, males needed to hunt, protect, and build structures, and females needed to gather food and care for children. Human brains adapted to defined "maleness" and "femaleness" so that we could effectively survive as a species. Our hormones developed divergently as well, as a survival mechanism. Though we all live now in a world of technology and material comfort our ancient ancestors probably could not imagine, our brains and hormonal systems—the prime internal determinants of our behavior—are inherited structures, flexible in superficial terms but inflexible when it comes to basic behavioral tendencies.

This idea is confusing for our present culture, which desperately wants males and females to be the same because it fears that biology and nature are somehow enemies of social progress. But males and females are not the same, and while cultures absolutely influence human behavior, the original tendencies of male-female behavior are only influenced, not reconstructed. Thus we notice that infant boys and girls as young as six weeks old act differently when pressured with loss or pain; we notice they do so as toddlers, as school-age children, and well into old age. We notice boys all over the world making twigs into weapons when they play, and we notice girls creating games that more directly deal with a talk-based interpersonal relationship. Both boys and girls are capable of most of the same responses—giving us the idea that males and females must be biologically androgynous. But the neurological and biochemical research over the last thirty years shows us that nature is quite powerful—millions of years of human development have created male-female diversity from even within the womb.

### Two:    Are We Protecting Our Sons from Moral Harm?

WHEN THE MEDIA POISONS OUR BOYS

*Failure to Connect: How Computers Affect Our Children's Minds—For Better and Worse,* by Jane M. Healy, Ph.D. (New York: Simon and Schuster, 1998).

*Screen Smarts,* by Gloria DeGaetano (New York: Houghton Mifflin, 1996).

In *A Fine Young Man* (chapter 8), I detailed the neurological and hormonal impacts of visual media on the growing boy's brain. The evidence of damage to the brain from developmentally inappropriate media use is frightening.

THE MORAL NATURE OF BOYS

*Real Boys,* by William Pollack (New York: Random House, 1998).

*The War Against Boys,* by Christina Hoff Sommers (New York: Simon and Schuster, 2000). This is a seminal work on our culture's neglect of boys' educational and moral needs.

GOOD SON PARENTING PRINCIPLES

Some of the cultures and subcultures, other than American, I personally have experienced are

    Italian (Naples)
    Irish (County Fermanagh)
    Israeli (urban and kibbutz)
    India (South Central)
    French (Paris and Quenet)
    English (London and throughout southern England)
    Turkish (urban and rural)
    Kurdish (urban and rural)
    Egyptian (urban)
    Nubian (rural)

American subcultures I have studied include:

    Hawaiian and Samoan
    Urban and rural United States (all regions)
    Native American (Southern Ute)

Some of the cultures and subcultures in which I have done scholarly research
are

    Australian Aboriginal
    Shavante (Brazil)
    Ndembu (Africa)
    Japanese (urban)
    Chinese (urban)
    Papua, New Guinea
    Native American (Lakota)

## PART TWO: NURTURING THE EARLY YEARS OF A BOY'S DEVELOPMENT: THE AGE OF OBEDIENCE (BIRTH TO SIX YEARS OLD)

### Three: Infancy: Nurturing Boys from Birth to Eighteen Months

DEVELOPMENTAL MILESTONES

There are many sources for and theories about developmental psychology. Adler, Erikson, Freud, Jung, Montessori, Waldorf, Piaget, and Kholberg are some of the best-known names in developmental work.

Just as I have studied gender and social patterns in thirty cultures in order to develop the Good Son Parenting Plan, I also have relied not on one developmental approach but on finding the best in all the approaches. Thus, students of developmental psychology will see some of Adler, some of Erikson, some of Montessori, and so on. I have not included any developmental information that I have not found represented in more than one developmental source.

HE IS DELICATE AND FRAGILE

See *A Fine Young Man,* chapter 1, for studies on male fragility.

Some experts believe that circumcision is an unnecessary and violent act committed against our infant boys. To look more deeply into this perspective, you might read *Circumcision: The Hidden Trauma,* by Ronald Goldman, Ph.D. (Boston: Vanguard, 1997).

## USING BEDTIME AS SELF-DISCIPLINE DEVELOPMENT

*Solve Your Child's Sleep Problems,* by Richard Ferber (New York: Simon & Schuster, 1985).

## CHILD CARE

In *The Wonder of Boys* (chapter 5), you will find additional material on child care, day care, and studies and standards regarding quality of care.

## THE ROLE OF THE ACTIVE FATHER

For a deeper look at these issues, you might enjoy *Fatherless America,* by David Blankenhorn.

## ADOPTION

If you have adopted a baby, there are many resources available to you through organizations such as the American Adoption Congress. Local organizations are very helpful for finding support and insight regarding the unique needs of the biological and the adoptive parents, and the adopted kids. Once such organization is Searchlight, in Coeur d'Alene, Idaho.

*Raising Adopted Children,* by Lois Ruskai Melina (New York: Bantam, 1998).

## NUTRITIONAL ISSUES

"Are estrogens involved in falling sperm counts and disorders of the male reproductive tract?" by Richard Sharpe and Niels Skakkebaek, in *The Lancet,* May 29, 1993.

"Environmental Hormones and the Male Reproductive System," by Ann Oliver Check and John A. McLachlan, *Journal of Andrology,* January/February 1998.

"Silent Sperm," by Lawrence Wright, *The New Yorker,* January 25, 1997.

"Toxicology of Male Reproduction in Animals and Humans," by De Celis, Pedron-Nuevo, and Feria-Velasco, in *Archives of Andrology,* 1996.

These resources help you get a better picture of the effect of endocrine disruptors on male physiology, but some of their scientific prose might be difficult. Here is some of the material in a nutshell: Bovine growth hormones succeed in making more meat on the cow by utilizing endocrine disruptors that increase estrogenic activity and decrease androgenic activity (testosterone). Estrogenic compounds make cattle fatter—testosterone makes them more muscled. From the cattle producers' point of view, more muscle means less edible beef. The producer needs an estrogen, not a testosterone, increase.

When humans ingest the meat (much of this goes for chicken and other hormonally enhanced foods as well), their own endocrine systems are affected by the hormones in the meat. Human females are estrogen based, and so the increase in estrogenic compounds in their system does not contradict their biology. Human males are testosterone based—the increase in estrogenic compounds does confuse their biology. This imbalance, endocrinologists believe, is the primary cause of increased male infertility and lowered sperm count. Because a human mother's fat stores hormones, the male fetus experiences estrogenic increases in the womb. Then he eats foods treated with hormones, and he lives in an environment filled with fertilizers, which adds to the problems. He eats apples treated with pesticides that utilize estrogenic compounds. Cumulatively, his reproductive system is affected.

### Four:    The Toddler Years: Nurturing Boys of Eighteen Months to Four Years

ATTENTION AS DISCIPLINE

*The Developing Person Through Childhood and Adolescence,* by Kathleen Berger (New York: Worth, 1991).

CREATING A FAMILY DISCIPLINE SYSTEM

For more material on discipline systems, see chapter 7 of *The Wonder of Boys.*

CREATING DISCIPLINE IN YOUR VERBAL INTERACTIONS

*The Moral Intelligence of Children,* by Robert Coles (New York: Plume, 1997).

RULES TO LIVE BY

The boy wants to learn self-regulation of his verbal aggression; keeping a non-cursing policy helps him. He'll experiment with cursing in adolescence, but he'll be less likely to be offensive then because he'll have learned politeness now.

He'll also grow up with a sense that some things are so reverent that they can't be abused by his tongue. Developing this sense of reverence, of even mysterious power, is a good thing to start in his toddler years.

FINDING THE SPIRITUAL IN EVERYDAY LIFE

*Emma and Mommy Talk to God,* by Marianne Williamson (New York: Harper-Collins, 1996).

*The Children's Book of Virtues,* ed. William J. Bennett (New York: Simon & Schuster, 1995).

Two very fine books on developing spirituality in children are: *Raising Spiritual Children in a Material World,* by Phil Catalfo (New York: Berkley, 1997), and *Nurturing the Spirit,* by Aline D. Wolf (Hollidaysburg, PA: Parent Child Press, 1996).

### Five:    The Boy Emerges: Nurturing Boys of Five and Six

LIMITING WHINING AND BACKTALK

*Backtalk,* by Audrey Ricker and Carolyn Crowder (New York: Fireside, 1998).

*Taming the Dragon in Your Child,* by Meg Eastman, Ph.D., and Sydney Craft Rozen (New York: Wiley, 1994).

*Winning the Whining Wars,* by Cynthia Whitham (Los Angeles: Perspective Publishing, 1991).

BUILDING SPIRITUAL LIFE

The report team was headed by Robert Hummer, a sociobiologist at the University of Texas at Austin.

In *The Wonder of Boys*, I suggested a detailed model for home-churching: the Who, What, Where, When, How, Why method (see chapter 7 of that book).

### Giving Thanks

Here are two "gratitude" songs we have sung in our house.

"The Thank-You Song"

Thank you, thank you, my heart sings.
Thank you, thank you for everything.

"The Johnny Appleseed Song"

The Lord is good to me, and so I thank the Lord
For giving me the things I need—
The sun and the rain and the apple seed.
The Lord is good to me.

PREPARING FOR SCHOOL

The best collection I've found of studies on when a boy should enter school appears in Moore and Frost's *The Little Boy Book* (New York: Ballantine, 1987).

### Be Aware of Brain Functioning and Early School Issues

*A Celebration of Neurons,* by Robert Sylwester, is a must-read on this subject.

If you have a question anytime during your son's upbringing about whether he has a learning disability, the Learning Disabilities Association can be reached at 610-458-8193. Children with learning disabilities have the right to an individualized education program (IEP).

CHORES AND ALLOWANCE

*Money Doesn't Grow on Trees,* by Neale Godfrey and Carolina Edwards (New York: Simon & Schuster, 1994).

*A Penny Saved,* by Neale Godfrey, with Tad Richards (New York: Simon & Schuster, 1995).

**PART THREE:   NURTURING THE MIDDLE YEARS
OF A BOY'S DEVELOPMENT: THE AGE OF CONVENTION
(SEVEN TO TWELVE YEARS OLD)**

### Six:   The Between Years: Nurturing Boys of Seven and Eight

HIS INTELLECTUAL DEVELOPMENT

*Attention Span Problems*

For insight into ADD and ADHD issues, see *Driven to Distraction,* by Edward M. Hallowell and John J. Ratey (New York: Touchstone, 1994), and *Ritalin Is not the Answer,* by David Stein (San Francisco: Jossey-Bass, 1999).

HIS MORAL DEVELOPMENT

*Look for Moral Fragility in the Boy*

"Head Start," in *U.S. News & World Report,* April 9, 1998, p. 7.
"Kids Killing Kids," by Jennifer Daw, in *Family Therapy News,* August/September 1998.

BEING A STRONG AUTHORITY

The mother's comment on creating a dictatorship is taken from an article entitled "Cultural Interpretations of Child Discipline: Voices of African-American Scholars," by Carla R. Bradley, in *The Family Journal,* vol. 6, p. 272.

HELPING HIM CHANNEL AGGRESSION

*Finding the Line Between Aggression and Violence*

The story from Salem, Oregon, was reported by the Associated Press on October 25, 1998.
*Helping Your Kids Cope with Divorce,* by M. Gary Neuman (New York: Times Books, 1998).

THE SCHOOL ENVIRONMENT

For a full collection of these statistics and references, see the first chapter of *A Fine Young Man.*
Ann Gross's tolerance teaching was reported in *Teaching Tolerance,* Spring 1998.
*Educating for Character,* by Thomas Lickona (New York: Bantam, 1991).

### Seven:   Pre-Adolescence: Nurturing Boys of Nine and Ten

MORAL TRAINING IN SUPERVISED GROUPS

Ethics in Action is an activities program for Cub Scouts that is designed to reinforce the character-building goals of the Boy Scouts of America. A series of fourteen Ethics in Action activities encourages Cub Scouts and their leaders to "think a little deeper" about values and about some of the decisions and their consequences that are normal parts of growing up. The activities also try to enhance boys' respect and concern for others by helping them see things from different points of view.

For more information, read the *Cub Scout Leader How-To Book,* No. LQ33832, available from local BSA supply distributors or by calling 800-323-0732.

SPORTS AND ATHLETICS

*The Cheers and the Tears,* by Shane Murphy (San Francisco: Jossey-Bass, 1999).

*Why Good Coaches Quit,* by John Anderson and Rick Aberman (Minneapolis: Fairview Press, 1999).

WHAT TO DO IF YOUR SON IS BEING BULLIED

*Before It's Too Late,* by Stanton Samenow (New York: Times Books, 1998).

SEXUAL MORALITY

*Beyond the Birds and the Bees,* by Beverly Engel (New York: Pocket, 1999).

SPIRITUAL DEVELOPMENT

One third-grade public-school Montessori classroom in Spokane, Washington— Mrs. Knight's class—developed a "second" pledge of allegiance. While they recited the normal Pledge of Allegiance, they also said this pledge.

> I pledge allegiance to the Earth
> and all life it nourishes,
> to all growing things,
> and to all species of animals.
>
> I promise to protect all life on the planet,
> to live in harmony with nature,
> and to share our resources justly
> so that all people can live
> with dignity and peace.

What a wonderful environment for moral education this classroom is. It teaches traditional democratic ideals through the normal pledge and requires these between kids to expand their sense of moral life.

THE RITUALS OF LIFE: THE FIRST RITE OF PASSAGE

For more information on all four rites of passage suggested throughout the next chapters, see part II of *A Fine Young Man.* Also, ICA Journeys is a national organization that specializes in rites of passage for both boys and girls. They do a wonderful job all over the country.

### Eight:   Pre-Puberty: Nurturing Boys of Eleven and Twelve

HIS BRAIN DEVELOPMENT

For further reading about specifics of brain development, you might enjoy some of the resources I listed in the notes to chapter 1, especially *A Celebration of Neurons* and *Brain Sex.*

HIS MORAL DEVELOPMENT

In *The Wonder of Boys,* chapter 8, I presented the stages of moral development as developed by Piaget and Kohlberg. You might enjoy pursuing these.

SEXUAL MORALITY

*From Boys to Men: All About Adolescence and You,* by Michael Gurian (New York: Price Stern Sloan, 1999).

Teen girls who want deeper insight into the emotional, social, and physical development of boys might enjoy *Understanding Guys: A Guide for Teenage Girls,* by Michael Gurian (New York: Price Stern Sloan, 1999).

INCREASE HONOR ACTIVITIES IN SCHOOLS

One of the finest public school ethics curricula I've seen is the one used in Missouri. The University of Missouri at Kansas City's School of Education is a good resource for finding out more. Landon School, a private school in Bethesda, Maryland, recently piloted a yearlong emphasis on ethics and honor that got rave reviews from kids and parents.

## PART FOUR:   NURTURING THE TEENAGE YEARS OF A BOY'S DEVELOPMENT: THE AGE OF MORAL INTUITION (THIRTEEN TO EIGHTEEN YEARS OLD, AND BEYOND)

### Nine:   Puberty: Nurturing Boys of Thirteen and Fourteen

YOUR SON'S THIRD DEVELOPMENTAL EPISODE: AN OVERVIEW

As your son makes his journey through adolescence, he will be seeking four primary developmental elements.

Identity
Autonomy
Moral Intuition
Intimacy

A great deal of *A Fine Young Man* concerns these elements during each stage of adolescence, thus I have not included all of them here in *The Good Son.* But if you are raising an adolescent, you might enjoy looking at these elements in chapters 3 through 5 of that book.

HIS ENCOUNTER WITH PUBERTY

For a more in-depth look at puberty, see *A Fine Young Man.*

## HIS EMOTIONAL DEVELOPMENT

The research at Harvard appeared in an article by William Pollack called "Raising and Loving Boys," in *Working Mother,* March 1999, p. 33.

## HIS MORAL DEVELOPMENT

Walter Williams was quoted in "Running for Precedent," by Jamie Tobias Neely, in *The Spokesman-Review,* January 17, 1999.

## RISKY BEHAVIOR DURING PUBERTY

Court Appointed Special Advocates is an immensely valuable national organization that publishes its findings on what our youth are facing. I got the NCASA material from the CASA press release of September 1, 1998.

In Houston, Texas, there is a model program for youth, the Fifth Ward Enrichment Program, which you can access at www.tyc.state.tx.us/prevention/5thward.htm, or at 4014 Market, Suite 105, Houston, TX, 77020 (713-229-8353). This program is one of the finest I've seen for giving boys jobs, missions, help to go to school, and a positive life.

## SEXUAL MORALITY

In your own ancestral culture, as in many tribal cultures, boys of thirteen and fourteen married and had children, but always in the supervised extended family environment of their tribe. They actually mated before they dated. In other words, marriages were arranged and intercourse occurred, but many of these young people didn't get to know each other until after years of marriage.

In our culture, we date before we mate, a very risky way of doing things. It may lead to more "true love" (this is highly debated in anthropological circles), but it also leads to more sexual and moral chaos because the young person is not supervised in discovering how to mate at such a young age.

## HOMOSEXUALITY

Good sources for further understanding the biological material are *Brain Sex,* by Anne Moir and David Jessel (New York: Laurel, 1987), and *The Wonder of Boys* and *A Fine Young Man.*

## THE RITUALS OF LIFE: THE SECOND RITE OF PASSAGE

The magazine *Healing Currents* included a wonderful and very practical article about a rite of passage called "Within the Embrace of Men," by Louis Carosio, November 1997, p. 12.

St. Mark's School of Texas does a wilderness adventure with its ninth-graders. When the boys are in fifth and seventh grade, they take smaller camping trips, which the boys think of as preparatory. Then, when the longer ninth-grade trip comes, the boys fill their packs, board the buses, say good-bye to their parents, and start off into the wilderness. Most of them find somewhere during the many miles of hiking and the camping and the other challenges that they face obstacles together, they face fears and pain, and they feel very bonded to one another during the process. For decades afterward, the grown men recall that ninth-grade rite of passage experience as a time of immense personal growth and attachment to fellows. For some of the men, friendships established or solidified on that trip are lifelong.

For further practical advice on setting up a rite, see *A Fine Young Man.*

### Ten:   The Middle Teens: Nurturing Boys of Fifteen and Sixteen

HIS INDIVIDUATION

Parent's Coalition is a C.O.P.S. program (Community Oriented Policing Services).

HIS INTELLECTUAL DEVELOPMENT

For the most recent data on how adolescent boys and girls are faring in school, check out the Horatio Alger Report and the Commonwealth Fund Reports. *A Fine Young Man* also includes statistics, findings, and database references in chapter 1.

HIS EMOTIONAL DEVELOPMENT

*Raising Cain,* by Dan Kindlon and Michael Thompson (New York: Ballantine, 1999), provides wonderful research and advice about building emotional literacy in boys.

*Through a Window,* by Jane Goodall (New York: Houghton Mifflin, 1990).

CREATING DISCIPLINE IN YOUR VERBAL INTERACTIONS

Dudley Weeks's *The Eight Essential Steps to Conflict Resolution* (New York: Tarcher/Putnam, 1992) is a good resource for working through disagreements with anyone, including your teen male.

PRACTICING CREATIVE DISCIPLINE

Associated Press, "Boy and his truck up a tree after tickets, tardiness irk dad," in *The Spokesman-Review,* September 6, 1998.

*Teen Tips,* by Tom McMahon (New York: Pocket Books, 1996).

PRACTICING IMMEDIATE ACCOUNTABILITY

Jay Nixon spoke at the Missouri Conference for Safe Schools in Kansas City in October 1998.

RULES TO LIVE BY

*A Parent's Guide for Suicidal and Depressed Teens,* by Kate Williams (Center City, MN: Hazelden, 1995).

*Toughlove,* by Phyllis and David York and Ted Wachtel (New York: Bantam, 1982).

*You and Your Adolescent,* by Laurence Steinberg, Ph.D., and Ann Levine (New York: Harper, 1997).

SEXUAL MORALITY AND ROMANCE

St. Augustine's High School in San Diego has a very fine chastity-based sex-ed program that focuses on the sacredness of fertility and the act of sexual intercourse.

I met Fadi Auro when I spoke at St. Augustine's.

WORK AND THE WORKPLACE

Wilson and Canada both are quoted in Geoffrey Canada's article in *American Educator,* Fall 1998. Canada's *Fist Stick Knife Gun* and *Reaching Up for Manhood* are immensely valuable reading for anyone concerned about our young men. Both are published by Beacon Press in Boston, 1995 and 1997, respectively.

In the National Campaign to Prevent Teen Pregnancy's publication "Not Just for Girls," Hector Sanchez-Flores writes: "The true definition of machismo: a person who is dignified, serves as a protector for his family, is nurturing, spiritual, faithful, respectful, caring, and trustful, and takes the responsibility to provide." This expanded definition of "macho" takes the word to its real meaning not only in Latino culture but, potentially, throughout all of American culture. By Sanchez-Flores's definition, we might say that the Good Son is quite macho indeed.

THE RITUALS OF LIFE: THE THIRD RITE OF PASSAGE

*Boy into Man,* by Bernard Weiner (San Francisco: Transformation Press, 1992).

Also see *Seven Arrows,* by Hyemeyohsts Storm (New York: Ballantine, 1985), a classic in male initiation rituals from a Native American perspective.

## Eleven: Pre-Adulthood: Nurturing Young Men of Seventeen, Eighteen, and Beyond

ENCOURAGING MORAL AND SPIRITUAL EDUCATION THROUGH TRAVEL

*Letters to a Young Poet,* by Rainer Maria Rilke, trans. M. D. Herter Norton (New York: Norton, 1934).

ENCOURAGING SERVICE ACTIVITIES

General Powell was quoted in the Big Brothers and Big Sisters publication *Duo Times,* December 1998.

TEACHING THE ART OF RELATIONSHIP

I learned of Steve McCormack and Kelly Morrison from an article by Susan Ager, of the *Detroit Free Press,* "Love Firsthand," printed in *The Spokesman-Review,* January 5, 1999.

*The Eight Essential Steps to Conflict Resolution,* by Dudley Weeks (New York: Tarcher/Putnam, 1992).

*Love's Journey,* by Michael Gurian (Boston: Shambhala, 1995).

# Index

# About the Author

Michael Gurian is a family therapist, educator, and cofounder of the Gurian Educational Institute at the University of Missouri–Kansas City Graduate School of Education. He is the author of eleven books, eight of them in the field of male development, including the national bestsellers *The Wonder of Boys* and *A Fine Young Man*.

Michael has served as a consultant to families, schools, community agencies, therapists, youth organizations, churches, criminal-justice professionals, the judiciary, the media, and policymakers. His training videos for parents and volunteers are used by Big Brothers and Big Sisters agencies throughout the U.S. and Canada.

His work reflects the diverse cultures (European, East Indian, Middle Eastern, and American) in which he has lived, worked, and studied. Before becoming a lecturer and consultant, he taught at Ankara University and Gonzaga University.

Michael shares a private therapy practice with his wife, Gail. They live in Spokane, Washington, with their two children.

Michael Gurian
P.O. Box 8714
Spokane, WA 99203
http://www.Michael-Gurian.com

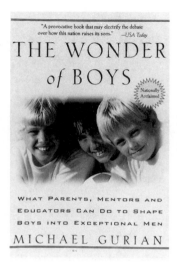

ALSO BY MICHAEL GURIAN

*The Wonder of Boys: What Parents, Mentors and Educators Can Do to Shape Boys into Exceptional Men*

NATIONAL BESTSELLER

"A provocative book that may electrify the debate over how this nation raises its sons."
— *USA Today*

"Full of good insights and advice."
— *Los Angeles Times*

"The Wonder of Boys will help future generations open the lines of communication between men and women by giving us what we need to raise strong, responsible, and sensitive men."
— John Gray, author of *Men Are from Mars, Women Are from Venus*

## Michael Gurian's
### *A Fine Young Man*

"This book is filled with stories and practical advice for parents and teachers of adolescent boys. Michael Gurian takes a thoughtful look at nature and nurture, and  at the role of culture and testosterone in the lives of boys. I recommend  it to all who want to raise fine young men."

—Mary Pipher, author of *Reviving Ophelia*

"Michael Gurian is a leader in the rediscovered field of helping young males to become successful men. His new book, A Fine Young Man, picks up where The Wonder of Boys left off. Gurian astutely provides advice and direction for today's parents, educators, and caregivers about how to understand and deal with problems facing today's 'fine young men.'"

—W. Brewster Ely IV, President
International Boys School Coalition